FEUDING
FAN
DANCERS

ALSO BY LESLIE ZEMECKIS

Goddess of Love Incarnate:
The Life of Stripteuse Lili St. Cyr

Behind the Burly Q:
The Story of Burlesque in America

FEUDING FAN DANCERS

FAITH BACON, SALLY RAND, *and the*
GOLDEN AGE *of the* SHOWGIRL

LESLIE ZEMECKIS

COUNTERPOINT · BERKELEY, CALIFORNIA

FEUDING FAN DANCERS

Copyright © 2018 by Mistress, Inc.
First hardcover edition: 2018

Library of Congress Cataloging-in-Publication Data
Names: Zemeckis, Leslie Harter, author.
Title: Feuding fan dancers : Faith Bacon, Sally Rand, and the golden age of the showgirl / Leslie Zemeckis.
Description: First hardcover edition. | Berkeley, California : Counterpoint, 2018. | Includes bibliographical references.
Identifiers: LCCN 2018019509 | ISBN 9781640091146
Subjects: LCSH: Bacon, Faith, 1910-1956. | Rand, Sally, 1904–1979. | Stripteasers—United States—Biography. | Burlesque (Theater)—United States—History—20th century.
Classification: LCC PN1949.S7 Z455 2018 | DDC 792.780922 [B] —dc23
LC record available at https://lccn.loc.gov/2018019509

Paperback ISBN: 978-1-64009-265-5

Cover design by Sarah Brody
Book design by Wah-Ming Chang

COUNTERPOINT
2560 Ninth Street, Suite 318
Berkeley, CA 94710
www.counterpointpress.com

Printed in the United States of America

For my boys
Bob, Zane & Rhys

The reason birds can fly and we can't is simply because they have perfect faith, for to have faith is to have wings.

J. M. BARRIE, *The Little White Bird*

Sally Rand

Faith Bacon

CONTENTS

FEUDING
FAN
DANCERS

PROLOGUE

IT HAD BEEN A TERRIBLE DAY. A TERRIBLE FEW WEEKS, MONTHS, *years* if she was honest.

September 26, 1956, was an unseasonably cold day in Chicago with temperatures in the 30s. It was evening and the roommates had been arguing for hours. Money, or rather the lack of it. The slender blonde had just returned from a futile trip home—if one could call it that—begging for money, her roommate would later say. But it wasn't to her mother that she had pled—and fled—but to an uncertain lover, still married, with a kind heart. He probably gave her a little cash, but not enough. Later, the one thing the roommate said that was true (and God knows there wasn't much) involved the blonde's lack of money. The years had caught up to her.

Looking in the cracked mirror of the hotel bathroom, she would have seen an aging face. What had happened to time? She had ridden off her looks for years. Now, vanished. Gone. Drunk up and drugged away. Not enough beauty to afford a drink at the bar next door. Desperate. End of her rope.

She was no longer part of the scene. She was rudely treated like a relic from the past, if given any attention at all. While Elvis Presley's "Heartbreak Hotel" climbed to #1 on the charts and Dear Abby's advice column debuted, she was relegated to offering her wares to whoever had enough pity to give a fallen star a dime. A job. That's what she wanted.

She was looking for an opportunity to climb back to the top, though it had been more than two decades since she had broken box office records. She had been dubbed "the most beautiful girl in the world." They would hang that title on her for the rest of her days.

She earned headlines and an arrest. Though at the time it was perfectly legal to appear nude under the lights of a Broadway production, she had "stepped out of line and offered a suggestion," which got a $500 fine and her name in print. From there her head swelled with the attention (and the need for what, love?) she had been seeking, or been pushed toward, since she was a child. On recalling the night in question and what she was thinking, all she could remember was "One Love" by Arlen and Koehler had been playing.

Burlesque straight man Lee Stuart and his wife caught her begging outside a theatre, looking like a "bag lady." It must have been a wrenching sight. Stuart had often been on the program with the incandescent blonde bringing down the sold-out houses. Sadly, she was far from the "Dancer Divine," dancing with only three orchids for cover "to the inhaling and exhaling of the audience" until it was time to discard the flowers, tossing them to the "palpitating audience." Stuart and his wife took pity on the former star and gave her some cash. Grateful, she promised to catch their show. They would never see her again.

For years her determination had kept her going through lawsuits, disappointments, a suicide attempt or two. And, of course, that feud. No matter how rough things had gotten—and Lord knows they had—there was usually a sliver of hope to penetrate nights of darkness and despondency. She had believed so hard for so long. Was it willpower that had gotten her through that awful dance school where she tried to teach movement and artistry to snot-nosed kids, whose mothers were even worse than their talentless children? The mothers would have reminded her of her own. And though the work was beneath her, she suffered when even that failed.

Some strength, some inkling of better days to come had gotten her through affairs and a marriage that wasn't much of anything. But she could feel her resolve slipping. Her hands weren't numb from the wind blowing off Lake Michigan. They were anesthetized from holding on so hard for so long. For nothing.

She wanted another fistful of fame. Even a finger-full of what she once had.

She lied about her age. Did anyone really believe she was still thirty-something? She was close to fifty. Her unlined, wide-eyed face had adorned the newspapers; now it was only her arrests, but even those no longer made the front pages. On chasing fame she had once blithely advised, "Try to get yourself arrested as much as possible." And she had. But that was par for the course for those working in the nude.

Back in 1934, while society doyenne Mrs. Harry Payne Whitney was cringing at seeing herself in the headlines (those of a certain ilk were *not* in the papers), accused of stealing her niece Gloria Vanderbilt from the poor little rich girl's mother (who was intolerably negligent), this luminescent blonde had reveled in her own scandalous headlines. Ink spilled for the most minor of incidents, like when her appendix was removed. Her every move had been broadcast.

"Dancer Wants Trial by Jury"

"War of Fan Dancers Begins at World's Fair"

"Held Up by Bandits and Rebuked"

Today she needed to eat. Her roommate was harping at her. They argued whether she should return to her family and beg for more money. What family?

There had been nothing for her in Erie, Pennsylvania. She had to be feeling so alone.

If no one else remembered, at least she knew she had once been a sensation who earned great sums, performing to standing-room-only crowds. "The Marilyn Monroe of her day," an inspiration for a legion of beautiful dancers, now down to less than a dollar in her stained pocketbook.

Perhaps she looked in the mirror and was finally honest with her reflection. There was no work. No romance. Nothing.

Time was running out.

Like numerous third-rate hotels, it would have had a long narrow hallway with a grimy window at the end. Imagine hazy light from the dim hallway casting uneven shadows over the pattern of the worn carpet. Neither light nor optimism could penetrate the broken souls in the cheap hotel. A last stop, a temporary asylum from dashed dreams and delusional schemes.

Impulsively—or had she been thinking of it all day?—the blonde raced toward the window. Her roommate yelled after her. A low-heeled foot clung to the rim of the ledge.

There was no time to turn back. Her roommate grabbed at her skirt, feeling the assurance of fabric in her rough hand. Then horrifyingly she felt it give—too fast—and the material slid through her hand.

"No!" she screamed as her troubled friend vanished from sight.

It was not an easy end to a life that had not been lived easily.

Ironically, 1956 was a leap year.

Part

ONE

ONE

CHICAGO WAS GETTING ITS GROOVE ON, LETTING THE WORLD know some little fire wasn't going to keep it down. The devastation wrought in the 1871 blaze was nowhere to be seen. The city had rebuilt itself quickly, skyscrapers rose, and the city was a thriving hub of activity. By 1890 more than a million people inhabited Chicago.

The World's Columbian Exposition of 1893 was meant to celebrate the 400th anniversary of Columbus's discovery of America. Set at the beginning of a serious economic recession when banks were closing, farms were unable to produce, and unemployment surged, the Exposition hoped to bring in much-needed income from visitors around the world. And it worked. Like most world's fairs it had a profound influence on popular culture, architecture, and American technical advancements. This one was fondly known as the "White City," partially because of the abundance of streetlights illuminating visitors as they strolled through warm nights enjoying the many amusements on the midway (also because of the many white stucco buildings). Sprawled over 600-plus acres along the lakeshore, it would attract some twenty-seven million visitors during the six months of operation. (Of the two hundred buildings constructed, only two remain today.)

The Midway Plaisance (vaguely meaning a pleasure ground) was said to be inspired by France's 1889 Universal Exposition that had taken Paris by storm. At over a mile long it was one of the main sources of income for Chicago's fair. People flocked to see the uncommon amusements offered, such as ethnic villages, sideshows, rides, and what looked like a gigantic bicycle wheel turning in the sky, the world's first Ferris Wheel. For the first time, the amusements at a world's fair were not mashed indoors in exhibition halls but enjoyed in the fresh air and sunshine.

This area was created by a music promoter named Sol Bloom, who introduced the term "midway" to our lexicon. Over four million dollars was spent on the sometimes lurid concessions and titillating sights offered there.

Little Egypt, a sinuous belly dancer (actually there would be more than one), made her appearance at the "Street in Cairo" concession, doing the "hootchy-kootchy" to raised eyebrows. The exotic cutie shook her hips to a ditty we now associate with snake charmers, improvised by Bloom. The publicity she generated, good and bad, would influence entertainment on and off the midway for generations to come.

With the eyes of the world on Chicago, citizens took a hard look at their city. At the time, Chicago "was an ugly, overgrown town of narrow uneven streets and cheap shoddy structures." A plan was put into place over the next few years to widen streets and line them with trees. Parks sprung up where slums had once festered. On the shores of glistening man-made beaches, bath pavilions made for convenient sun-worshipping welcomed visitors. Chicago would blossom into one of the country's most beautiful cities.

The exposition would have a lasting impact on not only Chicago but our culture. Out of these six months sprang Juicy Fruit gum, Aunt Jemima pancake mix, the automatic dishwasher. The combustion engine would inspire Henry Ford's automobile. Electrical illumination would soon brighten across America.

Because it was disproportionally slanted toward white folks, African Americans rightly protested their depiction at the fair. Where were their stories and their contributions? Their questions would largely be ignored.

Much of the art exhibited at the fair would be hung across the country in prestigious museums like the Smithsonian and Philadelphia Commercial Museum. But more importantly the exhibition had given millions of people, whether they attended or not, hope that in harsh economic times there was light at the end of the tunnel. Spirits were lifted by a jaunty tune and a swinging hip on the Midway.

The fair would close with a literal bang. On October 28, 1893, Mayor Carter Harrison, Sr., was assassinated by a mentally disturbed newspaper distributor, Patrick Prendergast, who killed the popular mayor in his own home.

Flash a g-string forward forty years and it is 1933. Once again the world's fair was sprawled along Lake Michigan and beyond, this time called the "Century of Progress" to honor Chicago's centennial. It was again a massive orgy of technical and scientific innovations that would engineer escape out of the Great Depression currently ruining everyone's fun.

The fair "promised abundance in a world of tomorrow that would be better than the world of today." The idea was that the country was on the precipice of a new day. The sun *would* come out tomorrow. And it was starting in America's Second City.

"From a shabby little outpost on the shores of Lake Michigan, to the glory of one of the mightiest cities on this old spinning globe, Chicago steps today with magnificent gesture . . ." noted Damon Runyan as the fair opened to much hype and expectation.

It was a scaled-down fair compared to the Columbian Exposition, by almost 200 acres. Chicago and the country were in the depths of an economic crisis that had shaken the beliefs of even the most stalwart of men. Life was hard, jobs and money scarce. Americans were hungry for something besides bread lines and dustbowls. The city was taking a risk throwing money at an event under such circumstances. The fear was it would in no way make its money back. Organizers had to reach the most common denominator in putting up concessions to attract the most people. What would draw both socialites and factory workers? Both foreign and native-born?

The fair was scheduled to run five months. There had to be wonders to leave even the most jaded gaping. The Sky Ride was an aerial tram that stretched across the lagoon and was longer than the George Washington Bridge. In the era before massive skyscrapers, few people had ever been that high. The rocket-shaped cars held thirty-six passengers, dangling 215 feet above the ground, at a cost of over a million dollars to build, and it wasn't even ready on opening day.

For those who wanted to stay grounded, there were leisurely gondola rides through the vast lagoon. With four hundred new buildings to see, the eighty-two miles of a "miniature world in itself" cost in the neighborhood of thirty-seven million dollars. The admission fee could in no way cover this investment. Nerves were on edge as businessmen strategized how to save the fair from being a humiliating, egg-on-the-face flop.

A variety of kitsch and tchotchkes were offered for sale: keys, playing cards, mirrors, cocktail shakers, tins, plaques, belt buckles, rings, pins, ashtrays, spoons. Because a dollar was hard to come by, there would be little to spend for trinkets. Vendors feared they would lose everything.

Still, the fair was positioned as a necessary "symbol of hope to this nation just emerging from some of the darkest hours of its history." The days of hopelessness and hardship would be wiped away as one passed through the gates into a world of wonder and delight, with endless divertissements to be enjoyed in the utopian future.

People of all classes, but especially the working class, sought to lift their spirits on the midway, hoping "their dreams of a more carefree way of life" were not only imminent but actually obtainable. Pointing one's gaze toward science and industry would thrust the country past economic uncertainty. The fair unveiled modern marvels such as a self-cooking kitchen, with dishwashers and electric mixers, automated faucets that promised women more free time. Clothing would become streamlined and less inhibiting. Life would be better for women. Machines would take up much of the work, which would allow for "leisure time" within reach of common folk.

The temporary art deco buildings of the fair were painted scarlet, rose, orange, turquoise, and teal. At night equally vibrant sapphire- and jade-colored lights washed the many paths and buildings. No more bland whitewashing, it was now a colorful world the citizens stepped into.

Once again the midway was populated with rides, a midget village, and every "specimen of mankind," including American Indians. There was the Cyclone Coaster, a freak show including a two-headed baby, even alligator wrestling. Something for everyone. For the tots there was an Enchanted Island complete with a magic mountain and castle. Nurses offered to take the youngsters in hand while the adults explored the more mature entertainments available.

There were cafés, cabarets, and eateries crowded with hungry souls searching for laughter. Music came from the many nightclubs. The Andrew Sisters and the Gumm Sisters sang, including an eleven-year-old who would later become Judy Garland.

Uncommon sights like incubators filled with premature babies were lined in glass boxes for viewing. For the predominantly white audience there were offensive portrayals of people of color, such as the Darkest Africa exhibition with African Americans dressed as "savages."

The mayor declared opening day a holiday, closing banks and federal offices. "Amid pomp and ceremony" on May 27, 1933, scores lined up waiting to experience a promising future.

Under flags and banners whipping in the breeze blowing off Lake Michigan, the first visitors eagerly pushed through the turnstile.

By December, Prohibition would be a thing of the past and the fair was looking forward to the profits from legal booze. With repeal came a sudden rise in public drunkenness. With inebriation came greater demand to see the girls.

Since its introduction, the hoochie coochie dance had become a staple of the burlesque houses. And Chicago was rife with them. Burlesque shows grew more popular during the Depression, lifting spirits for a dime. Downtown nightclub owners were hoping to entice the overflow of fair patrons who wanted to see more barely clad beauties off the midway.

It didn't work out that way. "They planned this Fair to bring business to Chicago into the Loop. But you could have fired a cannon down State Street and hit nobody because everybody was at the Fair," said one dancer. And the display of flesh at the fair was so tantalizing and respectable in the guise of science and innovation that there was little need to venture to a questionable club.

For the women dancing and exhibiting their bodies on the midway, it was considered both a modern occupation of this new world and an undignified way for a lady to make a living.

So little was thought of the dancers beyond sensationalism. In light of the era, the proliferation of blatant nudity on display at the fair is surprising. It seemed every concession—if they had a hope in hell of making a profit—offered, at the least, semi-nude women, in peep shows, as part of "games," performing in restaurants, amongst outdoor café tables, even on the ice rink.

"People come to see a show," warned businessman Charles Gates Dawes. And he was right. They might *ooh* and *aah* over the educational exhibits, but it was entertainment they wanted.

Certain prude members of the city protested the many unclothed beauties. To assuage the moral reformers, concessionaires joined in the argument that what they were presenting was art, and not to be trifled with.

One barker (a fast-talking, loud-mouthed man standing outside the concession singing an enticing spiel to coax visitors to hand over an extra dime or quarter to see the visions inside) inelegantly cried, "Of course many sins are committed in the name of art." Few cared about the sin.

For the first time in American history, an international fair would pay for itself—drawing nearly fifty million enthusiasts who ate, drank, played games of chance, strolled along the lakeshore, and experienced the many delights on display.

The fair would once again be host to "Cairo's Cutie," trotting out her wares some thirty years after her debut. Fahreda Mazar, supposedly the original 1893 Little Egypt, was again enticing audiences; no matter she was sixty-two and "graying." Donning "turkish trousers" and inhaling a cigarette, she compared her modest costume to that of the other nudes performing nearby. "I'd never go before an audience like that."

Fatema, another supposed original Little Egypt, was a *father*, not to mention a *grandfather*. (But that was "a great secret.")

Gazing at the midway's nude women was seen as an "American way of life"—and the fair was there to open a portal to those days where "laughter and fun" was the motto, and what better way than with a carnival atmosphere filled with exotic dancers.

These working women—though some later-day historians decry them as commodities, without taking into context their current times and what few opportunities women were afforded—were also seen as emancipated from husbands and families. They were a different, modern woman, streamlined of inhibitions, independent and unencumbered by not only clothes but society's judgment on what they chose to do with their bodies. Economically independent, they were hailed as the women of tomorrow.

It was into this chaotic, vibrant, multicolored world that Sally Rand burst onto the midway and forever into the hearts and minds of Americans with a most peculiar profession, a new one for her. Accounts vary as to how the stunt first came about, but all would agree it was a desperate ploy for attention. Sally Rand was a facile and ever-changing storyteller, easily adding and subtracting from the legend over the years to come.

At a time when the average yearly wage was $1,650 and the cost of a pair of silk hose was just 49 cents, Sally was offered $90 a week to play peek-a-boo with her nudity behind a pair of giant ostrich fans. It would be life-saving.

After 1933 Sally Rand would no longer be a struggling performer. She would be a "name on the lips of thousands" by dancing with "nothing but a pair of fans and a smile." She was twenty-nine years old, by no means a spring chicken, when she set foot on the fairgrounds. Her discipline and belief in herself, with a relentless drive to be somebody, would if not erase then soften the years of humiliation and dismissal.

A pair of seven-foot pink ostrich feathers hid the hard work and worry and struggle; they covered the consistent lack of funds, the years on the road and the toll it would take on marriages. She would see her name, one chosen by Cecil B. DeMille himself, immortalized, if not accurately, as the "original fan dancer."

With all the publicity in the papers there was a rush to see Sally perform, as it was feared the nudity would soon be exorcised from the midway because of the protests.

Astonishingly this "hick" from the Ozarks, as she called herself, "became the fair's enduring icon of optimism and hope." If a girl with no more than a pair of feathers could make it there, life held out infinite possibilities for other women on and off the midway. It was her unasked-for role as a symbol that would endear her to generations of working-class Americans.

Thousands lined up to hear: "Ladies and Gentlemen, I give you the one and only Miss Sally Rand." A spotlight penetrated the dark stage, illuminating Sally at the top of a set of red velvet steps, like Lady Liberty (but instead of a torch, this gal held fans in hand) promising to comfort the huddled masses.

The audience had eight minutes to play a game of guessing if she was nude. Though about seventy percent of the crowd was male, women eagerly sought to get in, wanting to learn what Sally had and if she was actually showing it.

What did this woman have that gave audiences hope? Made them feel uplifted in the current dark days? What kind of a career was this even, waving fans around? Sally seemed stunned that a "hillbilly" had started a trend that would become the hottest thing in the country. A fluke, a publicity stunt, it didn't matter. Her I-can, or rather I-will, spirit invigorated the crowds. In her determination to fan away troubles, the audiences felt better. They would pull through, she seemed to be saying with each flutter of her fans. If she could do it, this nothing from the Ozarks, surely they could too. A petite package of pert and pluck, standing five feet tall (she sometimes claimed another inch), weighing 105 pounds, Sally had a twinkle in her blue eyes, a set of deep dimples in her cheeks, and golden curls. She was vivacious and charming, ambitious and determined to write her future as she wanted to see it. She would save a fair. She would save America. And she would become famous doing it.

HARRIET "HATTIE" HELEN GOULD BECK WAS BORN EASTER SUN-
day, April 3, 1904, in a tiny village named after the deer that roamed
the wooded community in the southern half of Missouri. About
Elkton, she would say it was "so small they had to catch you to put
shoes on you . . . I'm still going barefoot." No one would really ever
catch this curious, magnetic child. Helen, as she was called, was born
with a yearning to be free and a desire for flight that would carry her
out of the Ozarks to worldwide fame.

The Ozarks covered much of the southern half of the state. Hick-
ory County with dense forests and prairie was a farmland paradise.

Helen's mother, Mary Annette "Nettie" Grove Beck, told her
daughter stories about how her mother, Mary "Mollie" Palmer, threw
"flowers for General Lafayette when he came to town for a visit" and
hid the "good quilts" in the fields during the Civil War. Missouri
would proudly boast of having "a higher percentage of participants in
the war than any other state."

Born in Kansas City, Kansas, Nettie moved to Elkton by seventeen to be a teacher. It was there she met William F. Beck at a party. A handsome man with a square jaw and straight nose, he had steel-blue eyes and brown hair and was a West Point graduate, now working as a post office clerk.

The Illinois-born William was eight years Nettie's senior, a former tailor before enrolling with the Army at twenty-three, an occupation he would return to in 1897. He was somber, strict, and religious. He sported a scar across his forehead and chin, presumably from his turn in the Spanish-American War, fighting alongside Teddy Roosevelt and the Rough Riders at San Juan. (Helen would vaguely recall sitting on the president's knee during a visit when she was four years old. She remembered the smell of cigar and the color of his gray tweed coat.) As former cavalry William was outdoorsy, as Helen would be, and taught her how to ride.

Besides teaching school, Nettie was a part-time correspondent for a local newspaper as well as a registered nurse. The couple was married in 1903. A year later she gave birth to daughter Helen. Four years later she gave birth to son Harold Lawton.

They were an odd couple. According to her grandson Sean, Nettie stood a commanding 5 feet 10, while William barely topped 5 feet 6. Helen would inherit her father's hot temper and learn the value of discipline over mind, body, and "order in life." She would never pull her eyes from what she wanted.

A happy child, Helen soon "arrived at the age to be giggly." Her father had no use for it, pointing out "the giggly girl causes grief." Perhaps grieving from the loss of two of his brothers in 1912, he was in a bad temperament.

When war broke out in 1914, William was sent off to France and his father, Grandpa Beck, a twice-married farmer, looked in on Nettie and her two young children. They would grow exceptionally close.

With their father gone, days in the sleepy village of Elkton were idyllic for Helen and Harold. The pair loved to fish, and Helen loved to ride a horse. There were long, humid days running barefoot amongst the trees and swimming in the Pomme de Terre River, which runs through the Ozarks.

Vast numbers of great blue herons settled around the river, flying over its cool waters. Ornithologist Otto Widmann wrote, ". . . there is probably no county in the state where some individuals cannot be seen flying from the distant nest to some favorite feeding grounds."

Nettie's dear friend Lucy Wilson pitched in to help Nettie, and it would be "Aunt Lucy" who took Sally to an event that would wake her like Sleeping Beauty.

In 1910, the magnificent Russian prima ballerina Anna Pavlova began a tour of America. Pavlova created a dance that "would tell the story of a dying swan with a fiery and majestic spirit, making an unsuccessful effort to soar one last time." The four-minute Dance of the Swan would become the inspiration for *Swan Lake*. It was created by the genius Michel Fokine, who said, "It was a combination of masterful technique with expressiveness."

It was a performance that those fortunate enough to see claimed it pierced the soul, stirred emotion, and fired the imagination.

Pavlova was a reed-slim dancer who used "every inch of her being to express the spirit" of the white bird. Dainty and frail, Anna was determined to overcome her defects, including weak ankles, by stuffing the toes of her shoes with wood—helping create the modern pointe shoe.

Helen was nine or ten when she experienced Pavlova and was so moved watching the ballerina soar across the stage that she "sat up and wept." She decided she would be a ballerina.

Besides Nettie, Pavlova would be one on a short list of women to profoundly influence Helen. Nettie had strength, Pavlova artistry. A self-reliant Pavlova lived for dance, not for love. (She died when she refused a necessary surgery, saying if she could not dance, she chose death.)

As a young girl Helen was well aware of her mother's staunch character, which she valiantly carried on while her husband was away. Nettie wanted so much for her children. She made sure to find Helen a dance class, though she could hardly afford it.

With images of a gliding young woman, fluttering her arms, an elegant head bowed, making "bird-like movements" as she crumpled and died, Pavlova's dance haunted Helen, who one day would take flight in her own personal homage to a different kind of bird.

It was a dark day when Nettie received a letter from her husband, now Captain Beck. William wrote that he had met a French woman and wasn't coming home. He was demobilized in 1919, but just weeks later, after applying for a passport stating he had "commercial business," he returned to France and a new life with a new woman. With the end of the Great War, William and Nettie divorced.

The abandonment by her father would leave Helen shattered. Absolutely heartbroken by her father's desertion, she was "starved for affection and attention." It would create a hole in heart that would never be filled. Nettie and the children were left to fend for themselves as money grew tight. Geography and lack of finances cut Helen off from her dance instructions. The Ozarks were not a cultural center by any means, and the Becks now had no mode of transportation to get her to a larger city.

The sad child sat on her bed looking out at the lake near her grandfather's farm. In the purple twilight, she watched the herons (along with ducks and geese) soar as the sun plummeted, casting bruise-colored shadows. Helen must have wished to be as heaven-bound as those great white birds. "I wanted to fly—to leave the earth, soar . . . to the sky."

At some point Nettie and the children headed north to Kansas City, because by the time she was thirteen, Helen was dancing in the chorus at the Empress Theatre. She was singled out and given a good review by the *Kansas City Journal*'s drama critic, who noted she had potential.

The "instant gratification" from the audience when she floated on stage filled her heart. She loved the applause. She felt the love. Helen had found her place.

Like the birds she watched on the lake, free to roam where they liked, Helen had a deep desire for flight that would never abate.

Her first escape came with the sound of iron tent posts being hammered into hard ground as barkers rehearsed their melodic spiel. It was that time of year when traveling carnivals and circuses made their trek across the heartland, pulling up in vacant lots on the out-skirts of towns where hundreds if not thousands poured in from rural communities to be entertained with feats of physicality and exotic sights.

These worlds unto themselves sprung up for a day or two, bring-ing a bit of magic, showmanship, a sparkle, and a lot of carny hustle.

On a warm summer night, Helen tiptoed out of her house to join the carnival. Though she probably looked younger than her fourteen years, she lied and said she was sixteen, convincing the carnival to take her with them when they left. Having practiced her charm on Grandfather Beck, she was expert at getting what she wanted. Helen slipped unnoticed from town.

And so began her love of the gypsy life, traveling by train, liv-ing out of a suitcase, seeing new things, living amongst the carni-val folk, the misfits and the outcasts, feeling perhaps she belonged somewhere for the first time. The sights and sounds would have been magnificent; the grunts of aerialists landing in nets, the roaring and snorting of the animal menagerie, a mix of displaced peoples like the freaks with their physical anomalies on display. It was a less judgmental, freer world. One in which she could become whoever she wanted to be.

Life as a carny would not have been glamorous, especially for a newcomer. It would have been grueling, dirty work, pitching in where she was told. Accommodations would have been cramped and shared with others. It wasn't long until she had had enough.

Back in Kansas City, she obtained a job at the Green Mill Café in Electric Park, an amusement park Walt Disney would use as a model for Disneyland. She danced and worked as a hat-check girl. Electric Park was modeled on the 1893 Columbian Exposition, with an alligator farm, shooting gallery, rides and amusements, and most likely her first exposure to *those types* of entertainment. It was lively and well attended, noisy from the arcades and cafés. There was also a parade of "living statuary" young women, "emerging from a fountain" as part of the attractions. No doubt in some form of undress.

Soon Helen was studying dance with Professor Peri and Georgia Brown and appearing in amateur productions. With a new name of Billie (sometimes Billye or Billy), in homage to her father William, she began dancing with the Bridge Stock Company.

Billie's dancing career was short-lived. A concerned Grandfather Beck found her (which gives credence to the rumor Nettie knew where she was all along) and hauled her back home. She was probably secretly relieved, as she later said, "I found many unscrupulous men in my path."

For a naive young girl, Kansas City would have been both intoxicating and frightening, a taste of a bigger world with all its temptations and dangers, where one had to tread carefully. And her first glimpse of women dancing with little clothing on.

Her schooling seems to only have been sporadic; she went part-time to a parochial school, First Christian Church School, in Columbia, Missouri. By 1922 she met and befriended another aspiring dancer, Lucille LeSueur, who also used the name Billie and lived in both Kansas City and Columbia (LeSueur later changed her name to Joan Crawford; the two would remain friendly). Billie also attended

Central High in Kansas City, where the actor William Powell had gone. She dated Casey Stengel, who would later manage both the New York Yankees and the Mets.

Yet Billie's restless spirit couldn't stay still. In 1918 she was in the chorus of the Al and Louie Bridge Troupe, touring for at least a couple years (presumably part of the reason for her sporadic education). During these years brother Hal appeared in several plays with her. Hal worshipped his adventure-loving sister. Brave, unpredictable, and unorthodox, they remained tied to each other.

Once again it would be the lure of adventure (and the chance for reinvention) that would spirit Billie away. Another carnival would start her on a magnificent career that would span more than forty years.

THREE

IRONICALLY, FAITH BACON ALSO HAD HER ROOTS IN MISSOURI. She would often make the rather implausible claim that she was a descendant of the eminent philosopher, scientist, and author Sir Francis Bacon. Except it was true. Her illustrious heritage included Peregrine White, the first baby born on the Mayflower in the harbor of Cape Cod, and she was related to author James Fenimore Cooper, who wrote *The Last of the Mohicans*. Her great-grand-uncle William T. Coleman was a vigilante during the 1849 Gold Rush in San Francisco. President Grover Cleveland was even related.

Faith's paternal great-grandfather, Henry Douglass Bacon, Sr., was born May 3, 1818 (or 1817), in East Greenville, Missouri. He became successful businessman who, among other things, helped found the University of California, Berkeley.

In 1835, he moved to St. Louis where he worked in dry goods, then moved into the iron trade. He married Julia Ann Page, daughter of Daniel Dearborn Page, miller, merchant, owner of considerable property in and around St. Louis, and at one time the mayor.

Four years later, Bacon and his wealthy father-in-law formed the banking firm of Page & Bacon. Their success led to the opening of Page, Bacon & Co.'s express office in San Francisco in 1849. Among the partners were Page's son Francis W. Page Bacon. The group would eventually open branches in Sacramento, Sonora, and Honolulu.

Business flourished until various factors—among them deception by Page & Bacon's New York correspondents and involvement in the financing of the Ohio & Mississippi Railroad—compelled the St. Louis house to close its doors. When the news reached San Francisco, a run on Page, Bacon & Co. resulted in suspension of business. Both firms were forced into liquidation. The failure of Page, Bacon & Co. served as a prelude to the San Francisco crash of 1855.

Henry Douglass devoted the next few years to settlements with creditors while he turned his attention to investing in mines throughout the western United States and Mexico. However, his primary interest lay in properties in California and Arizona.

In 1871 he purchased Marengo Ranch, more than a thousand acres of what is now South Pasadena. His son, Frank Page Bacon, managed the raising of stock and the growing of citrus, grapes, and walnuts.

With an office in San Francisco, Henry Douglass lived in nearby Oakland. He made generous gifts to the University of California, Berkeley, notably the Bacon Art and Library Building.

When he died in 1893, he was survived by his widow, a son, and two daughters named Carrie Bacon and Ella Etta Bacon Soulé. He divided one-third of capital stock in Bacon Land and Loan, worth more than a million dollars, amongst the siblings. The two sisters ran the company.

His son (Faith's grandfather) had been born April 4, 1848, in

St. Louis County, Missouri. Frank Page Bacon married "Mamie" Minerva Cooper and had eight children. After twenty-one years Mamie and Frank divorced, causing a scandal as divorce rarely occurred in high society.

According to papers, in 1905 the family company was dissolved because Frank Bacon could not agree with his two sisters about the investment of the monies. Frank got a share of the homestead, valued at $30,000, though he complained his sisters had removed some art.

His son, Frank Page Bacon, Jr., Faith's father, was born in 1886. At least by age thirteen he was living with his father, Uncle Soulé, Aunt Carrie, and at minimum two servants. He would grow into an extremely handsome man with a sharp nose, fine thick hair, and an aristocratic bearing.

Into this fractious, fighting, litigious family, Faith was born.

She was the only daughter of Frank and his wife, Charmion Cerry Hayes. Greek in origin, "Charmion" means "delight," and her family were Irish immigrants and farmers. It isn't recorded how the two met, but fifteen-year-old Charmion married twenty-two-year-old Frank Bacon, Jr., in 1909.

The young couple lived in Santa Rosa, in Sonoma County. Just three years earlier the entire downtown area had been decimated in the San Francisco earthquake. Frank worked as a chauffeur, and the young couple might have lived with Charmion's mother (and stepfather).

Charmion was pretty, delicately featured, and at sixteen little more than a child herself when on July 9, 1910, she gave birth to Frances Yvonne Bacon in Los Angeles.

It was a lot for a new couple to start life with a baby. What they were doing living in Los Angeles was anyone's guess. Movies weren't a thriving business yet. (In a few years' time Charm would list herself as doing movie work.) Charmion and Frank had to have struggled, because just two years after Yvonne's birth they separated.

Charm returned to her mother's home in Santa Rosa. Frank moved to Oakland. In 1914 Frank finally filed for divorce, citing desertion on her part. In the following years Frank found work as a salesman for Grandma Baking Company and as an agent for Bacon Manufacturing Vulcanizing Company (founded by brother Thomas).

Such was the stigma of divorce that by 1917, when Frank registered for the draft, he called himself a widower. After the war he settled in Antelope Valley outside of Los Angeles and farmed. Frank remarried in 1921 to Pearl M. Pollock and died 1937 at age fifty-one. He was buried in San Gabriel Cemetery. Daughter Yvonne would never mention him except to claim he was a physician.

In 1916, twenty-two-year-old Charmion married forty-five-year-old Carl Emil Sternlov, a Swedish immigrant. She would pad her age by two years on the wedding certificate. They were married in Los Angeles, and for a time he was a manager of a fruit farm. By 1919 he would marry another twenty-two-year-old girl and Charmion would be gone.

We lose track of Charmion as she grows into an adult. Perhaps she occasionally returned to her mother, who would have helped with the baby. Perhaps she drifted with a confused toddler in tow, seeking someone else to take care of them.

On September 22, 1919, at age twenty-four, Charmion entered into a third marriage, with thirty-three-year-old Roy Albert Rice. He was of medium build, balding with brown hair and eyes. He was a barber, though two years earlier he had been a chiropractor in Honolulu, Oahu. Chiropractic care was a relatively new practice; it wouldn't be legally recognized until 1931, and then only by some states. It was a third marriage for both.

Charmion and Roy were married in Washington State and settled in Portland, Oregon, for a time. In February of 1920, Roy, his new bride, and nine-year-old Yvonne set sail for Honolulu. Mostly likely Roy was returning to his chiropractic profession.

In Hawaii Yvonne would watch "dance orgies of the natives." Perhaps here Charmion was pursing her dance dreams, for later it would be said she was a "frustrated ballet dancer."

This marriage ended quickly, thrusting an ambitious, beautiful mother with an adorable daughter out on their own again.

In July of 1920, Charmion and Yvonne sat sail on the S.S. *Wilhelmenia*, a former transport ship for tourists, bound for San Francisco. State rooms held twin beds and hot and cold running water. Days on deck were passed playing games of bridge in the smoking room or watching movies. There was a masquerade ball, a turtle race, a ladies' lounge, and a social hall for reading and music.

It surely was not a stable life for a young girl. Yvonne would grow up to be nervous and high-strung. Of these years she would say little. The bond between Faith and Charm was toxic and, for the time being, impenetrable.

FOUR

BILLIE JOINED ANOTHER CARNIVAL THE SUMMER FOLLOWING HER first exodus from Missouri, and she ended up in Chicago at age sixteen, hired by the Adolph Bolm Chicago Ballet Company. The Russian-born and -trained Bolm had been Pavlova's dance partner. Billie would exaggerate that she helped "bring culture to the masses" when she toured with Bolm. A balding yet distinguished Bolm had been sidelined as a dancer by an injury. He choreographed to the music of Chopin and Debussy.

One of Billie's great exaggerations would be that she had made $2,000 a week at age sixteen as a "toe dancer." If that had been the case, she would not have had to make ends meet as a nude model and a cigarette girl in a club, which she did.

With the close of the ballet season, Billie was back under canvas, this time performing with Ringling Brothers as a "net girl and trapesist." (She continues to switch between the names Billie and Helen).

The circus was a patriarchal society. To enter as an outsider would have been difficult and taken months of training for Billie to become part of any act. Perhaps she helped out at odd jobs, or rode in the parade, as many pretty girls were relegated to.

Probably around 1920, she started a job with The Flying Wards as part of their trapeze act—a claim unsubstantiated, but not impossible. She always said she learned the high-wire act and that might have been truthful. She was athletic, with strong thick legs, and was fearless.

Under the smell of rosin and sawdust, mingled with the dampness of the menagerie, a waltz played inside the crowded canvas tent. Folks sat on blue seats, looking up at the famous troupe of aerialists. Billed as "one of the fastest and most sensational trapeze acts," siblings Eddie and Jennie Ward had started their dynasty in 1900. They were employed by many circuses, Ringling Brothers included, and probably this is how Billie crossed paths with them.

A self-taught performer, Eddie opened a school for boys and girls who wanted to learn the art of flying. By 1926 it was considered the best institution of its kind. Eddie and his sister learned the trapeze as children in their backyard in Bloomfield, Illinois, in order to help support their mother. Jennie was said to have exacting standards, a good trait in a profession where one mistake could be fatal.

For their thrilling double trapeze act, The Flying Wards performed without a safety net, with nothing but trust and skill to keep them from crashing to an almost certain death. In 1918, the Hammond Circus was traveling by train with twenty-six cars full of animals, performers, and equipment, including the Wards. It was pre-dawn when the train stopped in Indiana. The engineer in a following train had fallen asleep, and it plowed mercilessly into the Hammond cars at full speed. The trains burst into flames.

Eighty-six people died, Jennie among them. She was only twenty-eight years old. And pregnant.

By the time Billie found her way to the Wards, Jennie was gone, but not her legacy of precise and exact training.

Eddie believed the only thing needed to be an aerialist was muscle control and an ability to judge the distance from catcher to thrower. It took four years to make a flier, so it's uncertain as to what Billie would have been doing with the Wards besides training.

Billie traveled with the Wards to New York, where they parted ways.

By 1925, when she was twenty-one, there was an item in a Wisconsin paper about a party that featured child dancers. Billie Beck is listed as entertaining at the Riverview Country Club along with other dancers of the studio of Mildred Hagerty of Green Bay.

With work being sporadic, the hard years were just beginning for Billie, which would force her to dig deep within herself. "I did go broke, but I didn't care," she later recalled. "I did go hungry and I didn't mind." She was pursuing something, determined at all costs to succeed.

She might have looked like the era's ideal of a helpless female with blonde curls and blue eyes, but she was smart as a whip and unafraid. In the coming years she would have many experiences; she would toughen. Circumstances would sharpen her tongue. She cursed like a sailor. But she also became flexible, open to opportunity.

She believed women—and she in particular—could do anything. She would become unstoppable.

FIVE

FRANCES YVONNE BACON WAS REARED BY A MOTHER BOTH YOUNG enough to call herself "sister" and desperate enough to foist her frustrated dreams onto her daughter. Or maybe she wanted to fulfill her dreams alongside her daughter.

Throughout the years Yvonne stated she turned up in New York as a model's artist, posing nude at the tender age of thirteen. It is a chilling thought. It could not have been a young girl's own idea to pose nude for a group of strangers, most likely men. Maybe she posed alongside Charmion, or Charmion took a back seat and made available her nubile young child. (Charmion would be accused of worse in later years.)

Before Yvonne danced onto any known stage, in 1923 she won a scholarship to the Albertina Rasch Dance School in Manhattan, though she always claimed she had no formal dance training, she was just a natural-born genius of grace and dexterity.

Albertina Rasch was a Vienna-born ballerina, and her type of dancing was known as "simple," with an "emphasis on" costumes. Another fourteen-year-old who won a Rasch scholarship remembered Albertina as a "terror who would hit a student with a stick." Not too many years down the road, Yvonne would adopt her own simple dance, and it could be said she placed an emphasis on her nonexistent costume.

Called "Madame" by her students, Rasch mixed "high and low," from en pointe to jazz styles. She choreographed for George White and his *Scandals* and for the king of the Broadway revues, Florenz Ziegfeld. Her troupe of young girls would make their way across the Atlantic to Paris and the Moulin Rouge. (Sally Rand's brother Hal would dance with one of her troupes.)

Rasch would be an important connection for Yvonne. Madame would remain a significant figure on Broadway throughout the 1940s. Being her student would have opened doors.

SIX

THOUGH SHE ISN'T LISTED IN THE OFFICIAL CAST, TWENTY-TWO-year-old Billie claimed she was a Beauty Contestant in Ziegfeld's *Follies of 1922* on Broadway. The show ran for a little over a year, and perhaps she stayed for a short time, but any association with Ziegfeld had cachet, and she loved to remind reporters she had worked for Ziegfeld.

Ziegfeld's *Follies* was a magnet for an ambitious dancer like Billie, and his *Midnight Frolics*, which performed on the rooftop of the New Amsterdam Theatre, included acrobats from Ringling Brothers. The rose and green–colored rooftop nightclub was lush, tropical, and popular during the summer months in pre-air-conditioned times.

A large stage with a proscenium stretched thirty-four feet in width. An upper tier of box seats was suspended by iron braces. The terrace was filled with potted plants underneath evening skies. There was a glass runway; tables and chairs surrounded the dance floor.

One side of the theatre had glass windows that opened, letting in fresh air.

Billie's need to soar, not just metaphorically but literally, led her into an exciting new hobby.

One of her early boyfriends was "Houston Allred," probably Samuel Houston Allred, Jr., from a wealthy Texas family, who introduced her to his buddy Charles Lindbergh. Lindbergh would become a boyfriend, and at least by 1923 Billie had learned to fly planes. It was no small accomplishment to be a female pilot at the time. Billie received her transport pilot's license, the highest certificate available, meaning she was pilot in command on scheduled air carriers.

She thought nothing of flying herself to gigs. "It's the quickest, cleanest and most comfortable mode of travel." In an era of cinders and dust and slow-moving trains, she was right. "The time will come . . . when it will be no more distinction for a woman to pilot a plane than for her to be a good chauffeur." (By 1934 she would have 240 hours of flying under her belt.)

Romance didn't *seem* to figure prominently in these years. Though she would have various affairs, some discreet, others not so, she did not define herself through a lover and would make little mention of them over the years.

By 1923 Billie was working in the Gus Edwards Revue as a model, often in a bathing suit. As a young boy, the German-born Gus Edwards had sung from the balconies of burlesque houses. At seventeen he wrote his first hit song, "All I Want Is My Black Baby Back." He would go on to co-write many classic songs including "By the Light of the Silvery Moon."

With a partner he formed the "School Boys and Girls" touring company and would discover and nurture acts such as the Marx Brothers, Ray Bolger, Eddie Cantor, future *The Sound of Music* actress Eleanor Parker, Walter Winchell, and Helen Beck (switching again from Billie). The Paramount film *The Star Maker* with Bing Crosby was based on Edwards's career exploiting young talent.

Billie truly came alive on stage, feeling it was her home. It would be her deepest desire to become a great dramatic stage actress.

When the tour finished, she returned to Chicago and began posing (nude or nearly so) at the Chicago Art Institute. She also danced semi-nude at Ernie Young's Marigold Gardens, a dance hall and outdoor beer garden. These were learning experiences; while not failures, they were certainly not successes, dwelling in the shadow world of legitimate entertainment. She was mostly part of an anonymous fragment of the chorus. She would take a bit of this and a bit of that from each experience, always with an I-can attitude, searching for her moment.

She would rejoin the Gus Edwards Company, but it was again short-lived. This time when the company disbanded, it left her alone in New York.

She wandered hungry on the streets. In front of a large glass window she watched a couple dining inside a restaurant. Her stomach growled. After waiting for them to finish eating, she snuck in and took food from abandoned plates. It would not be the only time.

She was desperate. Put out of her four-dollar-a-week room, she slept in Central Park. Every day seemed to bring a new low point.

It was said she got a break dancing to *Scherezade* with Lew Leslie and the Blackbirds, a (mostly) African American revue on Broadway with Ethel Waters, Cab Calloway, and Bill "Bo Jangles" Robinson. She would remain a friend and admirer of Robinson. The show traveled to California, and so would she.

After a brief stint in Los Angeles, Billie returned to the East Coast with the Will Seabury Repertory Theatre Company. Seabury was a producer of the low-budget revue and would never have the stature of a Ziegfeld or a Shubert. He managed vaudeville acts, heavy on beauties who could dance. Billie was asked to step out of her shoes, unroll her stockings, and show her feet. The producer with the apparent foot fetish was looking for "artistic feet." He chose five girls, including Billie and Marian Hart. It must be assumed they both had the necessary "long narrow feet" he coveted. She was another anonymous body in the show, one of the "stepping beauties." It would not be enough for Billie. Later she would aggrandize her involvement, saying she had studied Chekov and Ibsen.

The jovial Seabury booked his company in Los Angeles. On board the train, the company smoke and drank and gossiped and thrilled at the opportunity to go to Hollywood. No doubt Seabury, or at least his actors, hoped they could procure work in motion pictures, which by now were doing a booming business.

A lifelong chain smoker, Billie talked incessantly (she had an opinion about everything) with a cigarette either bobbing out of her mouth or between her fingers. She usually pinched cigarettes from others.

Billie became a "sorta protégé" to Seabury. She would see he was a master manipulator of public relations. He was married to a showgirl in 1922, but she divorced him the following year because he could not stay faithful. He married his next showgirl, actress Margaret Irving, in 1923—in fact, married her so often, and in so many states, to prevent future problems should they plan to divorce. Which they would in four short years when he was "charged with domestic indiscretion."

The *Los Angeles Times* featured Billie and Marian Hart as "aviation fanettes" who flew themselves to gigs in their own plane.

After performing just one week in Los Angeles, Seabury fell ill (or used that as an excuse) and disbanded his company.

Billie was on her own again. Nothing ever seemed to work out.

Billie met Nils T. Granlund, or "N.T.G.," a burgeoning showman who would have a long career in the theatre. Granny, as he was known to the multitude of showgirls he discovered, took pity on the "hard luck" beauty and tried to help her find her footing in Hollywood. In the heat of a Los Angeles summer Billie had nothing but a heavy winter outfit. Granny bought her a silk dress, shoes, and a hat. All in white. She had her pride and would not accept the clothes as a gift, instead offering her services for three club dates.

Around this time she hooked up with Harry Richman, singer and cad about town, who would write a self-aggrandizing biography bragging about the multitude of showgirls, actresses, and socialites he bedded. He was an alcoholic, misogynist blowhard who had a fantastically successful career with hit films such as *Puttin' on the Ritz*.

Richman, who would breeze through his own fortune, slept with—according to him—every showgirl he ever looked at, and had legitimately helped many beauties' careers, including Joan Crawford's. When Billie was a dancer at the Winter Garden in New York, he convinced his horny buddy Joseph Schenck (who later ran 20th Century Fox) to give her a chance in Hollywood.

If Harry didn't accomplish the deed, he would have at least attempted to seduce Billie. Harry wrote that he originally met her when she was sixteen (he probably thought her older) and frolicking for attention on Brighton Beach.

With the help of her powerful friends, Billie would finally start to get somewhere.

SEVEN

IT WAS THE ROARING TWENTIES AND WOMEN WERE THROWING off the shackles of corsets and long hems. Cutting hair, taking up tobacco and cocktails, fighting for their right to vote, and thumbing their nose at a society that had kept them down.

Between 1924 and 1925, thirty-year-old Charmion and fourteen-year-old Yvonne left America for what Charmion hoped were greener pastures, possibly Paris. Though she was still a young woman, Charmion had to feel desperate; she was old for a performer, dancers especially. Since she had turned her back on at least three husbands, most likely she remained solely responsible, financially, for her daughter.

Not that she ever treated Yvonne like a daughter. Deprived of the right to call her mother, Yvonne had to act like her contemporary. It can only be imagined what else she was made to do to perpetuate her "sister's" obsession with youth. There was also the explanation of the absence of parents.

Charmion was probably looking for a new husband. If she wasn't interested in a suitor for herself, she pushed Faith into the man's arms, no matter his age, hoping to perpetuate a match. At some point Charmion fed Faith a steady diet of pills: to keep her going, to put her to sleep, to control her. The sleeping pills would eventually turn her into an insomniac. It was not an unusual custom at the time.

The trip was quick, maybe they explored employment, perhaps Yvonne danced with the Rasch troupe or some other dancers. Possibly they made connections and secured an engagement for the future. Whatever the case, they were back in New York in early 1925. Yvonne was cast as part of the ensemble in the musical *Bringing Up Father*, based on a popular comic strip, which opened at the Garrick on March 30. She was disappointed when the unpopular production closed April 18.

It would be natural for Charm to assume management for the underage Yvonne. Charm seized her "salary, and she never got money of her own. Whatever she needed, Cheri bought for her."

The Roaring Twenties were also the pinnacle of the showgirl era—a coveted, iconic image sought by young girls still in school, and oftentimes by their mothers who had missed their opportunity to stand on stage and be admired simply for being beautiful.

Showgirls were sought, hired, prized, and praised for the perfection of their figures. Barely dressed, impeccably made-up, exalted in their heavenly stature usually parading down a grand staircase, at least in a Ziegfeld show, elaborately beaded and feathered. They were considered the ultimate prize for a man and a role model for the women who attended the nightly revues, parading through gilded lobbies in their own more modest finery.

At the time the girls—and they were always called "girls"—were seen as modern, unafraid to flaunt breasts, make money, and exhibit themselves to the world in all their perfection.

The cult of the showgirl as gold digger—frivolous and out all night, leading a glamorous Zeldian existence (as in every flapper's role model, Zelda Fitzgerald), pursued by handsome young men in top hat and tails, escorted to the finest restaurants in chauffeured Rolls-Royces—filled the newspapers with their exploits and those of their admirers.

For others it was not only an admirable aspiration but a lucrative one, with possible fringe benefits that could include a husband and home. It was something Charm wanted. And if she couldn't have it for herself, she would have it for Yvonne.

On Broadway the revue, with its glorious or gaudy assembly of gorgeous young girls, was all the rage. "The Revue is one Broadway tradition that was great." They were humorous spectacles, parts "variety, vaudeville, minstrelsy, and burlesque."

It was upscale, prestigious entertainment—never mind the naysayers who complained about the naked girls—perfected in presentation by producer Florenz Ziegfeld, who crammed his stages with an abundance of showgirls. Sometimes a hundred thigh-showing, lace-wearing lasses.

Ziegfeld polished the revue, elevated it, and legitimized it (at least according to the mighty Ziegfeld publicity machine) so that by the 1920s the revue was a respectable, naughty extravaganza. Shows were many hours long; the vast stages were jammed with the most beautiful girls in the world, parading and posing in rhinestones and pearls, wearing enormous headpieces of feathers, silk, and jewels.

The reverence for these showgirls cannot be overstated. They were coveted birds of paradise. Myth and archetype. To be one carried special stature. To be chosen amongst thousands "carried a renown" like nothing that compares today. Showgirls were prized and prizes. These mannequins of the stage merely had to exist and the world fell at their feet.

It was a time and a place where these professional beauties were glorified and idolized for their looks alone. If they had the physicality of a Diana or the bearing of a Venus, their path was assured. Beauty set them apart from the ordinary. Beauty gave these young girls who poured into New York, often with hungry mothers in tow, an opportunity they would not otherwise have had.

Flawless of face and figure, filled with grace and charm, they followed a formula on stage and off. Talent was not expected. Beauty and charm was enough to carry a career.

"Scions of New York's most distinguished families" made their way to the showgirls' dressing rooms with notes and candies. Jewels were casually mixed in with bouquets of flowers and presented to the girls backstage.

It would be with great determination that Yvonne—and later Billie—would make their mark amongst this sometimes indistinguishable group of girls. They would both attempt to leap across the dark side of being a showgirl and instead use the opportunity it afforded them to their advantage.

Part

TWO

EIGHT

WHEN *ARTISTS AND MODELS* PREMIERED AT THE WINTER GARDEN in New York in 1925, women in the audience were wearing long blouses "adorned with collars, and cuffed sleeves, with two-tiered skirts." There would be nowhere near as much clothing on the stage.

The flapper brought a new body type to be shown. "The girls started getting slimmer, younger, and nuder"—perfect for the entry of Yvonne, who was cast in the show.

J. J. Shubert was credited for staging the entire production. One of three producing brothers, it was J.J. who had added a runway (nicknamed the "Bridge of Thighs") to the Winter Garden back in 1912.

Levi (later Lee), Sam, and Jacob (later J.J.) Shubert were Polish-born and three of seven siblings. The family immigrated to America with their alcoholic father. The three brothers would become legendary theatre owners, managers, and producers (often one and the same thing). The brothers were canny, barely educated, competitive, ladies'

men, in the right place at the right time to make—and change—
the girlie business. They often fought, which resulted in the brothers
communicating through third parties.

The brothers began producing in 1901, with over a dozen theatres
when Sam was fatally injured in a train wreck around the age of
thirty, leaving the brothers' burgeoning empire in the hands of the
detail-oriented Lee. J.J., an egotist and hothead, would eventually be
based in Chicago.

Onto the unusually large stage of the Winter Garden Theatre
Yvonne Bacon tiptoed. She is listed in several scenes and as one of
the models along with eighteen others, below an equal number of
dancing girls and an equal number of Gertrude Hoffman Girls. (The
dancing was choreographed by Gertrude Hoffman.) Yvonne was
probably in one of the bathing suits designed by Erté and Barbier
of Paris. George Barbier was a well-known and respected French
illustrator.

Anticipation was high, as the 1924 version of *Artists and Models*
had proven to be "more daring and vulgar than last year's."

No doubt this version would be even more risqué. The show
opened on a rainy night and ran a mind-numbing six hours. At four
dollars a ticket, there were no vacant seats with an additional 400
standing. It was a huge success and ran fifty weeks, hailed as a "sophisticated revue," "one of the best" ever produced by the Shuberts.
The audience loved the showgirls who "show everything." Nothing
new for the Shuberts, who had been the first to feature topless and
naked women.

The ubiquitous nudity in revues is what made them so extremely
popular with the sophisticates. Producers like the Shuberts knew it
drove hundreds into the theatre. *Artists and Models* might have been
"weak on content but lavish" in production value and that's what the
audience wanted. Glamour, froth, and fun.

The titillating spectacles were thought to be a rip-off of Earl Carroll's *Vanities* and Ziegfeld's *Follies*. Along with George White, all were competing for the lion's share of the ticket buyers, all trying to outdo the other with more girls, less clothes, more elaborate gowns, and funnier comedians. Audiences expected to be wowed and they were.

The men running the theatres were territorial and ruthless. Shubert hated Ziegfeld, supposedly after Flo reneged on a deal to permit Shubert to star his protégée Anna Held. The producers frequently dangled large salaries to entice key talent away from the other; it was constant filching of the prettiest girls.

Amongst the *Follies*, *Artists and Models*, *Scandals*, and *Vanities*, plus dozens more, the look and format was not dissimilar. Seemingly the only thing producers could do to beat the competition was push the nudity.

Theatres were giant gilded aviaries with their many exotic birds on display. Stars nestled in individual dressing rooms, while the showgirls shared an open room, gossiping under bright lights.

A receptionist in the alley screened guests before entry. There was a powder room where girls whitened their bodies before going on stage. The '20s saw the popularity of suntanning, but on stage a pristine, fair body was coveted. Giant safes held the girls' jewels given as tokens of admiration from rich strangers. An icebox preserved pricey orchids. Sloping walkways were built to save energy running up and down from dressing room to stage. Some theatres even had a full beauty parlor, gymnasium equipment, and a doctor on call.

Was fifteen-year-old Yvonne ready for the showgirl life? It was one of hustle, rehearsal, and competition.

Her day probably started with "breakfast in some chain rest or cafeteria," then dashing to the subway or tram to make rehearsal, probably accompanied by her mother. Was Yvonne ever alone? It is doubtful.

Explained one showgirl: "My time does not belong to me." Her day was filled with rehearsing, meeting people, appointments with photographers and costumers and dressmakers. Then a dash home, be it apartment or hotel, a brief rest, and then off to the theatre. She never ate prior to the show. It was near midnight when, hungry and exhausted, she was allowed a peck at a light supper before bed.

The showgirl had to "make hay while the sun shines." It was logical to hope she "jumps to some small part in a musical comedy" that would make her a star. Hollywood was jammed with former showgirls, including Barbara Stanwyck and Paulette Goddard.

To think, just a few years earlier the life had been substantially more difficult. Rehearsals didn't even pay. "A girl had to train for weeks and weeks, and then stood a slim chance of getting a job." There were multiple expenses. "Many of the girls had to buy the clothes they wore on the stage." They were oftentimes broke and could only hope for spare change from a stage door johnny to help keep them fed and rent paid.

Some joked that the reality of a romance with a showgirl was unsavory. They were often not "pleasant to kiss" as they kept their figures and pocketbooks by munching on cheap loaves of bread, pickles, and pickled onion.

The young sparrows crammed twenty-five to a room, wiggling in and out of costumes, swiping makeup. "Not very hygienic, but we have to slap so much of the stuff on that it's impossible to afford the cost of keeping your cosmetic bag full." So they stole from each other. The lighting was bad. It was either too hot or too cold. Rivalries existed that kept some sporting scratches.

But the girls were young and full of life and strong enough to maintain the pace with the benefit of friendships and laughter.

Yvonne was the exception, under the eagle eye of a mother who made sure Yvonne was isolated and dependent on her. Yvonne built a mostly impenetrable wall few could break through.

Artists and Models turned out to be a success, running almost an entire year. For Yvonne the tide had finally turned.

NINE

BILLIE'S NAME AND FACE APPEARED IN THE PAPERS FOR JUST about anything. Like a jack-of-all-trades she threw herself into anything that might get her hired (including ice skating), explaining, "a girl trying to break into pictures has to think of everything."

She said being an "extra in Hollywood is like a man on a raft in mid-ocean." And she wasn't going down with the ship. "If you're not noticed—you're sunk!"

Her dance instructor Ernest Belcher held her horizontal in his arms for photographers, giving her a lift above the other blonde blue-eyed starlets seen hustling to appointments down Hollywood Boulevard.

Belcher would be remembered as the father of actress/dancer Marge Champion. He taught son-in-law Gower Champion and was considered one of the most important dance teachers of his time, coaching many young starlets such as Cyd Charisse, Shirley Temple, and Betty Grable, and no doubt believed in Billie's potential.

Billie Beck signed a contract as a "soubrette" (a coy and some-times sexually aggressive stock character) for Harry Carroll's *Pickings* at the Orange Grove Theatre, posing in another full ballet skirt and backless dress.

She donned boxing gloves and high heels to demonstrate the "art of self-defense" for photographers, professing boxing kept her fit and trim.

Then a break. Billie was "picked from the surf" by film director Mack Sennett, or one of his scouts. A winning figure in a bathing suit, she had been doing high-dive stunts when she was spotted. The director needed someone to do a fifteen-foot dive, and Bil-lie sure could use the money. He would pay fifteen dollars. She agreed.

Mack Sennett filmed his slapstick comedies in Echo Park (Edendale at the time). Doing stunts for Sennett lent credence to her claim she worked in the circus. The Flying Wards were known for their daring dives, which Billie had no problem doing. She was also winsome and likeable, lucky to be starting her film career with the man who had nurtured Gloria Swanson, Charlie Chaplin, and Mabel Normand. She would work in several of his shorts, uncred-ited, but at least it paid for dinner.

In those days, as now, actors went from gig to gig, scraping a living even if they couldn't rent rooms. It was still the days of signs warning NO ACTORS ALLOWED. It would be some years before acting was considered a respectable profession.

She was cast in a couple films with director (and Sennett rival) Hal Roach, whose self-named studios were in Culver City. But it did nothing for her career, though she did pose with a lion (presumably live, though impossible to tell in photos) while wearing a long black wig and a skimpy costume.

Working for Sennett meant something, as nearly half of those he nurtured led directly to the Cecil B. DeMille "school where they rode directly to stardom under the insurgent producer's coaching and favor."

It was no surprise that Billie caught the eye of Cecil B. DeMille. A former actor, DeMille was enjoying directorial success in silents. His love of authority—his own—and hard work pushed his actors to take physical risks. He was a well-suited teacher to an athletic, ambitious Billie, who not only took physical risks but was a tireless workaholic.

DeMille had created an iconic image of himself as autocratic director in jodhpurs and megaphone. He made himself distinctive, and she would take note of the idiosyncrasies.

DeMille called Billie "the most beautiful girl in America" and put her under contract in 1925. She had a spark and spunk and a twinkle in her eyes with dimples to match. It was said Billie had "the figure of Venus and the mind of Minerva" with her "youthful spirit and her blonde beauty, and . . . personality that will get on in the world."

But the first thing to go was her name. There are two stories (as there always would be); the first, DeMille thought she looked more like a Sally. As for a last name, spotting a Rand McNally World Atlas he exclaimed, "That's it!" She was relieved he hadn't chosen "Sally McNally."

The other story Sally told was that *she* picked Sally because she thought the large "S" would look good in lights on a marquee, which is not unbelievable as she had been dreaming about her name in lights for so long.

Lonely, the newly christened Sally Rand wrote long letters to her mother and brother back home in Kansas City. Her missives took on an adoring tone, sharing the fragrance of flowering orange groves, the sound of big cars cruising down wide boulevards, not to mention all the opportunity springing up in Hollywoodland. The big movies that year were *The Big Parade* (starring John Gilbert), *Ben-Hur* (directed by Fred Niblo), and Charlie Chaplin's *The Gold Rush*. Opportunity and happiness seemed to be around every corner.

When not making movies, there were concerts to attend at the four-year-old Hollywood Bowl under twinkling stars, or loud and raucous nightly boxing matches, or perhaps a twisting drive in the hills along Mulholland Highway. Los Angeles was growing with its first million residents, most of who seemed to be making—or wanting to make—movies. If a movie star wasn't spotted hanging at every drug store, all the wannabe talent was.

In 1925 Sally's father was living in New York and married to his French woman with a two-year-old son and a newborn. They would have five sons total. Billie kept in contact with her father as best as possible. What the former Army man thought of a daughter out in Hollywood is easy to imagine. Despite her running away, family would remain of utmost importance to Sally.

She rented rooms in Glendora, east of downtown Los Angeles near Azusa, the location of many early films. She fell in love with "the luxuriant semi-tropical growth" in the valley. Orange blossoms perfumed the air, the weather was balmy.

Sally spent her time as many starlets of her day did, posing for ads such as canned milk or The Bootery, wearing "blonde kid trimmed with cocoa kid appliqué" slippers. In September she appeared in the "Southern California Forward" beauty pageant, chosen "to occupy positions in the spotlight of beauty." Sally smiled tirelessly for the cameras. For opportunity.

DeMille cast her in *Braveheart* with heartthrob Rod La Rocque. The diminutive Sally posed in an elaborate headdress, attempting to kick the top hat out of 6-foot-3-inch La Rocque's hand. Though she was nearly two feet shorter, her agile kick was spot-on. They would be reteamed for his film *Red Dice*.

All the while, DeMille's publicity director was carefully clipping Sally's consistent press. She made the cover of *Movie Monthly* looking like the modern flapper that she was, with short bobbed blonde curls peeking from underneath a cloche hat.

Like other flappers she was an expert at the Charleston and performed at the Venice Ballroom, hailed as the "greatest exponent of the Charleston in America." A small bit of hyperbole.

Looking especially fetching in an old-fashioned gown down to the ankle, Sally saw newspapers printing a song written about her entitled "Study of Sally Rand."

Sweet Sally Rand, the mischief in your eye
Was roused, I swear, by some divine romance—
Never by just a ballroom partner's glance!
Yet, Sally Rand, you poise as if to fly
In young alarm from possible mischance.

Her 1925 film credits would include *The Dressmaker from Paris*, playing a Fifth Avenue model, where she did little more than parade and dance in a breathtaking gown of multi-layered pink tulle, her hair in "Nell Brinkley curls." The film, starring silent actress Leatrice Joy and directed by Paul Bern, has sadly been lost. When *The Dressmaker* aired, Sally appeared in theatres before the film, modeling gowns worn in the movie. She also began a long affair with Bern.

Born Paul Levy, he was from Germany, not particularly attractive—at all—a director and film supervisor. Slight but cultured, he had dozens of affairs with the most gorgeous women in Hollywood. Former showgirl Joan Crawford, known to sleep her way to the top, had an affair with Bern years before he married Jean Harlow in 1932.

Bern would unexpectedly take his own life after a misunderstanding with Harlow. Many claimed he was impotent and humiliated after trying to make love to his new wife. Sally didn't buy it. Vehemently denying he would commit suicide, she scoffed at the rumors he was impotent. "I know for a fact he wasn't impotent." She would treasure a small compact he had given her.

She was included in a list of names that meant solid box office to exhibitors, when her name clearly did not. But she had the backing of DeMille and possibly Bern. More uncredited parts as a maid, a dancer, and a tourist came in 1926.

She was one of three actresses at the first-ever California Maid Exposition, a weeklong affair held at the Shrine Auditorium. Posing in a dark wig as a Spanish exotic with knife and elaborate hairstyle, Sally danced as part of the entertainment.

For two years she toiled in nothing parts and earned columns of publicity doing what she was told, appearing in cheesecake photos, one alongside of Jack Dempsey while she stood on stilts. She took small parts in features and shorts, mostly uncredited.

She also received her first negative publicity. Dancing for some "butter-and-egg" men, probably at a convention, Sally was doing the Charleston in a "one-piece costume" that brought condemnation by a church group who "claim she compromised the moral standing of Santa Ana business men."

For her jobs dancing the Charleston for businessmen she was billed as a "former Follies Girl." Then it was another film, *Sunny Side Up* starring Vera Reynolds, where Sally appeared as a short-skirted dancer.

Newspapers caught her leaping in the air in a one-piece dance suit with long flowing scarf, announcing "the dance of the butterfly" for a pageant. She danced for a children's event at the Los Angeles Monica Ballroom, off the current Santa Monica pier. It was the largest dance hall on the West Coast, allowing for 5,000 dancers to hoof across the wooden floors. Sally played hostess to a free event for those fourteen and under. Work, but disheartening.

She refueled with a visit to her mother's home in Kansas City while appearing at local theatres. It was announced she was being borrowed for Frances Marion's film *Paris at Midnight*. If she was in the Balzac adapted story, she once again was uncredited.

She filmed *The Last Frontier*, a post–Civil War western starring future Hopalong Cassidy William Boyd, and *Night of Love*, a Ronald Coleman film. Sally played a Gypsy dancer. There was a part in *Getting Gertie's Garter* starring Marie Prevost, a former Sennett Bathing Beauty, just years before Prevost's star faded and she died an alcoholic at age thirty-eight. To promote the film Sally posed for photographers looking out of place in an oriental costume with a long dark wig.

Between film assignments Sally headlined with vaudeville star Eddie Cantor for a week at the Orpheum, anything to get her name and face in front of an audience.

And then a break.

Along with twelve other aspiring starlets, she had been named a Baby Star by the Western Associated Motion Picture Advertisers. WAMPAS girls were deemed to have the best shot of becoming full-fledged movie stars. "The finger of destiny points to the most beautiful girls." Former WAMPAS Baby Stars included Clara Bow, Ginger Rogers, Fay Wray, Gloria Stuart, and Joan Crawford.

As a WAMPAS Baby Star, twenty-three-year-old Sally was promised, and given, massive amounts of publicity and a three-year contract in vaudeville (rather strange for someone touted as having a future in films).

Huge arc lights cut through the black night. Rain threatened to drench the tuxedos and silk gowns of the movie stars alighting from the Bugattis, Hispano-Suizas, and Rolls-Royces that lined Wilshire Boulevard in front of the Ambassador Hotel. The luxurious hotel sat on twenty-three acres and was just six years old. Inside was the vast and glamorous Coconut Grove nightclub with soaring papier-mâché palm trees with fake monkeys clinging to the fronds. From the high ceilings, faux stars twinkled down on a different kind of star. It was

Hollywood's nightly playground, with movie stars jamming the dance floor.

February 17, 1929, three thousands guests along with those unfortunates who couldn't get a ticket clogged the streets. There was pushing and elbowing to get into the lobby, with more bodies spilling down hallways looking to catch a famous face like Gloria Swanson or Anna May Wong in beaded gowns and feathered headbands. Hollywood royalty Douglas Fairbanks, Mary Pickford, and lovely Constance Talmadge were expected to attend. For ten dollars mere mortals could give the thirteen Baby Stars the once-over, though it was said demand was so high that tickets were selling at twenty-five dollars months before. (Ultimately $33,000 would be raised that night.)

The ballroom was decorated with "varied, colored striped buntings," lights suspended from them. In the middle of the room hung a "mirror-faceted sphere that turned and caught the rainbow-colored lights shooting across the dance floor." The stage had been swathed in festive gold and silver fabric for the occasion.

The master of ceremonies was director Fred Niblo. Niblo's recent success *The Temptress* had starred a luminous twenty-one-year-old Greta Garbo.

It was a marathon of a show, not uncommon at the time, when there was no rush home to watch a favorite television show or listen to a serial on the radio. There was no such thing.

Douglas Fairbanks played a badminton-like game, Eddie Cantor performed, the Duncan sisters sang, Babe Ruth made an appearance, Buster Keaton and Norma and Constance Talmadge performed a skit. Joan Crawford led a black bottom dance contest. Joan was always showing up for dance contests, and very often brought home the trophy. Sultry movie star Dolores del Rio preened in her glittery jewels. And then the introduction of the thirteen starlets.

One by one the girls stepped on stage through a silver star-shaped frame where a tiny pink and gold fairy held a wand. Niblo gave each girl a bouquet of flowers, and the audience scrutinized and cheered. It was an auspicious presentation for the young, gorgeous beauties filled with dreams of mansions and movie premieres. There was no reason not to believe their future careers were as golden as the audience surrounding them.

Over the clink of glasses and silverware, laughter and chatter, in front of hundreds of guests, Sally won a "baby blue evening wrap," her prize for selling the most tickets to the ball. It was a virtual cape made of ostrich feathers.

Relentlessly ambitious, hardworking, and smarter than most, Sally stood out. She wore a long white skirt and satin bodice. It was not particularly flattering, and she was criticized for being "over dressed" (ironically, the last time *that* would be said about her).

Noted for her "striking beauty," Sally danced for the crowd who included Jack Dempsey and Colleen Moore. For Sally the night was sweet reward for the years of struggle and identity-searching that had come before.

She hoped the event would lead to even more time in front of a camera, posing and smiling.

Sally had a romance on screen with Hoot Gibson, in his film *Galloping Fury*. Hoot remained a friend, as did many of the silent stars including Wallace Beery.

She was hustling from one end of Hollywood to the other, "flying from town to town." It was endless promotion. Later she would admit her road to success was not "short and smooth." It was also still years in the future.

Arrested in 1933, Sally would intimate it was her first time. But in July of 1927 a warrant had been issued for her arrest. She had been caught driving without an operator's card and failed to appear for the court hearing. There was also a small-claims action for failing to pay a dressmaker bill.

It was just a precursor to how the rest of her life would be. Hustle and harassment. She would learn to take it in stride.

Sally was cast as a slave to Mary Magdalene in DeMille's epic *The King of Kings*. She was having an affair with English actor H. B. Warner, who was playing Jesus Christ. (Warner is best remembered today as the cranky druggist in *It's a Wonderful Life*, who smacks the young Jimmy Stewart character in the ear.) Because of the subject of the film, and not wanting to take any chances on potential scandals, DeMille had everyone sign agreements of good behavior. Warner, fifty-two at the time, was suffering from a serious drinking problem and might have been hungover when he and girlfriend Sally arrived late to the set. DeMille, in no mood for it, shouted through his megaphone for all to hear, "Miss Rand, leave my Jesus Christ alone! If you must screw someone, screw Pontius Pilate."

Still more uninspired roles followed. In *Nameless Men* she was an "entertainer" in a nightclub, doing "intricate dance steps" (it sounded like her only scene); *Love Lorn, Crashing Through*, and a brief moment in the drama *A Woman Against the World* wearing teeny black lingerie. None were breakout movies, or memorable roles.

It is interesting to note that in July of 1928 Sally was in the silent film *Golf Widows*, playing a small role for Columbia Pictures. Hollywood and nearby Tijuana were the background about a pair of "golf widows" who were neglected by their husbands for the sport. One of the "widows," because of a misunderstanding, "is forced to enact a modern Lady Godiva role and go home in overalls." It would be the first mention of the noblewoman who would change Sally's career in a few short years.

Sally was pretty, she was working, she was multi-talented, she was a dime a dozen. There was nothing to set her apart from the other wide-eyed hopefuls crawling over the studio backlots looking for work.

So much for being a WAMPAS Baby Star. She had spent the year as "another mere dancing girl in the divertissement which precedes the showing of a picture." She continued to be pushed on the public. It was announced she was "one of the most popular of the screen's ingénues." An exaggeration if ever there was one.

She did have an interesting part in *Heroes in Blue* that was more her speed. Doing her own stunts, she drove a fire truck through the streets of Los Angeles and jumped from a four-story building that was on fire. When the flames came too close, she leaped into the net below.

There was nothing Sally wouldn't do.

And then there was nothing for Sally to do.

Chapter

TEN

AS A YOUNG, CONVENT-EDUCATED GIRL IN SAN FRANCISCO, GER-
trude Hoffman (sometimes Hoffmann) began dancing in vaudeville.
After running away she met and married Polish-born composer and
conductor Max Hoffman when she was fifteen or sixteen, and gave
birth to a son a year later. She would be one of the first and only
women at the time who was a "rehearsal director." (The rehearsal
director was usually a dancer who took charge of rehearsals.)

In 1906 she was cast in Ziegfeld's *A Parisian Model*, dressed as
a man and dancing with Ziegfeld star (and his common-law wife)
Anna Held. Two years later Gertrude was performing as the first
Salome in what would become a staple on the burlesque stages (even
performed by the doomed Mata Hari in 1912). Her Dance of the
Seven Veils would be the impetus behind numerous arrests, causing
a great scandal and reams of life-giving publicity. Her dance and
flesh-revealing costume would be copied by many, but she was the

first. A less shocking but equally memorable performance was her white peacock dance (Sally Rand would have a white peacock dance in the film *The Sunset Murder Case*).

Hoffman was statuesque and dignified, sandy-haired and slender, and someone who considered herself a serious artist. An admirer of Isadora Duncan, she believed in the power of the female body. A health and water promoter, she wrote for newspapers, experimented with physical movement, acrobatics, and mimicry. The intense Hoffman introduced America to the Ballets Russes in 1911 with her newly formed company.

By her mid-forties she had become the manager and choreographer to a group of girls known as the Gertrude Hoffman Girls (GHG). They were athletic and acrobatic, performing circus-like routines in casual clothing. Her avant-garde choreography included synchronized fencing. The girls often dropped from the theatre rafters wrapped in ropes to swing over the heads of the stunned audience. She injected into her sold-out revues "the edgy, the queer, and the sexy." The girls "frequently stopped the show with their aerial feats and stunts." Like a water troupe, swimming through the air, while dancing the Charleston and climbing up trellises. It was breathtaking. Many of her girls were as young as thirteen.

She often shocked dancers when she told them they would be performing bare-breasted. When they protested she assured them, "You have nothing to be ashamed about." The GHG were cast in the 1925 *Artists and Models* revue along with fifteen-year-old Yvonne Bacon.

Though Yvonne was not singled out, the GHG were. *Variety* proclaimed they "make the show." The girls were a "bacchanale which is far more thrilling . . . altogether out of the ordinary." Each twirling, twisting girl seemed to execute her own wild stunt, but in truth all was meticulously choreographed. The company was "comely, agile, tireless . . . " and a sensation.

Yvonne and Gertrude Hoffman took notice of each other, because by the next year, Yvonne had become a coveted GHG, which is a testament to her talent. She would have been well-behaved and disciplined. Hoffman put up with no nonsense. Her girls were not allowed to run wild. They weren't sophisticated showgirls with a reputation as gold diggers and late-night champagne partiers.

While at the Winter Garden Theatre, Gertrude placed a sign that read, PLEASE DON'T ASK TO TAKE US OUT. WE DO NOT ENCOURAGE STAGE DOOR JOHNNIES.

The GHG were interested in dance, not shenanigans. They were nonsmokers and nondrinkers. A troupe of girls had recently returned from the Moulin Rouge in Paris, and Yvonne—and Charmion—perhaps saw this as an opportunity to return to Europe.

Gertrude had strong beliefs about the presentation a semi-nude body while dancing. "I never thought of my body when I was dancing. And if the body is all of me, then I am nothing at all." Yvonne would heartedly embrace the axiom.

Yvonne would be at the Winter Garden in *A Night in Paris* in 1926. She would have been no more than part of a troupe of girls on stage with the singer. Her featured moment was coming though.

At the Winter Garden the GHG were given good reviews, but there were complaints that the "nudes, nudes, nudes, and more nudes" was distracting. One reviewer claimed the numbers were actually ruined by all the flesh. The girls were topless, and most likely one of them was our Yvonne.

Yvonne would have blossomed working with the other GHG in long, prosperous runs over two seasons with *A Night in Paris* and *A Night in Spain*. They were typical, extravagant Shubert-produced revues. *A Night in Spain* also featured Spanish musician and band-leader Xavier Cugat.

Gertrude and the GHG were most likely Yvonne's conduit to Paris and the Casino de Paris, where she would thrive amongst alluring acts, elaborate costumes, and sophisticated performers.

The year 1926 was busy for Yvonne as she was at the Winter Garden in *The Great Temptations*. The show was noteworthy only for the Broadway debut of comedian Jack Benny, but it did give Yvonne six months of employment.

Though we know little of what Charm was up to, we do know the devastating results of her meddling. Yvonne was growing up to be insecure and egotistical, spoiled and innocent. Shy and timid, expected to keep her mother's secrets, she would have no lasting friendships. Others noted she seemed to live in her own reality.

Tales of horrific backstage mothers, usually single, frustrated performers themselves relying on a beautiful daughter for their security and future, were common. Many of the girls toured with their mothers. Charm declared herself Yvonne's manager and collected her money and, eventually, her daughter's gifts of jewelry from suitors, doling out what she deemed suitable.

Probably because of her association with Gertrude Hoffman, Yvonne would again seek greener pastures in Paris, performing on the same stage as a charismatic singer by the name of Maurice Chevalier. She would claim to be his *première danseuse*. And she was given special billing.

She possibly had two stints on stage with Chevalier. But she was at least with him in part of 1926 at the Casino de Paris (not to be confused with the New York theatre of the same name). Yvonne and Charmion could have met Chevalier in New York, as he had recently flopped badly on Broadway.

The Casino de Paris 1926–27 season presented *Paris*, a review starring Maurice Chevalier and featuring Yvonne Bacon and Valérie.

Ph. Gilbert René
Mlle BACON

A teenage Yvonne Bacon from the Casino de Paris

Valérie was none other than Charmion. They are billed in separate acts throughout the program. How Valérie managed to be on the stage can only be guessed at. The forty-five tableaux, split between two acts, was possibly Yvonne's first exposure to tableaux, an art form that would change her life.

ELEVEN

OUR SWEET SALLY WAS A HIT WITH NEWSPAPER EDITORS BECAUSE "of her ability to do all kinds of dances and athletic stunts," which made for lively photos. However, it was noted Sally's athletic legs were "too big" for Hollywood.

Across the former orange groves, movie stages were being outfitted for sound. In earthquake country momentous change was shaking worse than the summer of 1920, when a series of quakes frightened the city.

Actors with thick accents, or those who barely spoke English, were losing jobs while theatrical actors were being enticed to come west.

Sally would assert it was a sibilant "s"—along with an Ozark accent—that derailed her career. It might have, but in a few short years neither a lisp nor accent would be noticed after she learned to speak in a carefully cultivated manner from teacher and author Margaret Prendergast McLean.

In 1930 Madame Maria Ouspenskaya, a Russian actress and student of Konstantin Stanislavski, would open a dramatic school in Los Angeles, and McLean would teach speech to Madame's students. It would have been sometime after that when Sally found her way to McLean and better speech.

But in 1928, the movies were through with Sally. Sally returned to vaudeville, where an accent or lisp didn't matter. She at least felt seasoned after her years in Hollywood. Wanting to be the director of her own destiny, she hired a pair of dancers from Los Angeles, a brother-and-sister team named Fanchon and Marco, to perform with her. They set out on the road to captivate audiences with Sally's "wonderful personality" in the show *Sally and Hollywood* that capitalized on her exaggerated Hollywood fame.

There were about ten men on stage with Sally who did "a toe dance, and adagio fantasie." The "diminutive and attractive" Sally in her "dance and burlesque numbers" pleased the audience.

The introduction song "I Wonder What's Become of Sally" had to leave Sally wondering the same thing.

Variety praised Sally for her "good singing voice" and for being an "excellent dancer." She took out a large ad with her photo, thanking her team for the show, obviously intent on showing Hollywood what they were missing.

She didn't fare well on the East Coast, with *Variety* noting "for all of her shapeliness and pulchritude, although she is too much legs on the personality business, has not enough of the real variety entertainment to register indelibly."

Sally wrote her mother about the wonders of Glendora, an oasis of palm trees, gnarly oaks, and avocado trees snuggled in the foothills of Los Angeles County, provoking mother Nettie and brother Hal to set up home there in 1929. Hal would also change his name to Rand and seek fame and fortune in the movies.

Sally remained mostly on the road and soon returned to New

York. She tried out for shows, claimed to have a spot waiting for her in *George White's Scandals* as a chorus girl. Then the stock market crashed, which left her, and many others, without employment and on the street. She was broke and grateful to a fellow Fanchon and Marco dancer, Perk Lazelle, for lending her money. (Perk would later act with Joan Crawford in *Mildred Pierce* and remained a pal.)

Sally made her way with the financial help of her mother and new stepfather, which would be repaid a thousand times over in the coming years. Sally's forty-eight-year-old mother Nettie, still very much an attractive woman with light hair and dimples, married forty-two-year-old Ernest G. Kisling in March of '29, shortly after moving to Glendora. They had met on a blind date and would remain married for thirty-three years, setting up home on twenty acres of orange trees they referred to as "the ranch."

Ernest was a kind man, completely different from Sally's father William Beck. An easygoing man, he had been a former stagecoach driver, and though he "didn't say two words," Sally adored him, considering Ernest to be the father she needed and wanted.

TWELVE

LÉON VOLTERRA'S CASINO DE PARIS COULD LEGITIMATELY CLAIM to be more popular than the Folies Bergère or Moulin Rouge. Situated on the site of Folie-Villa—built by the decadent Duke of Richelieu for King Louis XV and his mistress, the amusing Madame de Pompadour—the music hall was huge and its revues became known for "monumental sets and spectacular transformation scenes."

The lobby was "majestic and sublime." Twenty columns supported a ceiling full of naked woman. A huge, glass-walled swimming pool could rise and occupy the entire stage.

Cosmopolitan audiences from around the world came in droves to eat and drink in over-the-top elegance, hoping some of the sophisticated eroticism would rub off.

Paris was in the midst of the *années folles* (the crazy years). Cafés along on the Rive Gauche were meeting places for the many artists exploring surrealism and joining the avant-garde movement. On the Right, cafés and nightclubs dominated with the syncopated strains of American jazz snapping and striking through the air. The entertainment, thanks in large part to American import Josephine Baker, was nude, erotic, and free of bourgeois morals.

Yvonne would have her biggest billing to date, featured in two Casino shows, *Paris to New York* and *Broadway to New York*.

Again Yvonne and Charmion as Valérie shared the stage, this time together. Presumably they were a sister act (all the rage), no doubt hoping to be as sensational as the highly popular Dolly Sisters. The adored Dolly Sisters danced in elaborate feather and rhinestoned costumes, spending gobs on their matching furs, tulle, and beads. They too had worked with Gertrude Hoffman and Flo Ziegfeld and were luminous stars Yvonne would have admired.

Yvonne Bacon and Valérie performed "Les Choux Rouges et Verts" (red and green cabbages) and "Le Black-Bottom" (a dance similar to the Charleston). They are listed several more times throughout the bill, with Valérie having three separate numbers.

The photograph in the playbill of seventeen-year-old "Mlle Bacon" demonstrates that she has not yet become skilled applying makeup. She is plain and her hair blonde.

The photo of "Mlle Valérie," photographed by the distinguished G. L. Manuel Frères, shows a pretty brunette, or dark blonde, with shiny lipstick and heavily made-up eyes. Charmion looks chic and polished, staring seductively at the camera. She is definitely the prettier of the two.

In the show was a troupe of Lilliputians, and instead of the GHG there were sixteen Casino Girls and sixteen Lawrence Tiller Girls, both hugely popular dance groups at the time. Amongst the large and varied cast, Valérie and Yvonne received special billing, not as big as the always daring and decadent Dolly Sisters, but *Variety* thought enough to mention them.

"There is a great deal of splendor with elaborate settings and costumes and there is all the nudity that the police regulations permit."

With about eighty-two girls in the cast, it was a "brilliant show" and the talk of the town.

Yvonne "showed herself naked." To the audience "she was a sensation as she gradually removed one bit of clothing after another."

In one of their numbers, the Dolly Sisters waved giant ostrich fans. Paris acts and the Dolly Sisters in particular were often swathed in supple ostrich feathers, as was Josephine Baker, who that same year was shaking her skirt of bananas at the Folies Bergère.

Valerie and Yvonne would have studied the Dolly Sisters as they swept on and off the stage in their towering headdresses. The elegant Dollys conducted themselves as if they were royalty. They lived life with no thought of tomorrow, a mantra Yvonne would blindly embrace.

To be in Paris in those years was the stuff of dreams. The surrealists—Magritte, André Breton, Dalí, Man Ray—were expanding the constraints of expression in their nightmarish and illogical art. Music fueled raging dances and furious nightlife. Evenings were frenetic and fast-paced, enhanced by strong liquor. Women were smoking, drinking cocktails, showing knees as they kicked rolled-stocking legs, pursuing high jinks amongst admiring Parisians.

Charmion and Yvonne must have been dazzled by the champagne-filled nights after years of temperance and struggle. Part of a glittering cast of worshipped entertainers, they were—for a time—living the life Charmion had dreamt of.

Of course a showgirl's life was not all glamour. A typical day began with rehearsals by mid-morning. There was a short break when many of the girls roamed the streets to feast their eyes on the latest French fashions they could not afford. Then it was back to the theatre, late nights and never enough sleep. But when one is young and beautiful and flattered, sleep is inconsequential.

We know Charmion kept Yvonne from friendships, surely to maintain the ruse of being sisters. It would also keep Yvonne depen-

G.-L. Manuel Frères
Mlle VALÉRIE

Charmion's picture from the Casino de Paris, 1927

dent on her. After all, without Yvonne what did she have? Yvonne was the bait of talent, looks, and youth that Charmion could live on and through. Yvonne was the potential golden goose needed to sustain their fantasy world and pay the bills.

When thirty-three-year-old Charmion returned from France, it would be the last anyone heard of "Valérie." There was no further professional record of Charmion or her alias.

Returning to America, Yvonne was listed as "Francis" on the passenger log. She was seventeen years old. She had made a splash in Paris, and Charmion was probably contemplating their next move as she lay on deck of the S.S. *Minnekahda*. Not an opulent ship but the first all-tourist-class one, it was sleek and modern for two modern women. They couldn't yet afford the luxuries a Dolly

Sister salary provided, but they could put on airs and their furs and beads and regale their dinner companions with tales of prancing across the stages of Paris. They could make up any past and any future they dreamed up. The world felt like their oyster and why shouldn't they enjoy it, and if they bragged a little too much, and exaggerated a bit beyond reality, so what? They were headed back to Broadway.

During the crossing, the beautiful sisters would have been spotted strolling arm in arm along the wide promenade and chatting. They would have walked by the two smoking rooms as Yvonne at least did not smoke. Did Charm keep her eyes peeled for an available man in the lounge or the dining room that sat four hundred? It was a sure bet she wanted the security. Even though it was third-class sailing (fares in 1926 were as low as $170), they could enjoy the many concerts given on board.

Curiously the duo returned home with a new last name, that of Bacon-Morris, allegedly taken from a suitor Charm hoped would help Yvonne. There is also the possibility Charmion had already taken another husband. Whoever this Morris was, he was insignificant and soon out of their lives. They were headed for a hotel on 50th Street and Seventh Avenue with high hopes and champagne expectations.

Yvonne's time in Paris amongst glittering European showgirls would have solidified confidence in her body, a body she would showcase with little of the puritanical hesitation of other American girls. She was a bona fide showgirl. Yet, just as she was making a name for herself, she would choose to reinvent herself—perhaps ready to slide out from under the thumb of her mother and take center stage. It was time to let go of Yvonne.

Part

THREE

THIRTEEN

FAITH BACON WAS INTRODUCED TO THE WORLD IN 1928. IT IS THE first professional mention of the name she adopted for the remainder of her days. Perhaps she dropped Yvonne to distance herself from "sister," or going on eighteen she didn't want producers to know she had already been knocking around for years. It is surprising that she did not want to build on "Yvonne Bacon" and the experience she gained in Paris.

The same year Mickey Mouse makes his debut in *Steamboat Willie*, Faith begins her association with the man who would transform her life.

On August 6, Faith Bacon makes her first appearance on stage of the Earl Carroll Theatre. The show is Earl Carroll's *Vanities of 1928*. And like the rest of the country, Broadway is dancing without a care in the world, with little inkling of what's to come.

The *Vanities* had been Carroll's thorn in Ziegfeld's side for years. Since its debut in 1923, the *Vanities* were tremendously popular. The show followed the invariable blueprint of skits, songs, stars, and sirens as undressed as Carroll could get away with. Unlike Flo, who liked his beauties spectacularly overdressed, Carroll cared not for elaborate gowns. He wanted to blind with flesh. There would be eleven editions of the *Vanities* produced by Ziegfeld's former songwriter turned flamboyant and controversial impresario. It was only one of the reasons for the bad blood between the two showmen.

Earl Carroll was tall, gaunt, not particularly handsome, well dressed with a receding hairline. He was spectacularly successful with the women (on and off the stage). Besides a wife (living in France) he was currently involved with his leading lady Dorothy Knapp, the winner of the 1922 Atlantic City Bather's Revue, the forerunner of the Miss America Pageant (then only in its second year).

He was a Hugh Hefneresque polarizing figure. A photo of Carroll for his *Vanities of 1931* program shows him wearing a robe thrown over an open-collared shirt with snappy suspenders, his showgirls—the "Mecca of Beauty"—surrounding him. There is no mistaking he is the sun to all the orbiting beauties.

Born in 1893 in Pittsburgh, he claimed an exotic background, one that included selling Bibles in China. He worked his way up the Broadway ladder, starting as a program boy, moving to songwriting, directing, and producing profitable female-heavy revues.

In 1922 he built a magnificent, self-named theatre on Seventh Avenue in New York. It was modern and innovative. He had forgone the traditional box seats and conventional colors, instead painting his domain turquoise and gold, with pink, blue, and purple curtains. Always searching for ways to outdo the competition, he was the first to have an orchestra rise from the pit. Other and future innovations would include individual program lights at each seat and the game-changing introduction of microphones on stage. He made vast improvements to lighting and the counterweight system that hoisted lights, curtains, and scenery.

All the modernization was not just for the audience's convenience and pleasure. He built a room for the expensive orchids the showgirls accumulated from their admirers. There was a room for the crew to relax. He even had a room made of mirrors for performers to check appearances before sailing onto the stage.

History has largely dismissed Carroll as a playboy, gambler, and "flesh peddler." He was in reality much more. His magnificent theatre in Hollywood (which remains today) included a revolving stage and laid claim as the first to combine dancing, dinner, and a stage show.

He knew just the right amount of skin that would excite an audience, not drive them off. It caused jealousy amongst the competition, who accused him of being tacky, crass, and mediocre. Sour grapes.

There has only been one biography of the colorful impresario, written by the notoriously free-with-the-truth comedian Ken Murray. Murray had worked for Carroll, and at one point they had rival shows in Los Angeles, which explains Murray's disdain and venom toward his former employer. There was also the matter of a payment dispute when Murray performed in Carroll's *Sketch Book* of 1935. "Carroll gyped me out of $15,000," Murray complained. His book *The Body Merchant* was payback.

Murray does much to perpetuate the myth that Carroll was a secondhand version of Ziegfeld, "tawdry" and "slightly sleazy." Carroll was no more "sleazy" than Ziegfeld, himself a notorious ladies' man who had numerous affairs with his leading ladies and whom the papers called "disreputable."

Both Carroll and Ziegfeld waxed poetic that they worshipped the female figure, a form they admittedly judged and hired based on their ideal pair of breasts, perfect hips, and shapely legs. Both were competitive, egotistical, and brilliant showmen. Along with rivals George White and the Shubert brothers, Broadway was assaulted with ruthless promoters of beauty and flesh, each trying to one-up the other.

When Faith met Carroll, he was not only a successful producer but a convicted felon.

Back in February of 1926, the social-loving Mr. Carroll threw the party to end all parties with distinguished guests who included publisher Condé Nast, actress Shirley Booth, writer Irvin S. Cobb, Walter Winchell, and Harry K. Thaw, who had recently been sprung from an institution for the mentally insane—for the murder of architect Stanford White, after Thaw discovered the affair White was having with his wife, actress Evelyn Nesbit.

At the party copious amounts of illegal liquor were poured, including into a bathtub wheeled on stage where a "tipsy" seventeen-year-old chorus girl climbed in.

Days later investigators discovered Carroll had paid bootleggers for the illegal crates of booze, finding "fifteen nearly-empty liquor cases that were removed from the theatre" after the party.

On April 1 Carroll was arrested. He was found guilty of perjury and served time in an Atlanta federal prison.

After the prison stint besmeared his reputation, Carroll, with "obstinate grittiness," was determined to bounce back even bigger than before.

Carroll sent out a call looking for beauties for his *Vanities of 1928*. He held auditions late in the day that allowed for shopgirls, hoping to step from behind cash registers, to attend. Several thousand, usually under the watchful eye of their mothers, jammed the theatre and street waiting to be called. Over three weeks, 8,000 girls auditioned, 75 were hired.

No doubt Charmion held tightly to Faith's arm. Everywhere one looked the competition was fierce, usually in some degree of blonde.

The young hopefuls were paraded on stage, akin to a horse sale, with their overplucked eyebrows and their crispy peroxide hair. They lined up for Mr. Carroll as he paced past the birds in all the plumage they had managed to ruffle up. He strode at a fast clip, never catching their eyes. He worked off a quick sensory impression of beauty. In this manner he viewed rows of lined-up girls "at least ten times before he divides them into three classes"—his first, second, and third choices, with the third group being let go right away. The second choices were lined up and again he relied on instinct, dividing and dismissing. He settled on "100 nearly perfect girls" and began rehearsals. From there he whittled his selection down to the final fifty or sixty.

During this audition, one beauty in particular captured his attention. She was sixteen-year-old, raven-haired, dark-eyed Beryl Heischuber. As Beryl Wallace she would become Carroll's beloved companion, whose profile he later immortalized in a twenty-foot neon sign outside his club in Hollywood. Beryl was "a real knockout," "well-stacked . . . gorgeous hair . . . and lots of talent." She was a popular, "sweet kid" who Carroll was attracted to, though he was still dallying with showgirl Dorothy Knapp, and still married to Marcelle Hontabat, a former Folies Bergère showgirl (the two lived apart). Beryl would remain largely in the background while he continued making love to Knapp, who believed in the mantra of "beauty," having been told all must be beautiful, her thoughts, her food, her life.

Other stars of the *Vanities of 1928* included seventeen-year-old singer Lillian Roth (her struggle with alcohol would be depicted in the picture *I'll Cry Tomorrow* starring Susan Hayward). Carroll hired cantankerous comedian W. C. Fields, who had become a star under Ziegfeld in 1915. Rude and selfish, Fields knew his worth and demanded an exorbitant fee. According to Ken Murray, $2,500 was handed over to the bulbous-nosed comedian every Monday, followed by another $2,500 every Wednesday. Fields also received a $150-a-week royalty per sketch.

W. C. Fields was the clear star of the show, performing in "seven numbers." The forty-seven-year-old comedian did a hilarious sketch as a dentist, which would be immortalized in the film *The Dentist* and considered by many to be his "greatest sketch of all time."

The stage was loaded with talent, including twenty-two-year-old Louise Brooks and beautiful sisters Eileen and Rose Wenzel.

Carroll ushered the company into rehearsals that stretched from "eleven in the morning until five the next morning" if need be. Busby Berkeley choreographed the dances while a secretary took notes. Carroll dashed about in a "lemon yellow" jacket, headphones secured to his cadaverous skull as he directed the stagehands.

Girls dripped with sweat in the hot theatre. When they conquered a particularly challenging dance, he passed out silver dollars as reward.

With ten acts and a hundred girls, it was "the best *Vanities* of them all." It would run for 200 performances, and though Faith would not be singled out, she was in a smash success through February of the following year.

With excellent reviews and solid box office, *1928* would prove to be the greatest box office hit of all the *Vanities*. Carroll was just thirty-five years old.

Faith worked virtually nonstop for Mr. Carroll for the next three years. It was steady income, constant press, and a—if not *the*—highlight of her life.

Faith was at her most luminous. She was nineteen, blue-gray eyes, 5 feet 6, winsome and doe-eyed with a slim alabaster figure.

She would have worked hard. She would have been tested by Mr. Carroll. He was hands-on in every aspect of production. A scale was kept nearby to make sure his beauties didn't gain too much weight. He paid special attention and gave small perks like painting their names on dressing room doors. Several times a week he invited the girls—with their parents—to dine with him. He believed in "placing opportunity in the girl's way," seeing there was no shortage of "abundant opportunities to advance" careers.

There were no short days. Now instead of pleasing just Charmion, Faith would have to satisfy an exacting taskmaster. It was noted of showgirls like Faith, "seen from the audience, she appears to be the very incarnation of fragile femininity. But underneath her deceptive exterior she conceals the muscles, wind, and energy of a trained athlete, and she must be able to master complicated dance routines and spend long hours in arduous and exhausting rehearsals."

Faith was on her way to where she wanted to be: glorified, idolized, made to feel she was bigger and better and brighter than the shy girl inside. Becoming a showgirl was a glittery cloak of protection she would wear with pride. It would also serve as her rebellion, her way of thumbing her nose at her mother, at displaced days growing up on the go. She would use the persona of showgirl to shock, titillate, and enchant a legion of admirers. But before her great fame arrived, Faith would find herself thrown into the chaotic world of a bloated, backbiting show.

Fioretta was a romantic opera that would be the biggest flop in the history of Broadway (at least up until its time). It was written by newcomers George Bagby and Romilly Johnson. Bagby approached Earl Carroll, dangling the script and the money of his rich aunt Anne Weightman Penfield to entice Carroll to produce the operetta.

For his first attempt at an operetta Carroll cast girlfriend Dorothy Knapp, and Faith was part of the large ensemble. Traveling to Baltimore for tryouts, the company "took seven railroad cars" to transport "fifty-six chorus girls and the cast of 225 persons" plus "fifteen mothers of chorus girls" to haul a virtual Italian city of "beautiful buildings, the canals, the carnivals, and the gaiety of the 18th century." The show provided an opportunity for "gorgeous scenic effects," of which Carroll was a master.

Set in eighteenth-century Venice, *Fioretta* was a lavish production with the "highest paid chorus girls in the history of show business."

But before the show opened, Carroll would be embroiled in controversy. Multiple complaints were filed against him by chorus girls who were told they must "remove all clothing" so Carroll "could examine them for scars." When they refused, they were denied parts. (As distasteful as it might sound, this was not an uncommon or even unreasonable request at the time.)

As was his particular method to whittle down the competition, approximately 300 hopeful girls spent a week rehearsing "eight hours a day and returned for night rehearsal." At the end of the week Earl's stage manager, Herman Hoover (he would later run Hollywood's movie-star watering hole Ciro's), dismissed all but the top forty. It would be two of the girls dismissed who filed the complaint.

Carroll fought back, revealing it was part of a plot against him because he was "raiding the Ziegfeld, White, and Shubert shows to land popular beauties."

Broadway was—and remains—cutthroat. No doubt there was some truth to Carroll's claims, and yet nothing would come of the grievance.

In its first week the show earned $38,000, "which isn't bad for Baltimore." It needed to continue making $37,500 weekly to break even. The show moved to Philadelphia for three more weeks of sharpening.

Fioretta opened on Broadway on February 5, 1929, starring Fanny Brice, the enormously popular funny girl, and Leon Errol, known for playing drunks, who relished a scene in full armor, carrying a crate of oranges, tumbling down a staircase.

Theatre critic Brook Atkinson applauded Carroll's effort that had "outstripped his rivals in point of lavish display." The show was "the handsomest production seen on the local platforms in ever so long" and an "incessant parade of eye-filling wardrobe."

The chorus was dubbed the best dressed of the season. It was heady stuff for Faith and the other girls as they read about themselves. Hopes were riding high that the extravagance would sail into history.

It did, but not as expected.

The show was prematurely declared "a hit," and a radio version was broadcast for the "first time in history" while the play ran simultaneously.

Broadway critics were not tolerant of the "pretension" of the show with a story that was "neglected" and had "no action and hardly a laugh."

Faith was one of the "acres . . . of girls . . . in spangles, trailing skirts, and ostrich plumes." Dorothy Knapp was blamed for having "no vitality as an actress" and "faltering" in the lead. She was the "queen of the carnival in a tight gold gown" with a real ermine robe and a giant pink tulle skirt with satin bodice, flowers draped across the shoulder, and period white wig. Lovely to look at, but dull. Mocked for being "beautiful but dumb."

Fanny Brice was four days into her marriage with Billy Rose when she took the stage with her "burlesque" style of comedy. It would be partly thanks to her "engaging talent" that the show continued running at all. Despite its detractors, critics somehow predicted it had a "long life ahead of it," knowing audiences' propensity for stupid content.

Then Carroll had a fight with his patron and Bagby's aunt, Mrs. Penfield, who was "tired of paying" Knapp $1,000 a week "to do nothing more than look beautiful." (Carroll paid himself $2,500 a week.) Penfield wanted Carroll to replace the woefully underskilled Knapp "with a songbird who could sing." She was prepared to file a suit demanding a return of her money if Carroll did not abide by her wishes.

Some said Carroll, feeling magnanimous (after all, he had moved onto Beryl Wallace), allowed Knapp to quit. According to another story, Carroll caught Knapp canoodling in her gondola on stage with an actor (possibly the handsome and "swashbuckling young" George Houston) and in retaliation fired her.

The papers claimed Dorothy was withdrawing from the play and going the way of talking pictures, clearly an item to save her embarrassment.

Headlines taunted, "Beauty? Yes! But Not Dumb." Knapp's attorneys quickly filed suit against Carroll and Mrs. Penfield for $250,000.

The defendants countered that they were justified to be rid of Knapp, who "had no voice, and could not sing, could not dance or act, and that she was wholly incompetent for the title role."

It became a litigious stew with Knapp suing Evelyn Hubbell, Penfield's friend, companion, and dancing teacher (and a facilitator of funds to Carroll from Penfield). Another associate sued Carroll for allegedly persuading Penfield to back *Fioretta*. Everyone ran to their lawyers.

The judge dismissed most of Knapp's case, awarding her an insulting "six cents." Overcome, Knapp announced she was entering a cloistered convent. (She would not.)

By the time the show limped to an early close in May, it was said Mrs. Penfield had lost her entire investment of $350,000.

Worse yet, Romilly Johnson, heartbroken at the failure of his show, stabbed himself in the heart with a bread knife at his father's home. His "close companion" and co-composer George Babgy found his body.

It was Faith's initiation by fire. Gratefully her next show lacked any behind-the-scenes drama and Faith found herself "out of obscurity into the limelight" for her first starring vehicle in Carroll's *Sketch Book* at the Earl Carroll Theatre, doing "all the nudes," having been elevated to "Chief Nude."

She could think of nothing more interesting to tell *Variety* than she liked hamburger and egg sandwiches, in fact she was a "fiend" for them. To another publication she claimed to be a strict vegetarian. Whichever the case, she was disciplined and it showed in her figure. "I can't cook as well as my sister." A strict teetotaler—orange juice was the strongest thing to cross her lips—Faith had a dim view of marriage, professing she wouldn't permit a husband to get in the way of her career. "I'd be the boss." Then to assure the reporter she loved men, she claimed, "I'd marry a street cleaner if I loved him. Of course I don't know a street cleaner either."

With 400 performances, *Sketch Book* was a solid success. Faith was presented in tableaux totally nude. For her part she was completely at ease at the hundreds of pair of eyes trained on her. As showgirl, Faith knew she had become part of the "illusion that brought millionaires night after night."

FOURTEEN

AT THE RKO IN NEW YORK, "STAR OF SCREEN" SALLY RAND AP-
peared with the retired and over-the-hill sex siren Theda Bara. Sally
was attempting musical comedy. *Variety* called her "a very young girl,
pretty both in face and figure." What singing and dancing she did
"showed little talent," performing in costumes with "lavish use of
rhinestones."

Over the following year Sally continued making the best of it
on vaudeville stages with her own show including five male dancers
(reduced from nine), the Crosby brothers, and most likely brother
Hal. Her performance was compared to an "average dance floor
class." It was truthfully noted her name had "never meant enough"
in Hollywood. It certainly didn't mean enough in the theatre either.
She had fallen far from the headlines, and she already appeared to be
a footnote—another pretty girl who hadn't made it.

She was neither movie star, vaudeville star, nor a singer or dancer
of note.

She must have felt desperate. Quick-witted, she would have continued plotting and planning, hoping for that right moment that would thrust her center stage. Sally wanted fame and an acting career so badly she could taste it at night when she went to bed.

Sally had no qualms sitting around her dressing room nude, not even when others knocked. Once her dance partner Bob Crosby was shocked to find her cutting her toenails and having a conversation with him, all the while naked. Supposedly she was known to tease an audience by prying off a pastie and throwing it at them. Anything to get their attention. She wasn't prudish or ashamed of her body and didn't understand when others were flummoxed by her ability to be comfortably nude.

She appeared in court to testify about a fight that had broken out at the Hammerstein Theatre.

Sally and twenty-two-year-old Hal had been cast in the chorus of *Luana*, a musical comedy. Hal was slight and good-looking like his sister. During rehearsal Hal, who like Sally had inherited the fierce Beck family temper, was tap dancing by himself and causing a "disturbance" on stage. Dance director Jack Haskell ordered him to stop. Haskell blew smoke at Hal, called Sally a "prima donna" and Hal "a pest." While sticking up for her brother, Sally scratched Haskell.

Haskell went running to producer Arthur Hammerstein to complain. Hammerstein fired both Hal and Sally.

A furious Hal confronted Haskell. Another fight ensued where a heavy ring from Hal's punch tore the skin above Haskell's eye. Rand tore "epidermis from his elbow."

Haskell reported the latest to Hammerstein, who surprisingly turned on the dance director and gave him a wallop!

Now Haskell was out and the Rands were back in the show.

All three showed up in court looking like naughty school boys; Haskell with a swollen eye and scar above his nose, Hammerstein with his hand in a splint, and Hal with his arm in a sling. Undisturbed, Sally posed and smiled for photographers.

Stretching the truth, Hal told the court he was a "film star." *Variety* called him a "chorus boy."

Haskell testified about a fully stocked bar in Hammerstein's office and threatened to "tell of certain orgies that occurred in the producer's" office. The judge hastily adjourned the court before anything more salacious was divulged.

Sally and Hal would be cleared of charges. *Luana* limped through twenty-one performances before closing. One of the best things said about it was "the spray of chilled air" from the air-conditioner in the theatre. It would do nothing for the Rands' careers.

The funny thing about an economic depression was the rise of "low culture" entertainment. Even as revues grew more sophisticated and more expensive to produce, audiences appreciated the common touch imbued by the lowbrow comedians. People wanted a respite, hoping the theatre would provide them with not only a laugh but also fantasy cloaked in fantastically draped goddesses to worship from their seats.

In the 1930s Hollywood began producing bigger and more extravagant movies, many which are considered to be classics today. There was a definite movement to bring culture to the masses with an emphasis on decidedly American ideals and traditions. The "American Girl" would be the thing that would save the people from the gloom blanketing the country.

It was time to bring on the girls.

Ziegfeld would lose everything in the Crash. It would break him. "I can't do this anymore," he cried and eventually fled to California, hoping the film *Whoopee* would rescue him. Luckily it would be a success, earning $2.3 million. But Flo would remain teetering near bankruptcy; his mental state also suffered. The "Boss" was despondent and confused by the sudden turn of events.

Sally had only ever played a minor role in the girlie revues, and Hollywood had already said goodbye to her. She was forced to take any job she could during these lean years, mostly in vaudeville, disappointed that being a WAMPAS Baby Star had been no guarantee of fame. "The 1927 crowd" in particular "failed to click." It looked as if Sally's name "will be remembered for her work with Cecil B. DeMille" and nothing more. She was speeding toward oblivion.

She even participated in a trio of skits in a high school auditorium in Minnesota. Hardly star work.

"Freelancing in films" was a polite way to say Sally was no longer under contract and not making movies. She continued with her boy troupe, now down to three dancers, and personal appearances in theatres.

She danced in *Sweethearts on Parade*, a traveling burlesque show that stranded her in Chicago when it either closed or moved on without her. Strapped for money, she slept in alleys and on yachts that her bootlegger friends rented.

Things were becoming desperate.

FIFTEEN

LOUISE BROOKS WOULD RECALL HOW MANHATTAN IN 1930 WAS "the hottest place on the planet." Faith was in the midst of it, living with Charm at 140 West 69th Street, a beautiful apartment with nearly a dozen large rooms.

Charmion had grown younger; she now claimed to be twenty-eight, to Faith's nineteen. In the census both list their professions as actresses, Faith on stage and Charmion in the moving pictures. With the proliferation of films shooting in New York, Charm might very well have been an extra or taken uncredited roles.

With Earl Carroll, Faith found the perfect mentor with a blend of showmanship, prestige, and notoriety. He was both gentle and kind. Those who worked for him "were intensely loyal to him, and he treated them with great kindness." If you were good to him, he would be good to you. He hung a sign backstage that philosophized, I WOULD RATHER YOU WERE LESS TALENTED THAN LESS LOYAL.

Carroll not only dressed with flair, his office at the theatre was decorated with more than a nod to his time spent in China, with antique rugs and a Chinese chair. Perhaps as warning, a sword lay on his desk.

Carroll's love of the perfect female form resided in 33½-25-35-inch measurements (these measurements would sometimes vary up and down by a quarter-inch). Girls must be at least 5 feet 6, 121 pounds, with precise measurements for ankles, wrists, and thighs. He would often do the measuring himself.

In his unfinished autobiography, *Through Those Portals Passed*, Carroll wrote: "Girls are a commodity the same as bananas, pork chops, or a lot in a suburban development. They are the most fundamental of all commodities. Girls like to admire beautiful girls, and men unquestionably too, and they will all pay for this pleasure. Of course, this leads to my making money, thus satisfying my material as well as artistic desire."

It might sound harsh, but Carroll was merely making the most of his—and others'—successful formula. They were giving the audience what they wanted to see: an idealized version of the perfect female body. It was fantasy on top of illusion on top of fabrication. And all were complicit in the creation, including the women who found freedom in going against the norms to display their figures proudly. The performers did not complain about being exploited, because they were taking advantage of being put on a pedestal and worshipped. Using an impossible standard for women to aspire to, the showgirl created the "It" girl before Hollywood purloined her. The showgirl was mythologized, and the girls knew how to take advantage of it.

Whatever his real feelings about women, Carroll was revered by the dancers who called him "Mr. Carroll." He was constantly in motion during rehearsals, sipping mineral water and chewing sticks of gum while his secretary scribbled notes. He micromanaged every production, adjusting this, noting that. He was precious and uplifting. He wasn't a yeller. In fact he ended rehearsals by addressing his cast. "Everything is coming along lovely," he praised. "I'm perfectly satisfied."

As a producer he was tireless. "Meticulous" Carroll polished his shows. "I must be constantly preaching, pleading, ordering, and threatening." Earl felt chorus girls "think only with their hearts." They were "only concerned with their clothes, hair wash, manicure, and romance."

With deep-set eyes and a "sensitive face," Faith was one of thirty or so girls on stage in "one piece bathing suits," "rompers," and "gingham shorts." While other beauties sprawled on chairs in the theatre, a dance master put the girls on stage through their paces.

Equity salary at the time was thirty dollars a week. Carroll could not be called cheap. He paid a minimum of seventy-five dollars a week. Some of his girls earned up to $250 a week. And he let the world know.

To earn it, there were "brutally thorough long rehearsals"; girls were working "sixteen hours a day" until "fainting or desperate for sleep."

After Carroll chose a new girl for her "beauty and charm," he made sure they didn't overeat, or attend too many parties. A chorus girl's life "is not an easy one." If they stayed "bright, happy, vivacious" he promised they would have a great future, "either married, or with a great career, surrounded by friends, fame."

The alternative was oblivion.

The chorus girl "is free to make her own way and choose the road to happiness," Earl Carroll claimed. But was she? What did these very young women, some still in their teens, know about the hot white light of scrutiny, idolatry, examination, and gossip with a bewildering choice of men both predatory and honorable kneeling at their satin feet? They had little experience to navigate stage door johnnies, mobsters, and a voracious press. Many were gobbled up and used up until their beauty faded, or the next one came along. Carroll warned, "Beauty is a woman's most precious asset—and the least enduring."

The life of a showgirl had an expiration date. Every high kick, every pose came with a ticking clock.

Dubbed "the American Venus," Faith was Carroll's notion of every red-blooded man's "ideal of beauty."

He made "it a point to talk to each one and instill in her the principles of the profession." He believed, "Women of the theatre must always serve." Little different from the ideal woman of the time who served society, family, and a husband.

"I don't care about character. All I ask is that she isn't hard." Carroll wouldn't tolerate profanity and fired those who dared show up late.

At the end of a season, most girls were let go. "Only the most fortunate of them will ever play for me again."

Faith was told that "no matter what happens" to perform "with simulated lightness of heart." To look for opportunity and seize it. Anything she could do to step out of the chorus line and into the spotlight would bring longevity to an ephemeral career. She needed something to grab onto and soar above the rest.

Faith had an idea. Stepping from the chorus line during a rehearsal she spoke up, "Mr. Carroll, why can't we do a number where I'm covered when I move, and undraped when I stop? For example—let us say the orchestra plays a waltz, I dance around, but on every third note the music stops and I stand still and uncover." As long as she held still when the music stopped, it would be within the limits of the law.

Furiously chewing gum, Carroll was racking his brain how to, as Faith said, get "the audiences to see me from all angles."

Tableaux vivants were a staple in the revues, both with semi-nude girls and ones like Faith who wore nothing. It was a respectable way around the law, which forbade a naked performer from moving on the stage.

Faith maintained, "I think of my body only as a thing of beauty." Her physique, like other showgirls', was her meal ticket. It neither embarrassed her nor gave her physical pleasure. It simply was a "thing of beauty."

Tableau vivant was an art form dating back to the 1700s. Essentially it was a living picture portrayed by a live model. For Victorians it was a popular parlor game, but the popularity would fade with the advent of moving pictures.

In the early 1900s "the heroine of living pictures" was Olga Desmond. Olga, born in what was then East Prussia, posed completely nude except for white paint, so as to remind those assembled that she was not woman but an ancient statute. She called her performances "Evenings of Beauty."

"Call it daring or bold," Olga said, "or however you want to describe my appearance on the stage, but this requires art, and it (art) is my only deity, before whom I bow and for which I am prepared to make all possible sacrifices . . . When I go out on stage completely naked, I am not ashamed, I am not embarrassed, because I come out before the public just as I am, loving all that is beautiful and graceful." It was a sentiment that would resonate with both Faith and Sally.

During tableaux, it would be necessary for Faith to turn at some point. "I'd cover myself with fans while dancing and as soon as I'd reached the proper position I'd stop and hold them over my head." Revealing all.

They considered having fans made of daisies but settled on ostrich feathers, figuring those would cover her completely. As insurance Carroll called an attorney and police official to judge the dance during a rehearsal. It passed.

Earl Carroll's *Vanities of 1930*, with music by Harold Arlen and costumes by twenty-one-year-old Vincent Minnelli, opened July 1 at the New Amsterdam. In the ornate lobby of the art nouveau theatre, life-sized nude photos lined the walls. Ziegfeld had held his productions there since 1913. Now it was Carroll's turn. Inside the colors were "green, mother of pearl, and mauve."

A fireplace greeted guests in the lounge, then they were whisked in an elevator to the Aerial Garden upstairs where Ziegfeld had held his *Midnight Frolics*.

Billed as a "super-spectacle of sixty-eight scenes," the revue featured Beryl Wallace. Jack Benny ("almost a newcomer to the Broadway stage," according to the playbill) was one of the featured comedians. Another minor character was Harry Stockwell (actor Dean Stockwell's father), who would marry one of the chorus girls, Betty Veronica.

Outside the theatre Carroll had placed a sign: HERE NOW PASS THE MOST BEAUTIFUL GIRLS IN THE WORLD, the "NOW" a not-so-subtle dig at Ziegfeld.

The frivolity and feathers of this *Vanities* in particular was something the country needed. With a quarter of the workforce unemployed, and banks closing at a staggering scale (something like 9,000 by 1933, taking people's money, future, and hope), the mood was grim. Audiences wanted an escape. Comedy and beauty was a balm.

Faith appeared in the scene "A Field of Daisies," waving "two white" ostrich "fans, revealing her totally nude body." She danced to "One Love" by Harold Arlen. She tiptoed amongst a field of young ladies laying on the stage waiving fans. A gauze curtain hung between Faith and the audience, obscuring her nudity.

She returned for another number, "The Mysterious Stars," portraying Saturn. She also performed in several scenes with Jack Benny and comedian Jimmy Savo.

In Act Two, Faith was Neptune's daughter in the tableau "from out of the sea" with eight mermaids.

She danced to "Boléro," which had only just premiered in 1928. Composed by Ravel, the instantly "simple" but popular piece was said to have "irresistible power of bewitchment." And a gorgeous shimmering Faith was enchanting. She masterfully fluttered the giant white feathers in front of and behind her pale slim figure, smiling as she lifted one heavy fan behind her head while the other rippled under her chin. Her movements were fluid and minimal. Barefoot and dancing on her toes, she dipped and swayed her body with the fanning of the feathers. The audience leaned forward, glimpsing her lean arm, petite ankle, keeping eyes trained for a glimpse of more. Faith revealed when she wanted to reveal. Provocative, it was a small dance, intimate, achingly beautiful and private. With movements so elegantly executed, she was like an endangered butterfly cocooned in giant silken wings, landing only briefly on earth to everyone's delight. Deceptively spare and gossamer.

One reviewer sniped it took no particular talent to perform Faith's "simple" fan dance. What is important is the reference in the program acknowledging Faith as the creator of the fan dance; though fans had been used on the stage for years, none had previously been used to play peek-a-boo with nudity.

In *The Body Merchant* Ken Murray claimed Faith had a minor accident on stage. The merkin covering her pubic hair came loose and a piece of tape "dangled between her legs, causing the audience to gasp and . . . wonder if it were . . . a female impersonator."

A week after opening, it was standing room only.

•   •   •

The audience poured in for the 4:30 matinee on Wednesday, July 9. Among the crowd was the official censor, Captain James Coy, who politely made his way to his seat in the twelfth row. This would be his third time in attendance. Arriving with warrants in hand, Coy assured the probably apoplectic stage manager that "no action would be taken until the matinee was over."

Coy had been the chief witness at the Mae West trial for her 1928 play *Pleasure Man* when all cast members had been arrested.

As the lights dimmed in the theatre, a recorded voice welcomed the audience. "This is your unseen host, Earl Carroll."

Meanwhile a dozen policemen and several police sedans (as opposed to the more obvious police wagons) pulled into place on the street in the heart of the theatre district. At least one car parked at the stage entrance on West 41st. Crowds began to gather.

Word quickly spread. Some of the girls, maybe Faith herself, scrambled onto the fire escape to "boo" at the police below, who might have been worried they would be overtaken by the crowds. It was a chaotic sight, beautiful half-dressed showgirls waving while passersby below clogged the street.

Comedian Jimmy Savo finished his skit with several girls posed as mannequins in a store window that he undressed, "unfastening their garter belts and removing their long opera length silk stockings," actions that apparently "brought the" wrath of the police.

A police stenographer took notes throughout the show.

Vanities finished to rousing applause and cheers.

Any feelings of ebullience were quickly dampened when Savo and six others were served with warrants. Not one of the girls was more than twenty-two years old, Faith included.

Told to put on their street clothes and "come quietly," the seven were ushered through the 42nd Street entrance through a tunnel of 1,500 people, flashbulbs popping, into the waiting police sedans.

Dropped into a rear room at the West 30th Street police station, the group waited nervously for an hour until Earl's brother and the general manager, Norman, along with Earl's attorney showed up to pay $500 bail for each defendant.

Carroll himself had been issued a warrant but was out of town. He would turn himself in the following morning.

Faith paused to pose for photographers, smiling and clutching a bouquet of flowers, no doubt from an admirer. Free at last, the arrested returned to the theatre for the evening show. Word had spread and the place was packed. (The mannequin scene was omitted. It would be added back in the next day, along with changes and additions to Faith's "costume.") The show went on without a hitch.

Gleefully Ziegfeld commented Carroll had "a show so bad that it had to be raided." He was shocked, saying "it was one of the filthiest ever seen in New York."

Carroll shot back that Ziegfeld "was in no position to talk of purity on the stage . . . and one of Ziegfeld's best friends . . . instigated the raid." Carroll thought Ziegfeld's attitude "ludicrous in view of the fact that he has openly admitted that he is the father of nudity in the American theatre."

The arrests made the front pages, with pictures of Dorothy Britton (Miss Universe of 1927), Eileen Wenzel, Betty Veronica, Irene Ahlberg, Naomi Ray, Kay Carroll (no relation), and Faith.

While the girls loved the attention, they were outraged when their home addresses were printed (common practice, even into the 1950s). They complained they received unwanted phone calls and letters.

The publicity ensured the *Vanities* made a booming business. A pair of tickets was said to go for $26, double that if bought through a hotel.

On a rainy July 11 the eight charged appeared for a hearing in court. Somewhere between 500 and 1,000 spectators, photographers, and reporters jammed the streets in front of the courthouse. Faith, tall and slim in a tweed suit with a wide-brimmed lavender hat, arrived next to a dapper, spat-shoed Mr. Carroll.

Faith's eyelashes were beaded as if for the stage. A "double white fox fur reached to her knees."

Carroll charged the "complaint" was brought against him "to hurt him." He was a "victim of ulterior motives which will all come out." For nearly two hours the defendants sat "in the gloomy interior of Jefferson Market courtroom" listening to complaints against "vagrants and petty thieves."

Carroll sat next to his brother Norman. Carroll told reporters "we have an artistic show and if I please the public I feel that I am successful." Because it took twenty-five policemen to bring the defendants to court, Carroll suspected "we have been successful."

"It seems that my career is just one thing like this after another."

At one point, when the courtroom erupted into laughter, the judge ordered 200 spectators out. The room was still throbbing with bodies.

Contributing to the circus atmosphere, bailiffs asked to be photographed with Faith. Throughout the hearings the courtroom would be packed with dozens of photographers. Newspapers promised that Faith "excites much comment even with her clothes on."

On the stand, gray-haired Captain Coy offered to execute Faith's fan dance. Coy was a former circus performer, a "maharajah of Baluchistan," his job was to wash the elephants, a job that paid fifty cents a day. He must have had performing in his blood, as he had imitated Mae West at her trial. Now he mimicked Faith's performance using a straw hat.

Asked to be identified, Faith, when she rose, grandly bowed.

"That's her," Coy barked.

The defense attorney suggested that by sitting in the twelfth row of the theatre, it was impossible for Coy to see whether Faith was wearing a flesh-colored stocking or not.

Naomi Ray chewed gum, Carroll drummed his fingers, and Faith, reclining in her chair, powdered her nose. They acted like it was a lark. Some complained Faith was haughty. In reality she was anxious.

Coy described Faith's offenses: she "came down a long ensemble of girls with two white fans and made various movements. When she turned, I could see her nude body."

He admitted Faith was so skilled at the fans that he hadn't realized she was buck naked until she left the stage and her rear was seen.

Defense attorneys pounced. "While she was doing the dance facing the audience she so manipulated the fans that you couldn't tell whether she was wearing any clothing or not?"

Coy admitted, "Yes."

Faith was naked, he swore, "from the nape of her neck to the soles of her feet."

Earl Carroll claimed Faith wore a "chiffon arrangement."

The magistrate asked Coy if he was shocked by the sight of her nude behind.

"I certainly was."

"Were there no exclamations from the audience like 'what a shocking sight?'" the judge asked.

"Well there wasn't any general rush to get out of the theater," Coy admitted. The courtroom tittered.

Did the audience laugh?

"I don't know."

"Did you laugh?"

"I did not," Coy said. "I was too shocked."

Faith let out a "smile and a titter."

Coy exclaimed, "New York, with all its reputation for immodesty and brashness, is not yet so that women can be permitted to appear on any theater stage in a state of complete nudity."

Defendants' counsel argued it was artistic dance.

The argument over exactly what was obscene would be bantered back and forth for years to come in courtrooms across America with no simple answer. In this case, the magistrate was of the mind that nudity in itself was lewd and offensive. At the end of testimony, the defense argued nothing had been proven to show the scenes were indecent.

By the end of July, Carroll stated he wanted a jury trial and his lawyer brought up a previous case where the judge had decided "the question whether a play . . . is obscene . . . [and] tends to suggest impure thoughts is one that should be presented to a jury. The case should be investigated by men taken from various walks of life."

Faith wanted a jury trial because "judges' opinions are the result of experience gained in limited fields."

To combat some of the negative press, such as the one that labeled her a "fanny dancer," Faith gave interviews from her dressing room. She made sure to let slip that she was a descendent of Sir Francis Bacon.

Three pictures hung on her walls: one of herself, another of a sea nymph (perhaps inspiration for her role as Neptune's daughter), and "some religious picture." Faith stretched the limits of believability when she claimed to have been raised in a convent and was "intensely religious."

She said her hobbies were painting and cooking and someday she wanted to open a dance school for children.

To some she said she did not dance in the nude. To others, she bragged she had been posing in the nude since childhood.

The defendants were discharged, except Carroll, Savo, Kay, and Faith, who were to be held over for trial. Faith's anxiety ratcheted up. A "starry-eyed" Faith declared her dance was "art."

Faith had assumed she would be let go along with the others. She dropped out of *Vanities*, suffering, as *Variety* reported, a "nervous breakdown."

Faith Bacon escorted to court by Earl Carroll

Back in court looking weary, Carroll sighed audibly. He always seemed to look as if he was in need of a haircut. He was breaking Mae West's record for court appearances (his three to her two).

Faith was in the grand jury trial room for all of five minutes. Afterward she said she had danced holding a pair of newspapers for the grand jury, lifting her skirt just a little.

"I am a natural dancer." She lied that she had never taken a lesson. She claimed to teach at Carnegie Hall.

By August the grand jury failed to indict Carroll on "presenting an obscene and indecent theatrical production."

A radiant and relieved Faith hugged Mr. Carroll. She resumed her spot in *Vanities*.

Faith became "the top glamour gal on the most glamorous street in the world" with plenty of "eligible" bachelors "anxious to cover her nudity with minks and diamonds." Ironically, the one thing she had no particular interest in was the attention of men. She would act coy when asked why she wasn't married, because of course wasn't that the wish of every showgirl?

"I will not permit a man to spoil the beauty of my perfect body." There was good reason she was labeled a narcissist with answers like that.

Being an Earl Carroll Beauty opened doors. "Many were called but few were chosen." Faith had been singled out by the one man capable of elevating her to stardom. And it happened fast. Suddenly the name Faith Bacon was on everyone's lips. The new "It" girl. The one everyone had to see.

She was inspiration for more girls who were "looking forward to a life of fame and luxury," believing that if picked they would become "famous and successful."

The truth was often different.

Being a *Vanities* girl didn't mean a lasting career. Most worked three years before being replaced, topping out at age nineteen or twenty. By then they had better marry or parade into another career. Considered to be the most desirable girls in the world, they had better make hay while they could with "thousand-dollar bills tucked into vanity cases as their just due."

"No chorine, however, no matter how energetic or gifted, can expect to remain behind the footlights for more than ten years."

"At the end of that time she has either progressed up the theatrical ladder, married, or been forced into another career—usually that of manicurist or beauty parlor worker."

It was a sad reality.

"You don't have anything," said one former dancer. "I don't even know how to do anything." Being a showgirl did not prepare one for a future career.

Many of the girls did not plan for a time past the opening parade. For a moment in time they shone in the spotlight, young and breathtakingly beautiful, filled with admiration and the world at their fingertips. For many it would be a highlight of their life.

No doubt it was the same for Faith, who could adorn herself with the accoutrements of success, furs, jewels, apartments. Everyone wanted a bit of her. Faith was photographed, interviewed, given near-hysterical attention from both men and women. There was no hint that one day her style of entertainment would become passé.

SIXTEEN

BY THE TIME FAITH ARRIVED, SHE, ALONG WITH THE OTHER CAST members of *Vanities,* must have been exhausted. They had piled into buses and trucks after their last performance and sped to Fairmont in the wealthy enclave of Manhasset, Long Island, for a special command performance. They were promised "extra large sums" and a lavish gift.

Mrs. Virginia Graham Fair Vanderbilt, known as "Birdie," the wealthy divorcee of William Kissam Vanderbilt II, was throwing a party. As a woman with "unlimited wealth," her parties often made the papers. (This weekend party would cost $100,000.)

Faith would have marveled at the guests wandering about. Most had adhered to the white dress code, fantastically costumed as "sea gulls, aviators, friars, nuns, Indians, dazzling princesses, and snowbirds with iridescent icicle effects," while two full orchestras played. The guests eagerly anticipated the 2:30 a.m. performance of the "most risqué of all the New York risqué shows."

A temporary theatre had been constructed with walls lined in silver, flowers growing up trellises. A "multi-colored circular stage" was "bordered by a low green hedge."

Faith's fan dance was the highlight. She was described as "angelic looking" as she waved her white fans, wearing "discreetly placed" fabric. The applause was enthusiastic. Certainly she felt she had arrived, even though one paper misidentified her as "Faith Baker."

After the performance, Faith would have been able to wander through a specially made ballroom or along paths in the garden amid trees and bushes hung with lights.

Faith could easily have pretended she belonged amongst the rich bachelors, "elegant dowagers," and "debutantes" enjoying their privileged lives.

One can imagine Faith whispering in Charmion's ear in the wee hours of the morning, exhausted, draped across the bed while Charm drilled her with questions. Charmion would have wanted her to look for a rich husband or patron amongst the millionaires.

This was a world her mother aspired to. Thus was the power of the showgirl. Beauty as currency.

The year 1931 saw the completion of the Empire State Building. The economy was in terrible straits—over 16 percent unemployment—and the drought in the Midwest was causing serious food shortages. The average yearly wage was $1,850 when Al Capone was hauled into prison for tax evasion.

Faith saw the New Year in by signing with the top of the top, the pinnacle of the impresarios, the feather in her headdress. She scrawled her signature on a contract with Florenz Ziegfeld for his *Follies of 1931*.

She would go straight from Earl Carroll's to the apex of every showgirl's dream. When Ziegfeld, the "glorifier of the American girl," put a girl in a special number, she joined an exclusive club of a chosen few. Flo Ziegfeld was *the* destination for the showgirl. One can only imagine the betrayal Carroll felt when his angel abandoned him for his enemy. But Faith was ambitious and sought louder applause and a brighter spotlight at all costs.

In April, at a theatre benefit for the poor, Faith was introduced by society hostess-with-the-mostest Texas Guinan. Sashaying onto the stage, the blonde Mae West type, former chorus girl, and emcee for the night Guinan tried taming her raucous crowd.

Earlier in the evening ping-pong balls had been thrown into the audience, which were now being tossed back with much laughter, and wolf calls.

Out tiptoed Faith, nude except for her fans. She was absolutely gorgeous with long curly blonde hair below her shoulders, slim, and impeccably made up. On the stage at the same time were two of the most famous women of their day. After Guinan, Faith was the most publicized woman of her time.

Ducking ping-pong balls, Texas introduced Faith. "She's gonna do the same little fan dance she did at Earl Carroll's . . ."

"Her body's in full bloom," a heckler interrupted.

"Shut up," snarled Texas, "come on and give her a nice big hand."

Another jokester appears to ask Texas if she was going to perform the fan dance. "I would but the hand is quicker than the eye," Texas quipped.

We must take a moment and address this off-the-cuff reply. It is an astounding line in light of the fact that Sally Rand would later appropriate it as her own. "The Rand is quicker than the eye," she would say in hundreds of interviews, when asked if she performed nude behind her fans or not. But Texas said it first, and said it about Faith. For all we know, Sally might have been in the audience that night as she was still touring.

This rare footage of Faith on stage with Guinan shows her to be infinitely more graceful and skilled than any of her competitors in the coming years. Faith is alluring amongst the laughter and shouts in the theatre, which must have been broadcast for radio as there were microphones on stage. She is an absolute vision of loveliness. She is both vulnerable and serious, unable to joke with the audience.

Ziegfeld's *Follies* girls were specifically "choreographed to convey desire." Desire to be one and desire to be with one. With the label came relentless scrutiny.

For Faith, to be told she was wanted, coveted, worth something, meant all of Charmion's pushing, cajoling, and threatening had paid off with the title of the "most beautiful girl in the world." But Faith was always painfully shy, hesitant, and unable to really let herself go. She had too many secrets to guard.

"With the position as a Follies girl, came a promise. Once Flo . . . accepts her . . . that girl bears *forever* [emphasis added] a hallmark just as plainly as though a device were stamped upon her lovely arm." Branded a Ziegfeld Girl, she was "high quality."

Ziegfeld liked his beauties aloof. Faith was a perfect addition, both cool and uninterested in men. She was conveniently "unattainable and irresistible."

Ziegfeld alumni included Adele Astaire, who danced into history with her brother Fred. Paulette Goddard married Charlie Chaplin. Irene Dunne, Barbara Stanwyck, and Myrna Loy found fame in Hollywood, and Helen Hayes went on to become the first lady of the American theatre. And of course penultimate showgirl Marion Davies left Ziegfeld to become the longtime mistress of William Randolph Hearst, living a life of unimagined luxury.

Up-and-coming showgirls were hoping they would have the same sort of life as Davies, filled with travel and fame. They were promised their beauty would take them to the heights. The Zieg-feld girl in particular was distinctly American, fair and caucasian. During the Jazz Age especially the girls were a "symbol of liberty and independence."

Like Carroll, Ziegfeld ran "grueling" rehearsals, sometimes lasting so long the girls fainted. Hours were spent with costume fittings. More time on the subway and trams to and from the theatre. Usually girls tried to rent rooms near the theatre or stayed in hotels close by. After hours girls were invited to swanky parties.

Girls "demanded ermine, chinchilla, and pearls from Tiffany and Cartier." Celebrities visited backstage, including movie directors and producers.

The girls had to live up to their reputation as the most desirable girls in the world.

The one-upmanship backstage was a serious game.

"You see, getting a job depends on how we look, and what fash-ion sense we have," explained one showgirl. "The moment you walk in to an audition, the eyes are on the shoes, the fringe of your skirt, the line of your jacket, the quality of your stockings. Hairstyle is another major topic."

Ziegfeld made sure his girls were "immaculate." He insisted they were well dressed on the streets, had one good expensive suit, and did not wear too much makeup off stage.

It was as if the girls could not be trusted in their own tastes and styles. Instead they were representing others' ideals of beauty, which could only have contributed to insecurity and anxiety.

"A girl is only beautiful when everyone says she is beautiful," Earl Carroll claimed.

These arrogant men, arbiters of what the public thought was beautiful, were themselves dandies. Ziegfeld dressed the part of successful impresario, striding about in a black coat lined with mink, driven in chauffeured cars. He lived in a grand apartment, had three gold phones on his desk, and traveled by private train with his own chef.

Despite what he said in the press deriding Carroll, Ziegfeld too pushed nudity to its limit, while maintaining a holier-than-thou attitude. Burlesque houses of the '20s and '30s would defend themselves by pointing to the "legitimate" Ziegfeld shows with their brazen display of nudes on stage. Ziegfeld took a lofty stance; he was the "entrepreneur of sensual desire." What he allowed on his stage was tasteful and artistic.

Who got pulled off which stage and arrested was clearly arbitrary on the part of police, and oftentimes politically motivated. It was "selective enforcement."

By 1930 Ziegfeld was in trouble and so was his *Follies*. The man "who shaped the American perception of female beauty" was struggling. His fortune had been wiped out in the Crash of '29. Having lost a million dollars, he broke into tears. His wife, actress Billie Burke, gave him her money. It would not be enough to save him or his pride.

A small consolation for Ziegfeld was the pleasure he derived in snatching Carroll's "prized beauty," Faith Bacon, as payback for all the times Carroll bribed and stole talent from his stage.

Faith was about to become a legendary Ziegfeld Girl. What did Faith have that set her apart? Beyond physical beauty, the audience went crazy for this vulnerable-looking, bow-lipped cupid with a lithe figure and a hesitant smile—if she smiled at all. Her sensitivity reads in photos. An exploited Marilyn before there was a Marilyn Monroe. Troubled, damaged, wronged, and heartbreakingly lovely.

Her photos ran continually in the newspapers simply because she was "perfect." Faith and two other showgirls were held as examples of "vibrant" health. Earl Carroll was quoted as saying a showgirl must have "stamina," as was the case with Faith, "to withstand the heart-breaking grind of rehearsal after rehearsal."

Faith's witty repartee made her a favorite with reporters. She gave "the most humorous" interviews that were "shockingly frank." "The baby faced" beauty behind the feathers charmed even hardened reporters.

Tryouts for the show began in Pittsburgh. Faith missed a performance "due to a tummy ache, sore ankle, or something." Ziegfeld was not tolerant. He dropped Faith, calling her "unfit." She must have begged her way back into his good graces because she was returned to the show, but he punished her by nixing "a dance number more daring than the fan dance."

There was no cutting corners for his 1931 *Follies*. It would cost "Ziggy" a quarter of a million dollars. Bowing to public expectation, Ziegfeld was "content to bring on the beautiful girls in fewer and fewer clothes."

It would be the greatest showman's last hurrah.

The show opened July 1. "Bring on the Follies Girls" played as the thick curtains were pulled back. Rising from the depths of the stage, Faith was held in the palm of a giant hand. "Posed as a kind of water carrier without a jug . . . as free of covering," she held some sort of light. It was dramatic positioning.

Faith had multiple numbers. "Tom Tom Dance" (with fellow *Vanities* arrestee Eileen Wenzel) included a "herd of elephants, their trunks carrying scantily clad women." She was in "Clinching the Sale" with pal Harry Richman, and "Whisk Broom."

Her old dance teacher Albertina Rasch choreographed at least the "Tom Tom" number. Faith also reportedly swung nude from a cross to "Boléro" with the Rasch Dancers.

It was a huge cast, with specialty performances, including singer-dancer-comedian Harry Richman. Faith and Richman would spend time after the show in each other's company, sparking rumors of a serious romance as he escorted her about town. Faith would brush off the gossip. He was "good fun to tear a herring with after the show."

On the *Follies* stage Faith was praised for her "awe-inspiring undress." She made sure to tell reporters just because she wore few clothes on stage didn't mean she wasn't a regular church-goer.

Walter Winchell mentioned Faith in his column regularly. He found her "silence" "disarming." He was mesmerized when "slowly she moves, lifts her gorgeous eyes—looks at you, you, you, or even you!"

But Faith couldn't save the show. Most critics called the *Follies* too long and old-fashioned even if the beauties were lovely to look at.

Once the show wrapped there was talk of going on the road, but by November a notice of closing was posted backstage.

Ziegfeld's time was over. The Glorifier would be dead by the following year.

Faith at the height of her beauty and fame

SEVENTEEN

SALLY RAND PERFORMED AN UNCREDITED PART IN ANOTHER film for DeMille, who must have retained a soft spot for his discovery. Filmed in Fresno, *The Sign of the Cross* starred Fredric March and Claudette Colbert. She was "Crocodiles' Victim." A new indignity.

Sally was also having relationship problems. "Movie Actor Quits Wife Because Parents Object." Twenty-five-year-old "native of Arabia" actor Toofik Simon was leaving her because his "parents opposed my marriage to Sally Rand." Never mind that she was four years older and scratching out a living in nightclubs, not quite original, exciting, or, frankly, good enough.

Toofik was no star himself. He had played minor characters in a handful of pictures, including *Mata Hari* starring Garbo. His headline-making days soon petered out.

Everything Sally had been struggling for was slipping away: a movie career, stage work, and now a relationship. Not that her relationships with men would ever be a priority. It was always about work. It was always about Sally.

Then came an opportunity to return to toe shoes and tutu opposite seventy-four-year-old DeWolf Hopper. The well-respected and six-times-married actor was performing in his first nonmusical show. *The World Between* would be a "financial failure," and Sally found herself once again at odds, this time in Chicago.

Practically a second home for her, Chicago was buzzing with excitement in 1933. Buildings were rising along the lake in anticipation of the coming summer's world's fair, an event that promised millions of visitors. One could not escape talk of how the international eyes would turn toward Chicago. Opportunity was blowing its way into the Windy City.

Her previous publicity stunts had led to nothing, but that didn't stop her from picking the "coldest October day that Chicago experienced since 1906" to become a member of the Polar Bear Cub. She was photographed smiling and emerging from a frigid Lake Michigan.

A "desperate" Sally started dancing at a Near North Side nightclub (some called it a speakeasy) on East Huron. She had answered an ad in the paper for "dancers and exotics," a polite euphemisms for strippers, at the Paramount Club (or Club Paramount). Sally was twenty-eight years old and no ingénue. How many more times could she keep reinventing herself? It was a new low point. Sally later said it was this or "prostitution."

She introduced herself to owner Ed Callahan, known as Big Ed. Sally sized up the other girls on stage. She needed this job. Big Ed told the girls if they wanted the job to return with their costumes for the 10 p.m. show.

Maybelle Shearer was an actress and one of Chicago's leading costumers, specializing in showgirl outfits, with accounts at the club Chez Paree and the Chicago Theatre. It was from this shop that

Sally would spy a set of large pink fans made out of ostrich feathers, neglected and gathering dust.

Sally's seven-foot, forty-pound fans cost ten dollars, a small fortune for her.

She picked her music, "Clair de Lune," which she had danced to many times on the vaudeville stage. Arriving back at the club, no doubt nervous, sweating, and late, with an unfinished costume that was supposed to be a toga, she was informed that, as the new kid, she would be going on first. No time to finish sewing. Her fans would have to be her costume.

It was disheartening. The stage was postage stamp–size. A drunken piano player stumbled through her music.

Sally trembled as she maneuvered the heavy fans on stage. The place was hardly full and the customers could not have cared less. But she needed the money.

This story that she (more or less) repeated for the rest of her life, how she managed an impromptu fan dance, is absurd. The heavy fans would have been awkward, and to appear at all experienced with them would have involved hours of practice, not a mere afternoon already filled with trying to cobble together an outfit.

And her act was problematic. She admitted they were troublesome props. The flapping, twirling fans gave the spotty audience glimpses of her bare breasts and net panties. Truly, if she had not practiced for days, the audience would have seen a whole lot more than a glimpse of skin.

By the end of the dance she posed with the fans held high above her head, as bare as the day she was born, except for a "heavy coat of cream that costs" forty-two dollars a week. There was a smattering of applause that seemed more enthusiastic than the sparse crowd warranted. Big Ed told her she was hired.

"I haven't been out of work since the day I took off my pants," she said, and it was true. Thus began the myth-making of a girl who stumbled onto a career as a fan dancer.

She would develop her signature pose at the end of her dance, fans raised high overhead exposing her breasts, her lower half turned to the side with one leg raised to cover her crotch.

Big Ed would become a pal and counselor to Sally, grateful that her employment begat a steady stream of customers coming to see the winged creature who danced in the nude. Just weeks after her debut, business at the club picked up. The hours were horrible. There was a breakfast show at 4 a.m. But her stomach wasn't aching from lack of food anymore.

She would mythologize the dance. It was inspired by the herons that flew over the lake on her grandfather's property. "My interpretation of a white bird flying in the moonlight at dusk." "It flies up into the moonlight. It is dusk. It flies low. It flutters. Then it begins to climb into the moonlight." Other times it was a pair of birds.

And yet other times she told how the dance was not accidental at all. "I searched my mind for something that would hit the public fancy enough to make large financial returns possible." Which is patently false—she surely did not expect a large salary from the Paramount Club, the likes of which were end-of-the-line employment for her and other dancers.

Later still the fan dance actually began before her desperate tryout at the Paramount. It was "created in 1929, when I was attempting to invent a number which would resemble the movements of a bird." Or, "I have done this dance to get money to get back to Hollywood."

What was true was that getting back to Hollywood was always the goal, despite her limits as an actress. "I know I'm no Ethel Barrymore. I lack talent but I've made up for it with hard work." It was always acting that drew Sally.

She couldn't know she would be tethered to a gimmick she could not shake for the rest of her life. At times she would bow to the demand for it, other times she hurled it aside. She would learn to keep a smile on her face as she raised her fans above her head. Sally Rand and her fan dance were here to stay.

What Sally did find in the dance was freedom. She was finally free. Free of Helen and Billie. She would wholly and fully embrace Sally Rand. She was free to reach heights she could never have envisioned for herself.

By this point Faith Bacon had been making headlines for two years with her fan dance. Sally Rand meant nothing to her. Yet.

Sally settled into the Paramount, where the audience was not nearly as upscale as the crowds clamoring to see Faith on Broadway.

It was rumored "some hoodlum admirers" were actually responsible for getting Sally the job. Sally was friends with at least bootleggers, and everyone knew who was mixed up with the clubs in Chicago at the time.

Organized crime and its bosses ruled illegal liquor sales during Prohibition, and a "disturbing culture of crime churned insidiously around most nightclubs." A thriving gangster element would have had easy access to intimidating interactions with the women working there.

Sally, by proximity, would have numerous ties to a list of bad-boy criminals, and she would learn how to navigate forceful, violent personalities. In later years she worked for Jack Ruby at his Carousel Club in Dallas—"not a nice guy," she'd say. She also boasted Jimmy Hoffa as a friend. Sally could handle not-nice guys.

The Paramount was frequented by such notorious characters as Vito Genovese, who suggested Sally quit Big Ed and come work at his joint. Genovese was ruthless, vicious, and not to be trifled with. Not long after meeting Sally, he murdered, or had murdered, the husband of a woman he coveted. Once the husband was safely buried, Vito married the woman.

The owner of the Chez Paree, a glamorous nightclub and former speakeasy in Chicago, was supposedly strong-armed by Genovese into hiring Sally, even though the Chez booked much bigger acts such as Billie Holiday, Harry Richman, Jimmy Savo (who was arrested with Faith in *Vanities*), and Faith herself.

Genovese was just one of many underworld criminals Sally met courtesy of her new employment. Mildred Harris, Charlie Chaplin's ex, introduced Sally to "Machine Gun" Jack McGurn, hitman and bodyguard for Al Capone, who took a liking to her.

She relished telling the story of how Capone came into the Paramount one night to let her know he bought her contract and as of the next day she'd be working his club. Sally nodded in agreement, went home that night, packed her bags, and left for New York, knowing Capone wouldn't go onto another gangster's turf.

It was another of Sally's improbable but entertaining stories. Sally did not desert Chicago at this time, or any time in the near future. By the following year she was famous, and less able to be intimidated and bullied. Clearly she was often hired in a multitude of Mafia-owned clubs. The book *The Last Mogul* about Lew Wasserman—who ran the powerful booking agency MCA, based in Chicago, and booked his clients in Capone's club—claimed Sally worked for Capone's organization. Mobster Alex Louis Greenberg would say the same. Furthermore, Sally would herself become an MCA client. But again the tough cookie standing up to authority made for a better story, and no doubt she wanted to distance herself from any obligation she might have had to Capone or other gangsters in Chicago.

Sally bragged she hitched rides on the boats of her bootlegger friends as they went on runs to pick up illegal booze. Her friends bought the yachts from millionaires ruined in the Crash. Helping facilitate sales of the yachts, she earned between $5,000 and $10,000. If true, Sally would not have been quite so "desperate" to audition for a seedy little nightclub. The point is she knew bootleggers and gangsters and men who ran the city. The truth was, she was rarely fearful of anyone. On her own for years, she learned to make due and get along. She wasn't one to let a Capone drive her out of the city—although it made for an awfully good yarn.

EIGHTEEN

"FIGHTING WENT ON IN THE DRESSING ROOM EVERY PERFOR-mance," one showgirl recalled. No surprise "with sixteen different personalities crowded into one cramped room, there were bound to be conflicts." Sometimes the showgirls, many still teens, "fought savagely with kicking, scratching, and plenty of hair pulling."

If the fights weren't over men—and often they were—they were sparked by jealousies, competition, and pure survival. With the smell of talcum powder and pancake makeup in the air, backstage was a maze to be navigated carefully.

Girls complained that Faith, now the "famous fan stepper," spent hours "standing stark naked backstage" admiring herself in the mirror.

"My body is a work of art," she replied. "I am not ashamed of it."

And whose head wouldn't be swelled by the sudden celebrity and massive amounts of attention? Faith had become the showgirl everyone in New York City was interested in following. She had no higher aspiration at the moment. This sudden celebrity "takes particular joy in just being beautiful."

Faith missed out on much of the merriment, gossip, and confidences in the dressing rooms. Where it was natural to forge friendships, Faith would have none. Perhaps Charmion even hung around backstage meddling.

Faith had started 1932 with a tour of the *Follies*. Her nude picture in the papers was often painted over with a modest bra and panty.

Draped in "$2,000 worth of new jewels," Faith spent the summer months performing at N.T.G.'s grand cabaret the Hollywood Restaurant in New York. It was whispered Charm held onto the "jewels for safekeeping."

Though she was new to fame, a story lumped her in with other Ziegfeld girls, cautioning about the troubles of former "most beautiful girls." There was Kay Laurel who had died in childbirth, Mae Murray ended up homeless, and Eve Tanguay died arthritic in bed. Being dubbed beautiful came with no guarantee.

After her breakdown following her arrest, Faith never minded negative publicity again. If she wasn't in the papers for her performances or a rumored romance, a rivalry would do. It reminded producers she was a name people wanted to read about.

Jack Stanley Morris was a "playboy broker." He asked Faith to marry him. She wasn't interested. He eloped with another showgirl and was separated within a week, claiming, "I have always loved Faith." It was a rare mention of a suitor.

In fact papers hinted at the truth, that Faith was rarely linked to a man. As for love, Faith told reporters "romance has no place in the life of a classic statue."

Many an ardent suitor quickly discovered that just because a showgirl wore little clothing for a living, it did not mean she was receptive to a relationship. Those girls "are often as detached and cold in their devotion to the ascetic aspects of their art as any hardworking painter." Stage door johnnies dreamed of outrageous tricks to turn a showgirl's head, such as the young man who scattered diamonds across a hotel lobby at the feet of a smattering of Follies girls.

Faith expressed disdain toward any suitor. She was busy writing her memoirs (at age twenty-two). She would read aloud bits of *Remembrances of a Nude* to reporters. She had decided to write the "evolution of the fan dance" because it was "not a sudden inspiration." It is intriguing to wonder whatever happened to the sheaves of papers she was seen hauling about. Did she give up and toss them? Was no one interested?

Faith did have more pressing things to worry about. Charmion was "ordered to Arizona" for her health. Perhaps she had been ill for some time, one possible reason there is no record of any professional appearances after Paris.

Faith was frantic. Doctors were telling Charmion she had to leave "due to the cold weather affecting her."

At the time, consumptives were often sent to live in the West, in decidedly unglamorous locations (Arizona in the sweltering three-digit heat, or New Mexico with a foot of snow in winter). They "roughed" it. While the wealthy went to resorts, "the poorest . . . often ended their grim pilgrimages in Arizona." Denver was another place for those wasting away from tuberculosis; Charm would eventually move there.

Arizona, and in particular Tucson, the "tuberculosis capital," had more than a dozen sanatoriums. The disease had much to do with shaping the growth of the city.

Also known as the White Plague, tuberculosis is a bacterial disease that attacks the lungs. Before antibiotics became available in the 1940s, patients were prescribed fresh air, sunshine, and exercise. Charmion and Faith performed in smoke-filled clubs, breathed fumes from crowded dressing rooms, slathered on and off chemicals, in rooms cold, hot, or damp.

Perhaps Charmion was hooked on the pills she doled out to Faith, further weakening her condition. Faith would hereafter refer to Charmion as an "invalid."

If Charmion could not afford one of the sanatoriums, she could have pitched a tent in the desert floor, as some did. In either case Charmion made the move to Tucson and its arid climate—the first physical break between the two. Faith would visit and send money. She was there for her mother. Charmion would not return the favor.

It is likely because of Charmion's move to Tucson that Faith would meet a man who would attempt to save her. His name was Ed Hanley, and it would prove to be an everlasting and poignant relationship.

It's not unlikely that Faith herself, delicate and sometimes painfully thin, suffered the same condition as her mother.

Faith was stressed and physicians wanted her off her feet. But she couldn't slow down. "I have to have the money," Faith whined. It remained up to Faith to be the financial provider for her "sister." Without Charm managing her every move, Faith—who was said to live in a world removed from reality—would find it increasingly difficult to be self-sufficient.

NINETEEN

IT WAS A DAY FOR PAGEANTRY, SPEECHES, AND PATRIOTIC PRIDE. This world's fair was proclaimed the "Century of Progress" to celebrate Chicago's first 100 years and a century of advancements in science and technology.

The air crackled with anticipation and, more important, hope. There was optimism that as the citizens of America looked back at their past, they would somehow see into the future, and it would be a better place than it was at the moment.

The fair promised to bring jobs to hundreds and fill the city's coffers. It was May 27, 1933, and the country's economy was at rock bottom.

While bands played the "Star-Spangled Banner," the promenades filled with people; flags snapped in the breeze. Though the skies would cover over in a few hours, no bad weather dampened opening day.

Riding the massive floats, a queen of the fair waved alongside her fifty ladies. The mayor addressed the crowds, vowing that "for the next five months," Chicago, the country's second-largest city with nearly four million people, would be "the educator and champion host of the world."

Fireworks were launched from barges on Lake Michigan. A whistle blasted. Crowds streamed like a ribbon of fire ants up a faux gangplank, thousands marching through the entrance of a huge mock ocean liner with smokestacks that towered seventy-three feet in the air, eager and hungry to devour what lay across the "Atlantic," transported "in spirit" unto the naughty boulevards of Paris.

Flower and cigarette girls greeted the crowds surging forward. Clutching wide-eyed children's hands, parents pushed through the narrow streets of "the wicked city." The three acres designated for the Streets of Paris exhibit was a Disneyesque re-creation of France's capital, complete with a nudist colony (for surely Paris must have one) and the infamous Folies Bergère.

The smell of popcorn and fried potatoes wafted in the balmy air as shopkeepers hawked their wares for sale. "Direct from Montemarte!"

Waitresses with jaunty berets on their heads weaved through the laughter, carrying steins of beer, as music streamed out of the hundreds of open-air cafés. Now that President Franklin Roosevelt allowed the sale of beer and wine, there seemed to be a "bar every minute." Canopied sidewalks fought for space. Cafés "typical of Paris, like the Red Mill Café dotted with red-checkered tables, dance pavilions, theatres, even a swimming pool," enticed visitors in all directions.

"Merriment, camaraderie, noise, naughtiness" was the pledge of a visit to the Streets of Paris. It had been designed to help foot the cost of the fair, a whopping thirty-seven million dollars. The Streets of Paris offered adults mature entertainment, not seen outside the French capital, including peep shows displaying naked women.

Further down the road a barker called out, "Live models!" For a small fee one could take a class on how to sketch a naked woman. Ushered into a garret-like room that was purposefully stuffy and devoid of furniture, except wooden boxes for seats, one was handed charcoal and paper to sketch (or stare at) the nude women posing in front of them. Classes were surprisingly made up largely of women.

On the sidewalk, artists set canvas on easels. The Merry-Go-Round bar revolved in a slow circle. Vendors competed for every hard-spent dime and quarter. Fortune tellers and palm readers promised a better tomorrow.

There was a little something for nearly everyone. "Gigolos are provided to women who desire dining and dancing partners." There was an eighty-mile-an-hour cyclone coaster. A gorilla town, a freak show. It was "Harvard, Broadway, and Coney Island rolled into one."

There was so much to take it that it left the "brain whirling" at all the "undigested experiences," and this was just a small section of the fair.

There were compulsory visits to the Hall of Science, Washington's false teeth and the world's largest cow on display, a reconstruction of Fort Dearborn, the interior of Byrd's polar expedition, and prehistoric monsters.

There were states to explore. Florida had four acres of flowers; California grew giant redwood trees; Hollywood had prizefights, Leo the lion, and a replica of the Brown Derby Café. And if one wanted to travel to more exotic locals, there was Morocco and Belgium.

One could buy a postcard, or novelty item, or spend the day in the Seminole Indian village as the natives wrestled alligators, or gaze at the "lady with eight feet of red hair" and a "man who swallows practically everything," even a "petrified man" at Ripley's Odditorium.

One way to forget one's troubles was to eyeball the abundance of flesh on display. A goodly portion of the crowd was coming to see Miss Sally Rand.

•   •   •

To think, just weeks earlier Sally had been an anonymous failed actress waving her fans in a sketchy nightclub. Now, at 10:30 every night, the master of ceremonies stood up to introduce Sally and her "trained fans" as big as "sky scrapers."

Trumpets blared a welcome fanfare as a "lively red head" (perhaps the lights turned Sally auburn-haired) "pirouettes to the center of stage" as Debussy's "Clair de Lune" and Chopin's "Waltz in C Minor" played.

Finally proficient with her fans, Sally finished to thunderous applause. Some complained she was so engulfed by the feathers that only her lovely face was seen. They had come for the nudity, but the lighting was so dim she could have been wearing layers of clothing. She was not. She was nude except for a "strategically located patch" and liberal dusting of powder.

Sally had them lined up four deep for eleven solid weeks. In the first month alone, more than 70,000 would see her. It was beyond her imagination. "I never expected to make a living out of it," she marveled truthfully about her dance.

The cost of the fair was so high that it was not expected to make a profit. Until Sally Rand.

Because thousands poured in expressly to see her fan dance, Sally would be credited with saving the fair. She would become the image of the fair. She would be the picture people would think of for generations to come when the Century of Progress was mentioned. There was no Sally without the fair, just as there was no fair without the fan dance. It was a role that would cement her fame.

And to think she had originally been turned down for a spot on the midway.

As owner of the Charles H. Weber Distributing Company, Charlie Weber had the beer concession at the Streets of Paris. It was rumored his company was financed by Gus Winkler, an associate of Al Capone. It was also rumored Winkler was a partner in the Streets of Paris. Winkler would meet his maker in a hail of bullets in front of Weber's business in October of 1933. Sally had been "harassing" Weber to add her to a show at his concession. Though a friend, Charlie refused; after all she was just a dancer in sleazy nightclub.

She had worked for Ernie Young at the Marigold Gardens in 1923, but Young also turned her down for his revue at the fair.

Sally then heard about a swanky invitation-only dinner, at a cost of one hundred dollars a plate, hosted by Mrs. William Hearst, to take place the night before the fair. According to Sally's son, Sean, she was "insulted" that in a time of soup lines women were dressing up in expensive gowns and flaunting their wealth. Sally felt compelled to "put down" the society dames.

Sally also knew the value of stunt publicity. Besides, she had nothing to lose.

In one version of the retelling, Sally said it was Weber's suggestion she crash the party to get herself noticed, which makes little sense as he had the power to hire her in the first place. The other version she would tell (with slight variations) for the next fifty years had Sally turning to Big Ed Callahan for help.

"Ed, I can't get into the fair."

"Lady Godiva couldn't even get in to see those blue-noses."

A light bulb went off, and Sally "just came up with the idea" to portray Lady Godiva.

Again the truth was a little different. "The Chicago Artists Ball is considered practically no party at all without an annual Lady Godiva." In December the year before, Sally was paid twenty-five dollars by the Ball to be that year's Lady G.

At the time she told reporters she was bringing a horse, despite no former Godiva having ridden a pony to the Artists Ball. Sally was even photographed "rehearsing" astride her horse Mike while wearing a long blonde wig and two giant fans.

On the night of December 9 her horse was refused entry to the Stevens Hotel on South Michigan Avenue. Thinking quickly, Sally commanded, "Bring me a table and four bus boys." She was then carried around the room by "four slightly inebriated artists."

So contrary to what she would later tell, this was not her first encounter with the iconic lady.

Sally did what any publicity-seeking, socially conscious entertainer would do; she rented a stallion for ten bucks and hired a barge to take her and the horse on the river around Wacker Drive to the yacht landing at the Streets of Paris.

It would turn out to be a brilliant move, executed boldly, and one that landed her smack in the middle of history.

At the entrance, Sally was greeted by a "little man guarding the yacht landing who figured that a broad that arrives in a boat with a horse is supposed to be there." He waved her through.

Her horse wore a magnificent white and silver bridle and rubber shoes. A long white velvet cape was draped around Sally's determined but naked shoulders. It must have been comical to her. Everyone she encountered seemed to think a nude Lady Godiva on horseback belonged riding up the midway.

Once she was at the invitation-only dinner, the emcee gamely announced, "Lady Godiva will take her famous ride." And then it was "clippity clop" and a "nude Sally Rand" rode onto the ballroom floor with three thousand swells gasping and applauding.

She must have made sure to tell them her name. After causing a stir, she returned to her rooming house on Division Street. The next morning, as she claimed, a girlfriend called to say she was "on every newspaper."

With thoughts of employment on her brain, Sally caught the trolley for the fair. At the gates, she watched the gathered crowds who were searching and shouting for "Lady Godiva!" Confidently she approached the owner of the Café de la Paix on the Streets of Paris and said, "I'm the lady."

"You're hired. So go get your damn fans and be back here within the hour."

Sally having no money, he had to pay her cab fare. She eagerly returned an hour later.

And, as they say, a star was born.

Sally claimed she "*knew* she had arrived." But did she really believe this latest pursuit would be the one to stick?

Forces beyond her control would be on her side. Recently the papers had been spewing out rumors of a brewing tax scandal involving Mayor Edward Kelly. As distraction, City Hall decided it was time to clean up the Loop (the financial district downtown loaded with restaurants, stores, and hotels), hoping to deflect attention from possible revelations. They targeted salacious acts they deemed "lewd."

It was her opening night. Lines grew at the fair to see the nude fan dancer. And Sally was arrested.

She headed off to the police station, signed whatever she needed to, and returned in time to perform. The headlines pushed Kelly's tax scandal off the Chicago papers. If ever a politician needed a future smokescreen or platform to preach from, nudity would be the answer. For Sally and the Streets of Paris, it was a boon of publicity. There was a mad rush to see Sally—and see as much of her as was rumored—before she was expunged from the fair.

Sally's arrest might also have been a stunt dreamed up by the publicity man for the Streets of Paris. Arranged or not, her "obscenity" charge and visit to the clink would be a news event Sally would get used to. It never seemed to fluster her, especially as it whipped up interest in her like never before. And though she had at least two charges to her name prior to 1933, this was the beginning of a career filled with arrests.

With her first $1,000 earned, Sally bought her stepfather a trac-
tor for his property in Glendora. She had an idea to start an orange
grove business; after all, who knew how long this fan dancing would
last?

She was doing double duty at the Paramount. Following one
performance, Sally was greeted by a stern policewoman who insisted
that "either you put on some of this"—she held out gauze, tape, and
pins—or Sally was going to be hauled in.

Sally complained about the way it covered her. The policewoman
replied, "It covers the law."

Reluctantly Sally complied, but once she hit the stage, in a burst
of anger, she ripped off the gauze.

The debate whether Sally wore clothes under her fans is ludicrous
in light of the fact that judges were constantly pleading with Sally
to put on "a little something," be it mesh or gauze. She would insist
"cold cream" was enough.

"My technique . . . is to manipulate the fans so the audience will
think they are seeing things they are not." Some claimed she wore
body paint, or a body stocking. Unless forced to put something on,
Sally was nude, verified by photos and eyewitness accounts, including from her own son.

Sally complained clothes caught on the fans and "interfered"
with her dance.

She was fined twenty-five dollars, told she must wear clothes,
and warned that the mayor's office was keeping an eye on her.

She decided on a robe. She was warned not to take it off. She
said *she* wouldn't. Backing off stage, a stagehand unhooked her robe.
Technically *she* didn't remove anything. Sally was clever, temperamental, and stubborn.

One judge fined her while telling her she was a "beautiful artistic dancer." Her attorneys filed a petition to force the police to stop
harassing her.

The arrests drove in audiences. She was swimming in "sensational publicity."

Fully embracing her nudity and the attention it brought, she earned more money than ever. She worked multiple jobs at various nightclubs in the Loop. It was claimed she was making between $90 and $1,000 a week, but in a largely cash business, we will never know.

Sally Rand was on everyone's lips. Audiences gasped and screamed when she dropped her fans and stood behind a backlit scrim. Or performing outside, her bare bottom faced the band, who "got a completely different view" of Sally.

"Everyone adored Sally." She had a winning combination of healthy sex appeal and charm. As pretty as anyone's sister, she appeared wholesome and happy. Despite her nudity Sally Rand looked like the ideal of the American Sweetheart: petite, fit, curly-haired, with a bubbly personality. As the "metaphor for hope and optimism," Sally was everyone's darling.

Concerned members of society continued to file complaints against the "lewd and lascivious dances and exhibits," demanding all the nudes be thrown out of the world's fair. It was a very real threat, and Sally should have been concerned that her newly found fame could vanish at any second. It would never have occurred to her that *this*, this fan waving, would last a lifetime.

Police forced a rhumba dance at the Manhattan Gardens concession halted. Girls wearing gold paint, shorts, and bras had upset Mayor Kelly.

Objections kept pouring in until finally a 1:30 a.m. curfew was imposed. Entrance gates would close at 11:30 to crack down on the wildness happening after midnight with the lake-size amounts of beer being consumed.

Despite repeated threats, nudity was here to stay. Sally's success, and those of her sisters on the midway, ensured that unclothed women would be a staple at future fairs. A million visitors enjoyed the masses of nudies in the first two weeks alone. Millions more would look past today and its hardships and toward tomorrow where pleasure would once again be obtainable for all.

Thanks in very large part to Sally, the Streets of Paris pulled in hundreds of thousands of dollars every week. One of the places she worked was the Café de la Paix, where in a "huge amphitheater," divers illuminated by spotlights jack-knifed into a pool of water set in the center of the dining area. It allegedly made $2,500 a day. A french fry concession made $70 a day, the peep show raked in $500. The 82 miles of exhibits in the Streets of Paris were packed day and night. Because it was a mostly cash business, the Streets soon had to set up a "separate banking facility" because of the volume of greenbacks stuffing registers.

The fair tried to strike a balance between tantalizing and appeasing the peoples of the world who might take offense at too many bare bosoms. With Chicago hotels at full occupancy, the city couldn't afford to crack down too hard. There would be many half-hearted efforts and much vocal blustering in the paper that amounted to not much of anything.

Attorney Mary Belle Spencer hauled Sally and her fans into court. Spencer wanted the dance stopped. The broad-minded judge was of another mind. "People go to 'Paris' to see what they never saw before. If they're shocked, they can go home," he ruled. The judge even cited her stunt as Lady Godiva at the previous year's Artists Ball. "Sally Rand is well known around Chicago." He said of her audience that "a lot of boobs come to see a woman wiggle with a fan or without fig leaves. But we have the boobs and we have a right to cater to them." He banged his gavel and ruled her dance was not lewd.

By now a visit to the fair meant an obligatory trip to see Sally. Her association with this modern fair, with the sleek buildings devoid of ornamentation, ensured her association in people's minds as a symbol of the new woman. Standing unashamedly on her own, fans raised high like Lady Liberty's torch.

Reporters discovered Sally's indefatigable gift of gab. She was invited by numerous organizations to speak at luncheons and conventions. At one engagement for the Junior Chamber of Commerce she explained "the aesthetic and financial values" of her dance to the hundred members.

"I have not been put out of work since the day I took my pants off," she laughed, admitting it took "hours of practice" in front of a mirror to appear elegant, and hide her nudity. "The Rand is quicker than the eye," she joked. Next she varied her stock story, telling how the fan dance "evolved after I was asked to dance as nearly nude as possible."

She was introduced as a "graduate" of Columbia University. Pure fiction. Playing the sympathy card, she explained to the curious faces that she started dancing as a "sickly child." Tall tales flew easily from her mouth, just like the birds over her grandfather's lake.

Chapter

TWENTY

IT WAS ANNOUNCED THAT FAITH WOULD APPEAR AT THE
Hollywood-at-the-Fair concession. Faith was finally heading to Chicago, hoping for her share of accolades. Was it too late to reclaim her title?

Sally would have come to Faith's attention with the arrests that kept making the papers. If she had up to now dismissed Sally, this usurper had become a threat. After all, it had been *her* arrest for doing the fan dance that had made *her* famous. Faith had to be fuming.

At the fair Faith insisted on being billed as "the originator" of the fan dance and "inventor of the skin displaying act."

Was it curiosity or intimidation when Sally and some friends slinked into the front row for Faith's premier appearance? Afterward the group applauded and left. Faith might have been rattled. Sally decided it was time to switch her fans to "underfed ostriches," making sure her nudity was easier to see. Sally and Faith's "war" would be mostly played out in the newspapers, while they each tried to outdo the other—outrageous stunts and arrests and headlines became their calling cards for the public's attention.

For at least one reporter Faith was the better wielder of the fans, and he proclaimed hers "the best show on the grounds."

Headlines screamed: it was war. Both Sally and Faith declared themselves "the best nude in the business." Faith and Sally performed at many of the same clubs, sometimes within a week of each other.

After "Sally has asked her to take over the nude spot" at one club, Faith, not liking the salary offered, declined. "I'd be very happy to do it for nothing and pull Sally out of the red," she told reporters, "if she'd accept a six-year course in ballet from me. The ethereal fan dance has been made so ludicrous in her hands that part of the time I deny having originated it."

Just months earlier Faith had been "hiding behind a few beads" at the Monte Carlo de Casino on Broadway, where the tables were numbered and "a lighted wheel behind the orchestra was spun between dances to decide the distribution of favors to guests."

The mighty promotional machine behind the world's fair had already benefited Sally. The fair had "flooded the nation with publicity releases." Dozens of full-time reporters covered the goings-on, including Sally Rand, whose fame had achieved "staggering proportions."

It cannot be overstressed how much the national and international press turned Sally into a household name. Did she look back to 1923, when she had performed at the Marigold Gardens in Chicago for thirty-five dollars a week, in astonishment? She was making more money than ever—and everyone knew her name.

She had been in the right place at the right time. No matter how many fan dancers fluttered their way to Chicago, it was Sally the paying audience wanted to see. In their minds *she* was the original. It was a bitter pill for Faith, who needed to scheme her way in front of Sally. Faith tried to outstrip Sally. It became a battle of "belles being staged to see who can wear the least." Sally "used less of the fans than ever and brighter lights" to "combat Miss Bacon's more expert manipulating of the fans." Sally revealed more, believing nudity would swat Faith away like a pesky mosquito.

People would debate who was the better dancer. There were differences in their presentations. Faith performed in a "single dimension" as if a "wall" was behind her. Perhaps she felt she should remain at a distance, an object to be looked upon, whereas Sally performed as if she was in the "center of the floor," viewed close up and from all sides. She worked the crowd, begging for their love. "I'm up here . . . for *your* pleasure," Sally said. Every man in the joint felt as if Sally played to him.

Faith was aloof, deliberately keeping herself distant. It was second nature, Charmion had seen to that. Faith said the more nude one was onstage, the more one should give "an impression of aloofness and propriety." She was also quite nearsighted, so how much of the audience she could even see was questionable, which would have contributed to her appearing standoffish. In clubs where dancers were encouraged to mingle with the customers, Faith refused, as if she was better than them.

Sally laughed at any notice of being fancy, saying, "Sure I'm an Ozark hillbilly. Started going barefooted early and now I go barefoot to my chin."

Faith came across as more refined; she spoke softly, knew some French, was "nude and free on the stage, but timid and shy" off.

Sally was the proletarian's pinup. She empathized with the folks standing in long lines ready to hand over precious quarters to see her. She genuinely appreciated them.

Faith had less love for her audience. "In a night club, when I'm on the floor, I'm in a world apart from the people who are looking at me . . . I'm not conscious of the dopes sitting there."

Cruelly, twenty-three-year-old Faith was now reading she was a

has-been. It was false, she had not stopped working, but the taint of
something past its prime would stick.

There is existing footage of Sally dancing outdoors amongst tables as a "free attraction" three times a day. Her dance, wherever she
performed, was so popular she could not stop. Sally was rumored to
be earning $2,500 a week, far more than Faith, but that could be due
to the many places employing her at the same time. "Rumors of a
rift" spread about Sally and the managers at the Italian Village.

Sally was part of a vaudeville lineup at the Chicago Theatre.
She did two numbers, one skipping about in "billowing skirts."
In the second, the lights darkened for her fan number. She descended the stairs, disrobing completely. It was noted she was "not
a remarkable dancer."

The workload and stress got to her. She collapsed under the
"strain" of being arrested four times in one day at the Chicago Theatre. She was not getting enough sleep. It was probably around this
time that she began to take amphetamines to keep her going. Benzedrine had recently debuted and would earn Sally a reputation as a
nonstop talker and a whirl of unflagging energy.

Abruptly she terminated her engagement at the fair, saying she
was returning to the stage and screen. Sally still ached for the legitimacy of a serious acting career. She was tossing her feathers aside.
She signed to do the film *Search for Beauty*, starring Ida Lupino, with
Paramount Pictures. She ultimately did not appear in it.

Others said she quit the fair over a salary dispute. She was dis-
gusted by all the poor imitators on the midway waving their fans,
trying to infringe on her territory.

"I took the opportunity that came to me," Sally said. "Certainly
I am an opportunist." And now it was time to take her accolades
and return to her first love, the stage and films. She was returning to
Hollywood.

The day she quit the fair, Sally boarded a speedboat and headed toward the mouth of the Chicago River. The wind in her hair, the days of being homeless and starving behind her, she was relaxed. As the boat turned sharply, Sally was tossed into the cold water. She let out a scream. A young man on the pier dived in and rescued her.

Doing an abrupt about-face, Sally announced she was accepting employment at the Old Manhattan Garden in the Oriental Village at the fair at $750 a week.

In October, a New York judge wanted her dressed, threatening the license of the club and calling Sally's act "repulsive to public decency."

She was ordered to wear opaque foundation. Her dance was "indecent and immoral and cannot be tolerated by" the court. Sally openly wept. Wearing underwear would ruin her act. Sticking up for her (and for a potential loss of ticket sales), the manager told the judge Sally's act was "highly artistic, decent, and proper."

Defeated—temporarily—Sally donned underwear made of lace her mother had sewed.

Due to exhaustion and a growing temperament (no doubt due to the pressures, arrests, challenges, competition from Faith, no sleep, pills, and smoking), Sally increasingly fought with those she felt did not treat her properly. Many noticed she insisted she be treated like a star.

She fought with Sam Balkin, the manager of the Paramount Club. When she told him she was quitting, he docked her for missed performances. As he was handing over the cash, she claimed he purposefully gave her a black eye. She bit his arm. The next day she went to the police and demanded he be arrested.

Balkin showed his wrist in court and cried, "Look! She bites the hand that feeds her."

Brother Hal's temper also landed him in hot water. Along with Sally's maid Mattie, he was charged with resisting an officer, trying to protect Sally from a different arrest in October.

She replaced evangelist (and con woman) Aimee Semple McPherson at an event in Chicago because Aimee's prior crowds had been smaller than what an appearance by Sally could guarantee.

Her time in court piled up. There was a breach of contract suit against her manager. Sally settled for $2,500 and signed with the William Morris Agency. Then Sally received sad news; her friend Big Ed Callahan had quarreled with some connected men over liquor distribution and was killed. He would never get to see her astounding success.

She boasted Hollywood was hers to conquer. "The fan dance was a means to an end," she admitted, "and the end was Hollywood." Acting would give her legitimacy.

Wrapped in a fur, Sally told a group of reporters, "With every other dancer in the country picking up fans I've decided to cast mine aside." She wouldn't be allowed to.

There were so many imitators of "her" dance that she vowed, "I'll never do the fan dance in a theatre again."

Sally was loath to ever again be one of a dozen. She was not going back in the chorus. She had made herself a headliner, and even if it meant changing her signature number, she was determined to stay front and center. Perhaps too Sally felt the heat generated as Faith flapped herself dangerously close to stealing her crowd.

It was time for the Century of Progress to close its gates "in a blaze of glory."

The city had shown great foresight in putting on the fair. Over 40 million people had visited Chicago, spending $200 million.

"It was a great splash of color . . . upon a background of times in which grays were too heavily predominating."

When the popcorn dust settled, it was calculated the Streets of Paris had taken in more than any other concession—an astounding

$100,000 a day—in large part due to the appearance of Sally Rand. Sally's contribution was significant, not just to the coffers of the fair, but to American pop culture. Pushing her nudity, she created her own sexual revolution whereby the next generation of women were even freer, less dependent on a man for their value and their destiny. By taking off her clothes, Sally took off American blinders to the repression of women. It was a start.

Lucky "hundreds of thousands of visitors . . . gazed upon the alluring form of Sally."

Arguably Sally's most valuable contribution during the Depression was helping others forget their tough times. One stranger was so inspired he sent roses and a note saying her dance "had made the world a better place." She was beauty, grace, and hope during difficult days. By the time Sally and her fan dance came along, society's thoughts on women's independence were radically changing. So too was any thought of a woman having control over the displaying of her body. And here stood a woman, on her own, from a poor background, waving her way to the top. People fell in love with her—almost more as a symbol than a real woman. She was never described as sexy; it was always wholesome, charming, pert. She was nonthreatening. She was everyone's sister, neighbor, sweetheart. A cutie with dimples who was taking on society's mores.

Promoters pretended the nudity on the midway was an emancipation of sorts for women, despite the fact it was "increased liberation . . . at the cost of the further commercialization of beauty."

But no one exploited her beauty and nudity more than Sally, and doing so to benefit herself. She was not at the mercy of a man or institution. She was firmly aware that she "was an inconspicuous figure . . . before the Century of Progress gave her an opportunity."

Faith, on the other hand, most likely was absent from the close of the fair. She had been in an auto accident, badly spraining her back.

Doctors would not allow her to dance, but were optimistic that she "will be able to walk all right in a few days."

Employment at the fair had given new life to Faith's career as well. She was again sought after and in demand, though the shadow of Sally's great notoriety continued to dampen her feelings of confidence. She felt she had to do *something* to scramble back on top.

Part

FOUR

TWENTY-ONE

AT THE START OF 1934, FAITH WAS BEING BILLED AS "ONE OF THE world's finest exponents of the dance" along with other Century of Progress acts. She was back touring in vaudeville, hailed as the Century of Progress star. Confident she had inched her way ahead of Sally, Faith enjoyed packed houses and rave reviews.

Her act was a "louder and more blatant hurrah of nakedness." She used her body for shock value. "They have beautiful paintings of nude women, don't they?" she asked, ". . . so we should be able to put on a dance that is Art just as nude as we want to." She then thought about it. "I guess we're not that far advanced yet."

Chicago was not ready to give up the world's attention, and it was announced the fair would return in 1934. To appease the church groups, the Streets of Paris would be without the offensive "fan dancers and peep shows." A new corporation was taking over and decided to do away with all the "vulgarity" on the "midway." Bye-bye to the "freaks" and the "tawdry."

By summer, a cleaned-up version of the fair opened, putting long pants on the "rickshaw boys" who had previously run in shorts. So tame did the fair become, audiences were favoring the "ten burlesque shows on South State Street."

The fair abruptly did an "about face" and returned the nudies to the midway.

There was Mona Leslie, a "Dancing Venus" in platinum-colored paint, who dove into a pool only to rise, a harrowing ten minutes later, from the water on a pedestal. To perform her trick she hid in an underwater tunnel. Dorothy Dennis performed in black paint. There were nudes and semi-nudes in "practically every café, beer garden, or racy concession at the fair."

Faith had a new dance, "Falling Petal," sometimes called "Goddess of the Gardenias," at the horticultural exhibit, clad in a smattering of gardenias. While audiences sweated in the brutal heat Faith kept "very cool" in her abbreviated costume.

The owner of the Hawaiian Gardens confiscated Faith's fans, claiming he had paid "$1,500 announcing her appearance" only to have her sign at the Hollywood concession. She quickly ditched the Hollywood and retrieved her fans.

Hawaii was not yet a state when Faith and Princess Ahi shared billing at the Hawaiian Gardens. Princess Ahi was a Chinese dancer who sacrificed herself by diving into the mouth of a volcano. She and Faith were arrested and taken to the police station. Faith cried out, "I'm not nude. I've got tape."

In court an officer admitted he had been "tintillated" [sic] by Faith as she "stood in the spotlight and twisted and wriggled while all of her gardenias fell off."

In July Faith ran into more trouble with the law. Secret Service agents showed up in her dressing room at the Paramount.

They were there to inquire about a fake hundred-dollar bill she had used to pay her rent at 42 East Elm Street. She had given her landlord three bills, one of which was counterfeit.

In court for further questioning, Faith dressed somberly in black with a "black wagon wheel hat." She explained she had given her business manager/sister Charmion, living in Tucson at a sanatorium, her checks, which Charmion then cashed, sending her cash back, apparently including the fake bill.

No charges were pressed, but Faith's bad luck and run-ins with the law would not let up.

Fan dancing hit such a feverish demand, with women across America wanting to learn the art of it, that the New York School of Music added a class on how to fan dance. The previous generation's rage for ostrich feathers had dropped by the time Faith and Sally shook a pair on stage. Now they caused a boon for business.

The elegance of the art and the glamour of the fans mixed with fantasy and drama, and it seemed as if every dancer wanted to take up the practice. Dancers wanted to fly to the heights Sally and Faith had achieved. They wanted to be called winged goddesses. Yet, Sally wanted to distance herself from it. She investigated tire companies in Akron, Ohio. She had the idea for a balloon dance and thought maybe she could inflate a huge rubber ball with helium. Instead, someone figured a way for a balloon to fill as she waved it through the air, allowing the balloon to float over her head.

She would have seen the Firestone Tire and Rubber Company exhibition at the fair. They demonstrated balloon tires made from rubber. Sally had Goodyear make special light blue balloons for twenty-five cents.

She would claim to find, manufacture, and patent latex balloons that the U.S. Army wanted for aerial targets (another story was weather balloons).

The balloons were large, relatively lightweight, and impressive enough to help distance herself from an act already strangling her. Over time, the balloon act became gracefully executed. In the beginning it was oftentimes unwieldy, and when performed outdoors it frequently escaped from her grasp. Depending on the venue she either danced completely nude, wore a body stocking, or a Grecian-type chemise. On stage she positioned herself behind a dark net curtain glowing under her preferred midnight-blue spotlight, which helped create the illusion she was inside the giant balloon that varied between four and seven feet. Holding tight to her transparent balloon, Sally glided behind and underneath and behind it, usually to Brahms, "with all the grace of a woodland nymph." Sally "toyed and danced," flinging the balloon above her head. Holding it between her two outstretched hands, she gently tossed it in the air with little effort, as if it was a soap bubble. Slowly it bounced back to earth, and she kicked it up again. Gracefully she twirled herself and the balloon in circles, one hand gripping the tied end. Then with both hands behind her back she arched backwards and spun in circles. Next she lay on the ground and with the toe of her shoe kicked the balloon up. At the end of her eight- to ten-minute dance, she extended the balloon over her head, revealing her usually naked body.

But was this yet a further example of an act borrowed from another?

Rosita Royce was on the midway at the same time as Sally. Rosita's gimmick was training doves to remove her clothing. She was referred to as a "former bubble dancer" who first performed with balloons at age ten. The dark-haired beauty worked totally nude behind a transparent six-foot balloon. She had even performed in her hometown of Kansas City, where Sally could have caught it during one of her many visits.

Rosita explained, "It takes a lot of work to fill the balloon." She pumped up hers by foot on a bellows. "I am the only fan or balloon dancer who really is a nudist." She claimed her balloon dance was copyrighted and her lawyer was seeking a restraining order against Sally.

Rosita also had a feud with stripper Tirza—"the wine bath girl"—who performed under a shower of colored water. When her shower was clogged by gum, she blamed Rosita. The next time Rosita and her doves appeared, Tirza whipped out her BB gun and shot at the birds until they flew away.

The balloon act photographed more dramatically than it played. Audience reaction to Sally's balloon dance was mild. "It's just a dance, and they can take it or leave it." It looked like a return to fans.

Over 100,000 people strolled through the fair near midnight on August 3, 1934. A squad of police raided the fair, seizing gambling wheels. The Red Light Girls exhibition was closed, and Faith was "forced to put on pants." She was appalled. She had "become so used to the thought of appearing unclothed on the stage that the thought of having to wear a costume" was "simply unbearable."

Sally was packing them in at the Italian Village, alternating her balloon and fan dance.

Faith was in a vaudeville program at the State-Lake Theatre for several weeks, zipping between the fair and theatre.

She had an appendix attack at Colosimo's and vehemently refused to let doctors operate, saying she preferred to die rather than scar her perfect body.

Not much later she was rushed to the hospital and an emergency operation was performed, leaving her with a small scar she covered with body makeup. Her body would remain a temple. Untouched.

On All Hallows' Eve, October 31, 1934, the fair closed for good at 3 a.m.

Crowds with an overabundance of energy tore Sally's posters from the walls of the Italian Village. It was chaotic and the police had to be called to contain vandals breaking windows and destroying the buildings, as scavengers hunted for portable souvenirs.

Sally's meteoric rise at the fair was unprecedented. In two short years she had created a name that would last forever.

She had profoundly and forever changed popular entertainment. By promoting Sally Rand the "fan dancer" she flourished, becoming "the spirit" of the "changing notions of women and sexuality." It was noted other expositions at the fair "were theaters of power." So too was Sally's theatrical performance. She was the very symbol of a woman emerging from the Victorian era to grasp her destiny with her own two hands.

From a souvenir film one could buy of Sally at the fair: ". . . as the bubble . . . rises, falls, and floats away and returns . . . so too our hopes, dreams, and ambitions . . . "

For Faith, the bubble would slowly begin to descend.

TWENTY-TWO

SALLY MAINTAINED A CLOSE CORRESPONDENCE WITH HER MOTHER full of confidences, advice, and to-do lists.

Her mother would grow petulant when Sally didn't immediately respond to her letters. Sally explained that "in closing the Fair" she had been too busy to write. Performing twelve to sixteen shows a day for a "two year engagement" left her "very fatigued." She felt her mother wanted her to drop the very work that made their life possible.

For the past two years she had not slept properly. She worked, ran from gig to gig, gave talks, interviews, posed for pictures, showed up at court to fight arrests. She provided for her family back in California (and extended family elsewhere) and felt the burden of being the one everyone turned to for help. Sally reminded her mother that she had seen firsthand how hard Sally worked when Nettie had visited her in Chicago. Her father had managed a trip to the fair with his French wife.

Even grandmother Mollie would eventually see Sally's dance. "I think it was delightful," the dear little Quaker lady told everyone.

Sally's relationship with her mother was complicated. They were extremely close, yet often Sally was angry because "I am the one who must come to the rescue" even for distant relatives. She didn't "mind helping out." She remembered not too long ago being sick, alone, and broke, however she didn't want to be held "liable and responsible and spend all of the money that I have worked so terribly hard" for. She was furious when she sent money home. Sally felt in her marrow how fleeting "success" could be. She did not want to be hungry again.

She sent Nettie her "new bubble dance pic." She signed the letter "Helen." Just a couple months later she would sign "Sally."

Though for the next several years she would earn extravagant sums, it would slowly drip, drip away on expenses.

From the road, and she was now always on the road, Sally put together an act featuring other showgirls, perhaps to lighten her performance load. She had taken charge of the show at the Italian Village and was a natural producer, bossy, opinionated, and detail-oriented. She liked being in control of how she was presented.

Sally was busy with all-night rehearsals, teaching dances to the girls. She was on a track she could not get off. It was a relief to perform, for there she achieved a moment of "spiritual solitude." It's when "I achieve complete aloneness."

Sally, now a "marquee draw," was asked to perform in a film starring George Raft and Carole Lombard, both major stars at the time.

The film was *Bolero* for director Wesley Ruggles, an old friend.

The story was about a dancer, played by the roguish George Raft. Raft's character wants Sally, one of a "succession of alluring women," to be his partner. She refuses and Lombard steps in to fill her shoes. Their big number is sexy, including both sets of hands on Lombard's braless breasts.

Sally briefly walked off the set when she discovered she was wanted merely for her fan number. She claimed "she had been promised a chance to display her dramatic ability." She had no reason to think she would be confined to fan dancing forever. It was agreed some additions would be written in for her.

Sally is beautifully shot doing her fan dance, which testifies to the ability she had achieved wielding the enormous fans. Given top billing, Sally is marvelously effective. She does not remove any clothes nor does she dance naked in the film.

Though her part was small, she was paid $20,000. The movie would be a big enough hit that Paramount re-teamed Lombard and Raft the following year for another dance movie.

Sally used the money to purchase the land and home her mother and stepfather "were about to lose" in Glendora. The title was transferred to Sally, but her mother would continue to live there.

Hoping for more film work, Sally would be disappointed. She wouldn't make another film for four years. Hollywood remained a fickle lover. She feared Hollywood, feeling she had "no security" there. After all these years it was still a "struggle." Memories of being a hopeful starlet, hustling to be famous, would be tainted with the memory of rejection.

Meanwhile others were claiming to be originators of the fan dance. One absurd claim was from a dancer with flashing black eyes, named Fay Baker. Baker claimed she ran into Sally and Faith and all three had lunch and came up with the idea of the fan dance. Baker performed hers while tap dancing.

Faith moved her Dance of the Gardenias into the Chicago clubs. Though she would return to her fans and defend her title, it seemed she was looking for her own "balloon dance," something that would keep the headlines fresh and the crowds coming.

She would have thought her inclusion at the Fair would bring her the kind of national recognition Sally enjoyed. It did not.

Faith wore a big diamond ring on her wedding finger. In publicity photos she wore fur coats, tailored suits, and good jewelry.

Though modern-day historians say that immediately following the Chicago fair Faith faded into oblivion, it is far from the truth. She continued to work, mostly in Chicago and New York, constantly lauded for giving an artistic performance.

Working too hard, she had a return of ill health. She was pale and "consumptive." Faith downed cod-liver oil to "build up her frail body."

Faith, and to a degree Sally, were dancing against time. Though scores of women were picking up fans, the dance was becoming dated.

Mae West and Sally Rand were the record earners amongst women entertainers of 1934. America was now rewarding confident, sexual women.

The economy was incrementally turning around. Unemployment fell from a soul-wrenching 25 percent to a hopeful 17 percent.

Gone was Ziegfeld, dead at age sixty-five. The following year Earl Carroll would declare bankruptcy, and George White had turned his *Scandals* into movies. It was a changing landscape for the showgirl.

Vaudeville was dying. The kind of venue that would employ a fan dancer was left to the burlesque houses, which emphasized the taking off of clothes. More people were flocking to movies to be entertained.

Our fan dancers continued to wave their plumage in cabarets, restaurants, vaudeville, and burlesque houses.

Many times they danced before the showing of films, like Faith in Chicago at the Ritz before the film *Gold Diggers of 1935*.

Sally was in New York with her bubble dance as "*Moonlight Sonata* and a Brahms waltz" played. *Variety* called it a "strip bubble dance" where her chiffon "dress slips" and she is "exposed."

Initially engaged for two weeks, Sally stayed eighteen, smashing records at N.T.G.'s Paradise Café. Another three-week tour turned into three months, with an average ticket price of two dollars. She played Boston, Akron, Los Angeles, Chicago, and Wisconsin with her troupe of flawless showgirls who danced and roller-skated on stage. Many she hired were former *Follies* and *Vanities* girls. At the end of the show, Sally made a little speech from the stage promising a new dance the following year.

She again swore she would "abandon fans" and play Shakespearean roles. In particular she had her sights on the role of Portia. "When this time of earning has passed, I'm going to France," she grandly announced. She didn't say what she intended to do there.

Popular with ladies groups, she spoke on a variety of matters, including her dance and "the bare facts of beauty" in front of six hundred. She gave cooking classes at colleges. She was charming, intelligent, and funny. Causing a near-riot at an appearance at the Illinois state legislature, she talked about art for art's sake. At the Youngstown YMCA she spoke about "the economic dangers of communism in America," wearing a chic yellow scarf, marine-colored suit, and hat. She spoke of adversity and landing in a flop show in Chicago that forced her to conceive of her fan dance. "Dancing is a more normal form of expression that touches a primitive urge in all of us."

Hoping to change the public perception of her, she appeared buttoned-up and ladylike in hats, gloves, and high collars when in public. She hated being referred to as a "stripper," pointing out she neither teased nor removed her own clothes. Instead, she designed her act so her clothes appeared to be removed magically. One minute they were there and the next they were not. (In reality, at some point in her dance she moved toward the curtains where a stagehand would stealthily pull her gown off without being seen. In later years, her son handled those duties.)

Sally reconnected with Jack Dempsey when both were judges at a cocktail mixing contest at the fighter's new restaurant in Manhattan. Sally Rand was a celebrity who drew crowds.

"I had . . . the ability to give an illusion of ethereal beauty. My merchandise was my dance." Acknowledging she had to keep up with the times, she sought to "change merchandise."

Her bubble dance continued to garner less-than-stellar reviews. It seemed to lack skill and hampered her actual dancing. Some complained the ball was constantly up in the air, leaving her bare and lacking any "mystery" or "allure." At venues that had already been witness to her bubble and fan dances, she performed a Leda and Her Swan routine (something Faith would do later as well). By awkwardly strapping wings to herself, she painted an "ungraceful picture." Some sniped she "has dropped far below her fan-dancing standard of popular appeal." "Brief and uninteresting," *Variety* opined, this was the "weakest" of her acts and quite "meaningless."

Asked if she contemplated marriage, she admitted, "I haven't time to think about marriage now. I am much too busy."

She kept up a punishing schedule of one- and two-night stands, performing seventy-one out of seventy-eight days. Not every engagement was pleasant. One night in Florida, dancing close to the audience, a young serviceman managed to lift her dress and bite her on the behind.

Another time in South Bend, Indiana, a mischievous fan shot nails at her, bursting her bubble and piercing her lower eyelid. She reprimanded the offender, and though it isn't recorded what she said, Sally swore like the proverbial sailor. "She would get in your face." Tough and temperamental, she had come too far to let pranksters mess with her. "She was a great lady, but a bitch-on-wheels" when crossed.

Banned from a stage in Providence, Rhode Island, she prevailed on a local reverend whose parish was in the same district as the theatre. The reverend would not relent. There would be no Sally Rand for his brethren "even if she came on the stage wrapped in the back drop."

"He was cruel and most unreasonable," she said. She too could quote the Bible. "Let him who is without sin amongst you cast the first stone." She showed letters from other Catholic priests defending her. The answer remained "no." He explained, "Your performance would cause sins of thought on the part of members of my flock."

Sally sighed, "It's just a shame that there are narrow-minded persons who can't differentiate between art and indecency."

She made her way to Skowhegan, Maine, in August to perform in *Rain* as the tarnished prostitute Sadie Thompson opposite Humphrey Bogart, who was a year away from his breakout performance opposite Bette Davis in *The Petrified Forest*.

Lakewood Theatre had the reputation as a "jewel of America's resident stock companies." Plays presented there hoped to make the leap to Broadway.

The community was ideal for the outdoor-loving Sally with tennis courts, fishing, and water sports in a lush setting of lakes and pine-covered mountains. Most likely Sally shared a bungalow with another actress, as that was the norm.

Critics noted "her voice as clear and well-placed." The audience stood to their feet and cheered, forcing her to take five curtain calls.

She would revisit Sadie Thompson again in 1941 at the Woodstock Playhouse, and cartoonist Al Hirschfeld immortalized her in a drawing as the South Seas siren.

In August Sally contacted the police, frantic. Her "red-headed sweetheart" was missing. She had police search for two days for her bearded, green-eyed fiancé Charles Mahan. He had disappeared after he left Cheyenne, where Sally was, headed for Chicago in her big

Lincoln sedan. After he reappeared, Sally refused to talk about it. His disappearance would remain a secret. They would be over as a couple by the following year.

Sally focused on her grove-to-consumer orange business, but grumbled to her mother about the bills piling up; a $600 mortgage payment, $600 for spraying, and taxes, fertilizers, groceries.

Sally sent money home, but not without protesting. She was constantly "in debt." It seems she said, "I'm working to pay the fan ballet!"

She felt bad that her mother worried, but said, "I put forth every effort and the result is far from what it ought to be." Large sums of money slipped through her hands. She couldn't remain on the road earning money and supervise what was happening in California. The road was difficult and not always profitable. In Wisconsin she had to "reduce my company to a point where I could just break even."

To reporters she remained lighthearted. Eating a hearty breakfast of ham, eggs, cereal, juice, and muffins, she announced, "I want to change the public's conception of me." Said while wearing a negligee.

By all appearances she was successful, with a Filipino servant (all the rage at the time) named Alfredo, and two Pekingese dogs, Snoofy and China Boy. The public was fascinated by why she wasn't married. She had "two minds about marriage," noting "I have the primitive urge for marriage and children." But "the thing I'm doing requires a certain freedom. I should have married very young." She was thirty-one. A future husband would have to be "very understanding" and would have to "grant me a certain amount of individualism." One who could deal with all the criticism, like from the Boston city censor who ordered her to put on more clothes. She was outraged. "Does he want me to carry fans in my toes?"

TWENTY-THREE

SO POPULAR WAS THE FAN DANCE THAT SOCIAL REALISM PAINTER Reginald Marsh did a bold nude painting called "Fan Dancer at Jimmy Kelly's." A frequent visitor to the burlesque houses, the artist could conceivably have been in the audience when either or both Sally and Faith were performing. The woman he paints is blonde with a huge feathered fan. She is exultantly nude, with breasts bared, and is posed in Sally's signature pose, her knee raised for modesty. The chunky thighs give credence to the belief it is more Sally than slim-hipped Faith. There are leering men in close proximity to her fans. Jimmy Kelly's was a popular restaurant in Greenwich Village owned by an underworld figure who regularly employed fan dancers to entertain customers. It is not unlikely that both Faith and Sally were employed by him at one time or another.

Sally kept breaking records and was held over at the Biltmore Bowl (at the Biltmore Hotel) in Los Angeles. She had a deal where she took any cover charges over one dollar, netting herself between

$3,000 and $4,000 a week. Her final week she made $5,000. Sally was squeezing every ounce out of her popularity. She didn't even mind—too much—the one drunk who rushed on stage and took her bubble. At least it made the paper.

Elsewhere pranksters harassed her with rocks, cigarettes, slingshots, anything to pop her bubble. A young man was caught with an air gun and slingshot. "Aren't you sorry you tried to do this?" Sally confronted him.

"I wouldn't have been caught if I'd gone down the other aisle."

Nothing deterred her, neither hooligans nor a snow-covered Columbia, South Carolina. She simply threw on a fur coat for a performance on the State House lawn.

She rolled with the punches. Once when the truck containing her balloons failed to show, she scoured a local toy store, buying up what she could. Her shows always went on.

Sally was photographed in Wild Bill Cummings's speedster at Daytona, driving over 100 miles an hour on the course. She was fearless and undoubtedly impressed Cummings, who had been the 1934 winner of the Indianapolis 500 and would later die tragically in an auto accident.

She continued to read scripts in search of a great play or movie. In the meantime there were more world's fairs to captivate.

A total of 100 million people would attend the world's fairs in America from 1933 through 1940. Many of them would see our two dancers.

Sally arrived in April at the idyllic seaside city of San Diego for the '35–'36 California Pacific International Exposition. Old pals Fanchon and Marco were booking acts and signed her for three weeks as a free attraction. She would alternate between her fans and balloons.

Many exhibits from the Century of Progress would be transported to San Diego along with some of the same popular acts.

Again nudity was front and center.

Sally danced with thick white makeup painted over her body (which sometimes made her itch) and wore a beautiful blonde wig as her hair was actually "stubby." Her awkward ballet dance (half the time without her balloon) was performed nude around a pond with a splashing fountain that sprayed her. She was reveling in her nudity. The "dance" was secondary. Performing two shows a day and two a night at the Plaza del Pacifico kept her busy.

Another attraction causing a stir was the Zoro Garden Nudist Colony, promoting a healthy outdoor lifestyle, or more likely trying to get away with showing as much flesh as possible. The colony was populated by hired help with gorgeous figures, as opposed to real nudists. For an admission fee one gazed upon half-clad girls playing volleyball and sunbathing. As can be imagined, it was not without its protesters, including women's civic and religious groups.

The nudists, in probably another publicity stunt, protested Sally's arrival when she refused to visit them. The nudists held placards that read "Sally Rand Unfair to Nudism" because Sally was claiming her form of nudity, not Zoro's, was art.

"I like to be as naked as possible," Sally said. But clarified, "I'm against organized nudism." Or anyone who took away from her appearance. Maybe that is why her "dance"—and it seems unfair to call it that—was really more showing off her body. "All the nudists I saw," she sniped, "had scratches all over their rear ends."

No matter how much she dismissed them, Sally must have taken a peek (there were strategic holes in the fence surrounding the exhibit), because by the time of the Fort Worth Frontier Centennial Exposition in June of the same year, she was promoting her own nude show. So much for art.

Sally was never above taking a good idea and making it her own, never capable of crediting anyone else.

Again she was a target when "rowdies peppered her with pebbles," leaving her cut and bruised. She had to retreat to retrieve a spare balloon to finish the dance. A guard was placed at her act but could do nothing about the swarm of bees that next attacked.

Sally spent time away from dancing, flying over the city. She gave a multitude of interviews and lectures. However, she wouldn't allow morning interviews as she hated getting up early.

She visited Paramount studios in Los Angeles and ran into her old boss Cecil B. DeMille. She smiled. He smiled. He wasn't quite sure who she was.

"Don't you recognize me dressed?" she quipped.

"I hear you're looking for a girl to play Calamity Jane in your new Gary Cooper picture." The director admitted he was. "And that she is supposed to be the toughest, most glamorous, most beautiful woman in the West. Have you thought of me?"

Coyly, DeMille answered, "You're the best possibility for the role, yet." Jean Arthur would get the part.

Sally's name drew the crowds. However, it did not always add up to financial success. It was assumed the San Diego Expo was a walloping success. But privately she worried because it had been "quite a flop." She needed "new publicity impetus," and for the first time she was "under 'canvas'" touring with a bevy of girls, charging promoters $600 for her show.

Life on the road was never easy. "Six ministers in Cheyenne and the Bishop in Denver and all the mealy-mouth old maids raised hell about me being an immoral person and totally improper."

A "freak western wind" blew her stage down. Management had to send for a new tent, which was expensive. Sally rallied the troops and had the whole thing repaired and up by opening day, only to have another storm hit.

There were sheets of wind and hail. The hail "gathered in pockets" that pushed down the tent until it burst. Luckily the ground dried out by showtime, Sally reassuring management "that hot or cold weather or dry weather, rain or snow, the show would go on and it did." Twelve thousand people saw her over five days. She felt the entire community took her into "their hearts."

Life in the spotlight came with a price. "He that is first, must perpetually live in the white light of publicity." Sally was perhaps throwing in a dig at Faith, who still publically insisted she was the originator of the fan dance.

In July of 1936, Sally was in San Antonio posing in front of the Alamo. She was there to perform in the Fort Worth Frontier celebration. Fort Worth and Dallas each had dueling fairs celebrating 100 years of Texas. Fort Worth had two things going for it. First, it had won Sally's presence.

She did have outrageous competition for publicity. Local stars and Siamese twins Daisy and Violet Hilton, attempting a comeback of sorts, staged a marriage in front of a paying crowd of hundreds. Daisy was noticeably pregnant at the time her sister Violet married a homosexual member of their vaudeville troupe.

Luckily for Sally, her picture appeared hundreds of times in the newspapers. The "sheer volume of publicity" she generated meant booming business for the fair. She threw out the first pitch at ball games. She gave interviews and speeches. She was admired as "one of the sharpest and shrewdest women." She admitted she was in negotiations to buy thousands of acres so she could become a resident of Texas.

Texas declared November 6 "Sally Rand Day."

Fort Worth's other secret weapon was Billy Rose. Rose, the lyricist of "Me and My Shadow" among other popular songs, was still married to funny woman Fanny Brice (they would divorce in '38). He was an impressively diminutive 5 feet 2, pot-bellied and likened to an "urchin." Like Sally, Billy made up for his stature by smoking and talking nonstop.

Sally rehearsing her balloon act at Casa Mañana, 1934

Rose hired Sally to perform at Casa Mañana, his enormous outdoor amphitheatre that held 4,500 and had the world's largest revolving stage surrounded by a moat and dozens of jets sending a curtain
of water 40 feet in the air. Portions of the stage were exposed steel,
which amplified the brutal summer heat and had to be cooled off before each performance, not to mention how unforgiving the surface
was on the dancers' feet and legs.

The publicity-hungry Rose plastered thousands of billboards
across many states, vowing to "put on a show the likes of which has
never been seen by the human eye."

The talent included Ann Pennington performing as "Little
Egypt," bumping and grinding so wildly that beads from her costume landed in patrons' soup bowls.

Before and after the show hundreds of guests danced to two orchestras on the extra-wide stage.

Billed as "America's No. 1 Stripper," Sally performed two shows a night with her fans under a midnight-blue light to a waltz, making sure to turn her bare backside to the audience. After Rose complained her dance was "dated," she switched to her balloon dance.

One afternoon after walking in a light shower after a storm, Sally returned to her dressing room and flipped the light switch. The electrical shock that followed burned her thumb, bringing her to her knees. She continued with her show that night after a brief visit to the hospital.

As Rose's headliner, Sally wore no more than her usual makeup, "carefully applied by her 'male maid,'" which had the thickness of "plaster."

Though Sally had loudly protested the nudists in San Diego, she now decided to incorporate her own "Nude Ranch," knocking the Hilton sisters off the pages with her posse of naked cowgirls. At her exhibit, a giant sign was displayed, SALLY RAND'S DUDE RANCH. Except the "D" was crossed out and replaced with an "N" above it. Sally advertised for girls with perfect figures, though the candidates could be of any height. She settled on fifteen girls.

The girls "cavort behind glass wearing as little as the law allowed." They were outfitted in gilded cowboy boots, holsters, guns, and green bandanas around their necks. Ten-gallon hats kept the sun off their faces, and except for g-strings they were nude. Each girl displayed a rubber-stamped "SR" on her bare thigh.

The girls tossed beach balls, played with bows and arrows, or sat on horses in front of an audience who paid twenty-five cents to view the "athletic gyrations."

Hostess Sally was dressed in full cowgirl garb. And though technically Sally didn't own the concession, she received a share of admissions. Open only during daylight hours, *all the better to see you, my dear*, it was blatantly exploitive, using Sally's name to great advantage.

One columnist complained the nudists "looked to me as though a bath wouldn't hurt." Still the crowds lined up.

Sally quit Casa Mañana on November 1, two weeks before the close of the fair, taking Rose's "best dancers" with her. Despite the lines, the fair would lose $97,000.

The Nude Ranch would be closed for unpaid bills to the tune of $41,350. The owner left town and Sally departed with her 10 percent royalty.

Despite the crowds Sally brought, fairs were having an impossible time trying to replicate the financial success of the Century of Progress. The exhibitors at the Lower Rio Grande Valley Fair were distressed to find they made no profit from Sally, partly due to her negotiating skills. They did not receive a cut of her ticket sales (also there was the matter of a stand collapsing, repairs, and medical costs to deal with). And church groups still protested her nude appearance. The local Calvary Baptist Church called her "immoral" and an "insult to the decency of . . . womanhood."

It was indeed a bumpy ride.

TWENTY-FOUR

INTO 1936 FAITH CONTINUED TO SHUTTLE BETWEEN POPULAR joints like Colosimo's in Chicago and the Paradise in New York for long engagements, always headlining. With nonstop work she believed she would remain at the top, earning more than most, dazzling audiences as a "high priced attraction." If she wasn't yet thinking about what came next, she was enjoying needling Sally in the press with her "original" fan dancer label. However, she spent the majority of the time defending her right to be nude because her act was "artistic."

In New York she attended a Ziegfeld Girls meeting at Sherry's, a ritzy hotel on Fifth Avenue. Also in attendance was Gypsy Rose Lee, at the height of her ecdysiastical powers. It was unusual for Faith to hang with the girls, but it meant something to be a Ziegfeld alumna. Perhaps she longed for camaraderie and support now that Charmion wasn't supervising her every move.

At twenty-five she declared, "I've achieved success in my art— I've reached the top in my field. In a little while I'd like to quit." Her time at the Chicago fair was exhausting, and now she was shuttling from club to club.

She was added to *Broadway After Dark,* a revue at Loew's State Theatre. She had plenty of work, if fewer headlines than Sally.

Faith was sensitive about her past. When reporters asked her probing questions she turned angry. "I am a native of California" was about all she would say.

As Christmas decorations were hung along State Street, Faith was set to perform at the State-Lake Theatre in Chicago. It was cold. The "feather dancer" posed with a fake bird on her head. Novelty acts such as tumblers, glass blowers, and a trained seal filled the bill.

"The Show was called 'Temptations,'" she described the night, "and all the girls were supposed to be temptations, you know, temptations of man. One was power, another was wine, another was pearls, and so on. I was beauty."

Faith had already dazzled them with her Bird of Paradise act when she climbed on top of a specially made glass drum to pose in the nude.

The curtains parted.

"I was wearing a special spray, which brings out the better points of the body, and there were lights shining on me up through the top of the glass box." It would have been a stunning effect, her slim pale body illuminated from below.

"Well . . . I crashed through the box." Pandemonium broke out on stage with girls "screaming for a doctor and running around." The trooper that she was, and in shock, Faith climbed out of the broken drum and danced over the shattered glass. Then she collapsed.

Someone picked her up from the stage, covered her eyes, and warned her not to look at her legs. She was taken to the hospital and underwent surgery without anesthesia.

After spending a month in the hospital, she was left with "deep and ugly scars" on both legs. "It was two months before I could dance again, and I still can't toe dance. I even had to learn to walk."

It was a painful recovery, compounded with worry that she could not afford not to work because of her invalid sister she supported.

She was probably encouraged by some acquaintances she was socializing with to file a lawsuit against the theatre asking for $100,000.

As Faith recovered, the Chicago police closed in on a "gigantic ambulance-chasing" racket involving hundreds of doctors, lawyers, undertakers, and hospital workers.

The gang operated when a person was hurt in a car accident. Once he or she was taken to the hospital, an informant contacted an attorney who then finagled his way into the hospital and handed the victim a contract to sign, allowing the attorney to go ahead and sue various organizations.

The eight accused ringleaders included forty-six-year-old Lucien Plant, his wife, Dorothy, and her daughter, twenty-seven-year-old Elizabeth Dickinson, who was Faith's friend and at whose apartment Faith was now recovering.

The group, accused of swindling not only accident victims but insurance companies, was arrested at several apartments that had multiple phone lines, "extensive filing cabinets," and "short wave radio sets tuned to the police broadcast" to learn about collisions as they happened.

Police discovered the victims, some "crippled for life" after innocently colluding with the gang, only "received a few dollars" compensation while the crooks collected the majority of the insurance money.

Faith was in the apartment at 720 North Wabash—suspiciously furnished as an office with a man working the "short wave radio receiver"—when the police raided. Because she was still recuperating from her injuries, police delayed questioning her. She would be swiftly exonerated, but the kind of company she was keeping would do much to hasten her downfall. She began a habit of initiating annoying and trivial lawsuits.

Chapter

TWENTY-FIVE

THE DREAM OF A THEATRICAL CAREER GNAWED AT SALLY. IN 1937 she undulated into the role of Tondelayo in *White Cargo* at Provincetown, Massachusetts. Her character was a seductive half-Egyptian and half-Arabian woman. Certainly not typecasting, but stunt casting.

Though she yearned to be a serious actress and wore a sarong in the part, Sally made the audience wait as she changed into a long gown and hat for her curtain call, acting the grand dame of the theatre. The cast was not pleased or impressed by her airs.

The usurper who "used to hold my fans," as Faith called Sally, was destroying Faith's peace of mind as she grew increasingly bitter. Not only did Sally command a higher salary, she received publicity for nearly everything. "I'm an artist," Faith defended herself. "Rand is a business woman." Faith must have smiled when newspapers called Sally "chunky" while she retained her lissome figure.

Faith wasn't without her supporters. She was still noted as being the "most daring of all nudes," cursed with being "the most perfectly formed girl in the world."

Recovered from her accident, by February of 1937 Faith returned to Colosimo's with more tap dancers and tumblers. She continued with various dances, one where "she comes on the stage wearing three orchids . . . and sheds them in a somewhat sensational manner that almost knocks your eyes out." Because the "management wouldn't agree to pay for the three orchids daily," Faith bought them herself. She could afford to. Engagements were lined up.

She purchased lakefront property in Beverly Shores, Indiana, promising to build by the spring. Beverly Shores was a planned community in the early 1900s. Nothing came of the development until 1933 when sixteen structures from the Chicago world's fair—including several from the Homes of Tomorrow exhibit—were brought in. It was gay- and artist-friendly. Perhaps Faith hoped to find her community there.

While at the Stratford Theatre in Chicago with a girl revue, she readied a show at the High Hat. Trying to escape the fan, she performed the "dance le nudite" and "purple flower dance."

Coyly pulling aside her "wine red velvet negligee," she showed a reporter a six-inch scar above her ankle. She felt permanently damaged. She explained she had to sue because "beauty is my livelihood." It was all she had to support her "invalid sister."

Stressed by the pressure to continue supporting herself and Charmion and Sally stealing what should have been her thunder—not to mention prestige—Faith's complaints grew louder. Her publicity stunts turned self-serving and outrageous. She was becoming a difficult star that club owners began to complain about.

Faith said she didn't mind the most recent crackdown on burlesque, as she felt audiences were "more interested in the artistic side" of the show, which is what she presented, not crude stripping.

Faith must have a "strictly ethereal atmosphere" to perform. She was still claiming she had been raised in a convent and thus was more virginal, above the squalor of the burlesque world. "I never bump or shake anything at anybody. If anything shakes it is a normal, natural thing and belongs there."

With an upcoming date in court for her suit against the State-Lake, her attorneys assured reporters they would insist she dress in a "sober conservative street suit" when she appeared in court.

Scheduled to appear in Oklahoma City at a fashion show for the Campfire Girls, Faith was forced to withdraw after dozens of protesters discovered her plan to model a long robe and then discard it to reveal a nightie underneath. All Faith could say was "I really dance."

She was brought to the Great Lakes Expo in Cleveland to perform at the Showboat, a floating attraction on the lake anchored in front of the midway. The Showboat was losing money, and Faith was expected to boost revenue.

After protests at her appearance, a censor was brought in to watch her peel off her flowers. He told the owners she could perform "as long as you keep that violet-blue spot on her. That covers her as completely as a bearskin coat." The spotlight that hid most of her nudity and the scars on her legs, of which she was self-conscious.

The dance was approved but giant nude posters of her were not. *Variety* noted she had almost as much publicity as Billy Rose's divorce from Eleanor Holm.

The general manger, bowing to the church groups trying to have Faith kicked out, claimed she was a flop even though the Ohio governor was enthusiastically suggesting folks catch her act. Contradicting the general manager, the operator declared a 50 percent increase in revenue since Faith started her three dances a day. Still papers would rather print she was a flop.

The producer fell into debt, failed to pay taxes, and the show closed early. Faith was unfairly blamed.

Bad luck seemed to trail Faith like shadows from her fans.

Before a two-week engagement in Erie, Pennsylvania, someone slit the top of Faith's convertible and stole suitcases containing her swan costume and fans.

Faith, "one of the brightest stars ever to shine in the Ziegfeld firmament," trudged on with more grueling engagements. It was life on the road, scrambling and hustling, dodging suitors and sending money to Charmion.

In Memphis following a show, Faith and two male comedians, Bob Gifford and Lew Parker, were held up by "two armed white men." They stripped the pants off the men, no doubt to hamper being followed.

"It was a terrible experience," Faith said. "One of the bandits slapped me so hard my head still aches." They made off with her purse, which had fifty dollars in it, and twenty-five bucks from each of the men. To add insult to the robbery, the "bandits" reprimanded Faith, taunting that she was a "naked she-male." Whatever insult that was.

Sally too would have her share of robberies over the years, a very real danger of working in a mostly cash business. The women were targets, especially when photographed in expensive jewelry (as Faith often was).

Before the end of the year, Faith settled for a paltry $5,000 from her lawsuit with the State-Lake Theatre. She calculated it was approximately $192 per each of twenty-six stitches. It was a definite blow to her ego.

It was a mixed bag of a year: work, robbery, work, controversy, accolades. With enough work and raves, she wouldn't yet feel as if she were just hanging on.

TWENTY-SIX

SALLY WAS A FORCE, PRODUCING, DIRECTING, PUBLICIZING, AND performing in her big All-Star Revue with fifty other acts. When not designing the scenery and costumes, she was staging the show. She even booked the acts, once finding a six-foot-tall store clerk and putting her in the show.

Sally's smiling face beamed from newspapers, endorsing shoes, beauty creams, Carter's Milk, dry cleaners, Nehi soda. Being in the business of beauty she felt she "must at all times look pleasing to the eye."

During the dead of winter in 1937, she played Boston, cocooned in a long fur. There was never enough time, madly dashing in and out of taxis, trains, cars, and planes. It was all-night flights just in time to make curtain.

Sally and her current crop of girls, the Rangettes, gave a fulsome staged show promoted as "free of risqué entertainment." Never mind the nudity. A lot of the young girls had mothers in tow as the show traveled.

Her appearance in a St. Patrick's Day parade in Cleveland left a Catholic bishop "humiliated" especially as "she rode in an open carriage next to a float decorated to honor the blessed mother of God." Sally would shrug it off.

Despite the arrests and protests from clergy, Sally was not offensive to most, because *she* was not offensive. She was ladylike (except when swearing), never vulgar, and generally given the chance could charm anyone.

The love of Sally's life was a young ensign just out of the Naval Academy. Sally always had a weakness for a man in uniform because of her father, who she continued to idolize, even if it was mostly from a distance. Jimmie Thach was handsome and five years younger.

Thach's history would be dramatic. His father was an attorney for Capone who turned on his client, helping the government send Al to prison for tax evasion.

Thoughtful and shy, Thach would prove himself to be a brilliant tactical innovator in the air. He was a wingman for Edward O'Hare, a naval aviator of note, and Medal of Honor recipient for his tour in WWII. Thach would also be a WWII hero, developing a flight pattern for his squadron. The film *Battle of Midway* re-creates how Thach bravely and strategically shot down five Japanese planes.

It was probably during her Hollywood days that Sally and Jimmie began an affair that would carry on for several years. They would break up during the war after having spent the night together at his Hollywood apartment. When Jimmie escorted her home, a furious Nettie answered the door and "got in his face," telling the startled young man that "if he had enough guts to go with his lack of brains . . . he'd make a good officer."

Thach would marry someone else. Sally and Jimmie stayed in touch, remaining fond of each other.

Lasting romance would be difficult for our fan dancers, who could not remain in one place for long.

Sally said she had no interest in marriage, instead hoping to "retire a rich old maid" by the time she turned sixty.

Faith boasted she was so beautiful she couldn't marry because she needed to protect her "super-perfect form."

"I love my body so much that I can never allow any man to touch it."

Mr. Carroll had once sent Faith flowers with a note stating, "you're so afraid of men I suppose if you ever have a baby, the father will be a rose."

Because she had been bullied and pushed into the arms of inappropriate men, it would be claimed that in order to have sex she had become a lesbian "out of necessity." Though clearly she did have affairs with men.

Lesbianism, at the time, was not thought to be normal. It was a secret she would have guarded closely, and it seems when the hints in the papers grew, and speculation as to why she was single ramped up, Faith would suddenly give interviews exclaiming, "I want a man—a man to love! I want a husband, a home, a kitchen, and what goes with it."

A fellow showgirl blamed Charmion for keeping "Faith on sleeping pills, and her life consisted of sleep, eat, dance, travel . . ." With Charmion a safe distance away in Arizona, one of Faith's female lovers would take over managing her career.

Faith, who lived in an ethereal world, "wanted delicate flower treatment, and for her taste, men were too rough. Women were softer, and she had no patience to wait for a gentle male; neither could she teach one to be tender with her, she was too timid. Therefore lesbian affairs were chosen."

Chapter

TWENTY-SEVEN

IT WAS 1938. EARL CARROLL MOVED TO HOLLYWOOD AND OPENED a successful nightclub. He took with him girlfriend Beryl Wallace. It would be Beryl's neon profile twenty feet high that lit up the sky outside the new Earl Carroll Theatre.

Beryl made *Life* magazine at a party at Ciro's wearing a pre-Madonna bridal veil, panties, and bra. The party was hosted by the mysterious millionaire from Waco, Rex St. Cyr.

The average wage was $1,730 a year. Sally and Faith were making far better than most.

Using the Century of Progress in her advertisements held a distinct advantage for Sally. She was landing engagements at world fairs, as Faith was beginning to be associated with the seedier aspects of stripping.

Faith defended herself vigorously. "I am not through by any means. My career has yet to reach its heights. My ambition, you know, is to do a series of Sunday evening dance concerts with a symphony orchestra. I want to demonstrate my own technique. I'm a natural dancer."

It would be an astounding year for Sally in terms of the volume of her output, which was nothing less than herculean. The employment varied: fairs, basements, ballrooms, nightclubs, talks, and lectures. Sally reveled in being a full-fledged celebrity, even though with the accolades and perks came harassment and pressure.

Sally even squeezed in time to campaign for John Nance Garner, the Texas democratic running for president in 1940.

Billy Rose brought *Casa Mañana* to Broadway with a "stunning line of show and chorus girls that any theatre-with-tables ever will assemble." It was a three-hour show with sixty chorus girls and a cage filled with snarling tigers. Sally, though only thirty-four, was called "matronly." However, it wouldn't prevent one male patron from fainting at the sight of her performance.

"Oh dear," his wife exclaimed and called for help. "What!" said the waiter whose eyes would not budge from Sally's figure. "And miss the rest of the act?"

In Dubuque, Iowa, Sally was given only $200 cash instead of the $350 promised for an appearance the year before. She sued for the remaining money. The operators claimed there wasn't enough money from the few who attended her performance.

Sally insulted friend Gypsy Rose Lee by omitting her from a "best undressed list" she had compiled for the papers.

There was and would be weird lawsuits over the years involving Sally directly and indirectly, including a libel suit regarding a letter to her from an AFA union official after she was refused a spot at a benefit.

She attempted a daring act in Boston that brought disastrous results. A piano wire was rigged to fly her in what sounded like an innovative twist on her fan dance. Her insurance was canceled because the company considered it hazardous work. Her insurer was correct. An iron bar holding her broke, sending her crashing twenty feet to the floor. The audience thought it was part of the act as she "hobbled" out to take a curtain call.

"How to be intelligent though educated" was the topic of her lecture at Harvard for 1,500 freshmen. She wore a gown and admitted to being nervous. She joked she was astonished at the recognition and reception she received just for putting on clothes. (Sally could wink at her profession, something Faith could not.)

Other universities such as the University of Kansas engaged her to talk, but not the University of Colorado, which canceled her appearance, saying she "doesn't fit into our picture."

John North, a Ringling Brothers relation, considered her reputation so poor he would not allow Sally to perform for his family-oriented circus.

It was announced she was discarding her fans (again) for a four-picture deal with Standard Pictures.

Sally walked on stage in a blue tailored suit and a maroon felt hat. She moved slowly, poised and serious, occasionally stopping the pianist and giving direction in a soft, carefully cultivated voice. That was how methodically she rehearsed, though she had been doing her fan dance for years now.

Sally pushed her tiny frame. She was always seen with a lit cigarette—a maid even waited off stage with one. She drove herself high on Benzedrine. Sally "screams like a banshee," one reporter noted. She was a "nervous, quivering bundle of energy." Her mood was highly changeable, she interrupted conversations, snatched cigarettes out of the hands of others, behavior most likely a result of her amphetamine habit.

One reporter spending time in her dressing room observed she was "headed for a nervous breakdown." The pace of her life was too much. Her schedule would have crushed a lesser performer.

Her chemical-induced vigor was frantic. Talking on the phone, she ordered her maid about, while turning for her "male dresser." She said she was "weary" of her fan dance. She wanted "to be a real actress."

Yet fan dancing enabled her to buy land in New Mexico, Montana, California, Connecticut, and back in Elkton, all "tilled by a Rand relative." With "two automobiles" and a home in Long Island that she eschewed for "an expensive midtown hotel" in New York, Sally was making it without the help of a man.

She was careful to keep hidden her increasing debt and unpaid taxes. She shouldered enormous expenses that kept her on the road, while praying and searching for a play or movie to relieve the monotony of the fan dance. She never seemed to be in love with it. It was more harness than liberator.

Tethered to her feathers, she complained there was nothing "new." "I keep right on doing the same thing, touring is very repetitive." She believed God had a plan for her and she just had to hang on until "something good comes along." If she made another picture in Hollywood "everything will be hotsy-totsy." Belief in herself and her God kept her aloft.

Everyone knew she prayed before her show and was warned not to interrupt her. She kept a copy of the *Christian Science Monitor* nearby.

It was July 12 and Sally was performing in Los Angeles. The sign outside the Paramount Theatre enticed, "See Sally Rand in her sensational fan and bubble dances." On a whim Ray Stanford, a handsome twenty-six-year-old farmer, and his twenty-two-year-old girlfriend Hazel Drain decided what the heck. They paid sixty cents each for front-row seats.

Under her "number thirty-seven, or midnight blue" spotlight Sally presented the first of her two dances. Holding a seventy-two-inch yellow balloon, she danced behind a transparent curtain. When the balloon got away from her, Ray pushed his camera through the curtain and took a picture. The click of his camera made her blood boil. She didn't object to posed photographs, but candids, which caught a mere moment, did not tell the whole story, and she was afraid they might be vulgar. "My work represents so much to me that it is extremely detrimental to have poor pictures."

She left the stage determined to get those frames of film. Backstage she threw on a robe and flew out into the audience. Spying the fleeing couple she hurried up the aisle in pursuit.

A pissed-off Sally "took Stanford by the scruff of his neck and demanded the camera." Ray and Hazel refused. In the ensuing scramble the camera was smashed, the film exposed, a shirt ripped, Stanford's suspenders snapped, and there were scratches and a bite left on Drain's arm.

Hazel showed Sally her black-and-blue mark and threatened, "This will cost you plenty."

The couple filed battery charges against that "nude dancer." Sally claimed Ms. Drain had bitten her.

A date was set for trial, but Sally received a continuance because she was performing on the straw-hat circuit two plays, *They Knew What They Wanted* and *Rain*, plus other fan dancing dates.

In August she was stung by a wasp, which was nothing compared to the lawsuit Faith filed against her.

Distracted and overwhelmed with work and travel, Sally, in Philadelphia, missed her court date for the Stanford/Drain suit.

An unhappy judge issued a bench warrant for Sally.

From the nineteenth floor of the hotel room Sally was staying in, she posed in the shower for reporters, nude except for a shower curtain. She promised she was on her way to Los Angeles to take care of that court date. To pay for her lawyers she had performances booked along the way.

By mid-October she was finally headed West when, traveling through Pennsylvania, Sally lost her Pekinese, China Boy. As she told police, she had pulled the car over for a quick fifteen-minute nap and the dog had jumped out.

She did not know what to focus on; there was the bench warrant and trial, Faith's lawsuit to answer, her lost doggy, her refusal to name the man she was in love with, and a bunch of work dates she had to keep to pay for everything. How could she juggle it all?

Finally, in Los Angeles on October 17, she was held at court until bond was posted. She got into a tiff with a policewoman who wanted Sally to pose for a picture with her. "I won't have my picture taken with a policewoman," Sally said. "I'll jump out of a window or I'll pose standing on my head but I won't have my picture taken with a policewoman."

The insulted policewoman threw her in the bullpen. Sally burst into tears. One of the few times she broke down in public. It was all just too much.

A few days later Sally was in Oakland performing. She did not dare turn down any jobs with multiple attorney bills to pay. Her car broke down, and she had to buy an airline ticket to return to Los Angeles.

Headlines screamed, "Whatta Surprise! Sally Rand Wears Girdle Into L.A. Court." Sally made a show of adjusting her girdle. The girdle was strictly to hold up her stockings, there was nothing wrong with her figure, she explained. Wearing a "modest blue wool dress" for trial, she repeated how sorry she was to have missed the October date. She took "copious notes" during jury selection, no doubt directing her attorneys, who were asking potential jurors their views on privacy and "abbreviated costumes." Prosecutors told jurors Sally had been "descending into a theatre audience to maliciously, unlawfully, and willfully bite scratch and tear" at the defendants.

One of the exhibits presented was Hazel Drain's white sweater with big smears of pink lipstick on it. Sally pointed out "she didn't have a mouth like a gorilla." Besides, she wore red lipstick. Sally showed the pots of white paint she used all over her body, even demonstrating painting it on her arm. She would have gotten paint on everyone if there had been a fight.

Sally wanted to perform for the court in the nude. The judge refused. "I fail to see what purpose could be served."

During a recess Sally posed for dozen of photographers who had purchased toy balloons and a fan.

The jury was entertained by Sally, Hazel, and their lawyers as they ran around the courtroom re-creating the theatre aisle and what had taken place.

Sally claimed to a jury that included "nine gray-haired women" she could not have scratched anyone, because she kept her nails short so as not to puncture her bubble. "I was defenseless."

Sally was convicted on both counts of assault and fined $2,000 (about her weekly fee) and sentenced to a year in jail, all reduced to a fine of $100.

A "glum looking" Sally complained the loss of her privacy hurt worse than the fine. The judge reprimanded her that if she was taking a private bath and someone burst in taking photos, that would violate her privacy. What Sally did in public was not private.

Sally was furious. "Apparently I'm to have no such thing as privacy."

Judges often felt themselves between a rock and a hard place in sentencing Sally. One said he was stymied: "Everything I say just seems to result in more publicity for Miss Rand."

The matter would not be resolved until 1945 when a $150,000 suit brought by the couple was officially dismissed because time for trial had expired.

Sally claimed, "It sears my soul, all this is bad publicity." Yet she never shied from it. The bad publicity made her even more well known, but ultimately cost her time and money and peace of mind.

"Sally has so many of these personal appearances to make in court." It was a big fat distraction, and now she had Faith to contend with.

TWENTY-EIGHT

OPENING AT THE ORPHEUM ON BROADWAY IN 1938, FAITH WAS given most of the credit for the $7,800 ticket sales.

During a frigid winter in Boston, she performed at the Crawford House, three shows a night doing a short routine. Though applauded heavily she declined an encore, upset at the lack of production values.

In Oakland performing at the Roosevelt Theatre, Faith visited uncles Thomas P. Bacon and Robert Bacon and chatted about her illustrious heritage with roots reaching back to Sir Francis Bacon. (Uncle Thomas was an Oakland civil leader who bred horses.)

Faith was desperate. She sought new publicity. She looked around and there was Sally, always in the headlines, always the "fan dancer."

She told reporters, "Sally always admits I originated it when I'm around."

Her long-simmering resentment finally caused her to file a $375,000 suit seeking damages and an injunction barring Sally from doing the fan dance. Faith accused Sally of stealing the dance after

Rand worked for her as fan holder at an N.T.G. revue in 1930 (Faith would cite several different clubs, perhaps innocently mistaking where she had first encountered Sally).

A short time after her *Vanities* arrest in 1930, Faith explained that Sally was helping out a comedian on a vaudeville bill when Faith let Sally hold her fans. From the wings every night, Sally observed Faith performing.

Out of "the kindness of her heart," Faith showed Sally how to "manipulate the fans to cover the nudity." At first she hadn't minded Sally doing the fan dance while she was in the *Follies*, but when Faith wanted to tour in vaudeville no one wanted to see her.

Jimmy Reda, an Italian immigrant with his own orchestra in the 1930s, was one of many who corroborated Faith's claims of being first. He had been playing with Faith in Chicago and watched her maneuver her fans.

However it happened, it was fully two years after she saw Faith perform that Sally claimed the dance as her own invention.

"All she does," Faith complained, "is walk around and let the people gawk. It breaks my heart to see my art treated like that."

"The fan idea is as old as Cleopatra," Sally shrugged. "She can't sue me for that." The bitching grew personal. "Faith and the Egyptians did the fan dance 5,000 years ago."

"Ostrich feathers!" Sally thought it a joke. "It simply depends on who is behind the fans."

It was like "Webster suing somebody for using words in the dictionary."

Faith said her own dance was "one of ethereal beauty and that woman turned it into an animated French postcard . . . I only wear talcum powder."

"A little talcum is always welcum," Sally joked. "But I don't put talcum on bacon. Just pepper."

Faith called the press to gather in her agent's office at Radio City.

"Fan dancing is my baby"—she jiggled her leg—"and nobody is going to take credit as the originator of it, only over my dead body." She wore a chic tweed jacket, skirt, and shoes, all in green. From a slim ankle dangled her gold anklet. She refused to tell what name was on it or even where it came from. Her hair was newly "champagne blonde." She was also sporting bangs. "It's something new I'm trying."

She made sure to mention she was currently performing in N.T.G.'s show *Midnight Sun*, with various dances including the fan. "It's always requested."

She boasted she was one of only three who could dance on their toes barefoot. "I do my dancing in bare feet, because whoever saw a statute wearing a pair of high heels?" Faith deplored Sally dancing in heels, citing her history. "Fan dancing is an off-shoot of statuary."

Faith was indignant. "I figure her use of my dances has netted her one million dollars." Faith said it was hard to get booked with her fan dance (not entirely true as she was regularly working) because everyone wanted to see Sally, who had "stolen" her dance. The papers got into the catfight, printing the catty headline about Faith, "Once Broadway's Prettiest Woman." Ouch.

Faith extolled the merits of dancing nude, saying she preferred it. "I am going to see if the authorities won't make a concession in the name of art." Then she suggested "a committee" should preview nude dances, believing hers would be deemed art and Sally's "vulgar" dance dismissed.

She spent the rest of the time with the press rehashing her past resume, the arrest with Earl Carroll, the years posing nude as a teen, and her ambition to "dance concerts." All this, she believed, set her apart from Sally.

In a court in Hollywood that October, Faith demanded Sally be deprived of her fans.

Sally in slacks, checkered coat, and yellow bandana at her deposition was in no mood for photographers and attempted to keep the press from the courtroom. In a foul mood she refused to state her legal name.

Faith's attorney J. E. Rosen asked Sally, "How long have you performed as a nudist?"

She clarified she was a *ballet* dancer, not a *fan* dancer, throwing a wrench into the whole suit.

Rosen asked her if she danced in the nude.

Sally told him he could find out by paying to see her dance. She admitted to meeting Faith sometime after 1929.

Faith would reiterate that Sally had watched her from backstage, stolen and copied her act.

Perhaps on the advice of her attorneys, perhaps because she could not afford to continue further, "charges were never pressed" and Faith dropped the suit. It would, however, continue to gall her. Both continued with their fan dances, each trying to upstage the other, Sally with different feuds in the paper, Faith with acts even more daring and nude. Both would continue to be hounded by police, arrested and made to defend their art, both grasping at publicity to propel them in front of the other.

Sally would ultimately admit, "When you get something that's economically successful you grab the bull by the horns and ride it to the bitter end."

Sally went back on the road, an engagement in San Francisco at the Music Box. The bitterness between the two remained. They would eye each other from a wary distance, making the occasional verbal swipe.

Chapter

TWENTY-NINE

FAITH POSED FOR PHOTOS LOOKING GORGEOUS IN A "SILVER FOX cape" after her first transcontinental flight in 1939. "Flying is like dancing: the plane stopped three times and each time it stopped, I would wake up to listen to it go whoosh when it took off. Then it got very bumpy, and I almost got thrown out of bed."

She felt she was soaring again.

"When gangsters were kings and Alcatraz was too good for them" was how the film was promoted. Hollywood had finally called. Faith would make her only cinematic appearance, in a low-budget film entitled *Prison Train*.

The film was about a racketeer, a murder, a kidnapping, and a jailbreak on a train. Wearing black lingerie, Faith played a character named Maxine who works in a club owned by a gangster. She's neither remarkable nor terrible in her few seconds of screen time.

In the film was Dorothy Comingore, who would portray Susan Kane in *Citizen Kane*. The film ran just over an hour and was nothing more than "routine general fare." It would do nothing for Faith's career, and there would be no more feature films.

Not yet thirty, Faith closed the decade at the '39 world's fair in New York for N.T.G.'s exhibit "Congress of Beauty," alongside the "Sun Worshiper's Colony" that was exploiting the trend for nudist colonies, with topless women on display behind a railed fence for the men to gape and photograph like dangerous animals at the zoo.

For the forty-four million who attended, there were revues and exhibits with naked women to photograph or sketch.

Faith's new dance would be "Afternoon of a Fawn." Her costume would be "eight autumn leaves" and of course her fans. She would start the dance asleep on a "bed of moss." She promised the dance would be "startling" and was scouring the country for two real fawns. The bit of publicity she dreamt up would cause her no amount of headaches.

It was about 2 p.m. when heads turned as the beautiful blonde emerged from her luxurious tenth-floor apartment at 70 Park Avenue and slowly walked up the street barefoot. In her hand she held an apple and wore a see-through "Grecian type dress."

She wasn't alone. At the end of a leash she held a skittish deer. The fawn was unused to the leash or the people and noise of New York City, and it cowered.

Her "pet" was Sir Francis Bacon, reminding all of her heritage. "This tiny deer was a freak, never grew much more than two feet," and supposedly followed her wherever she went, including to the theatre. Today he was not being so cooperative.

Faith said she was training Sir Francis to eat the leaves off her costume on stage.

Followed by "four publicity men" Faith managed only a block. "Bleeding slightly," the fawn refused to budge another inch. Crowds gathered. A policeman arrived.

Faith explained she was "taking my fawn for a walk . . . to my rehearsal."

She was "a nervous wreck." She had been trying to get herself and the fawn into a taxi. "I was never so pushed and mauled in my life." She complained about the crowds when her "leaves started to slip" from strategic places and "all those people kept staring."

"I was never so embarrassed." The police were "mean" asking her if she was "running away from a fire" as they escorted her to the 35th Street police station and charged her "with causing a crowd to collect."

Bail was set at $500. She casually laid down a $10,000 diamond solitaire ring (she would get it back).

A police lieutenant told her to refrain from further stunts or "you'll be leaving the rest of your jewelry here."

"Can't I even walk my baby around the block?"

She was assured she could not.

In court she looked demure and chic in a hat, pinstriped blazer and skirt, holding a small wicker purse that held her offending Grecian costume. She was prepared to put it on in court.

Faith was exonerated of any wrongdoing. The American Society for the Prevention of Cruelty to Animals received "several hundred" phone calls protesting Faith's use of the fawn.

The police were no fools. "You probably engineered the arrest for a very obvious purpose." The officer did concede, "I think you're a nicer girl than Sally Rand."

At the Tower Theatre Faith danced nude. The theatre told her next time to put on tights. She told the manager she would like to get arrested. He said she was "hungry for publicity."

She left her dressing room with her robe wrapped tightly around her. It was a Saturday night and the house was packed. At her entrance she dropped her robe and danced onto the stage. To the horror of management, she was not wearing tights.

When police asked why the manager didn't remove her from the stage, he said, "She would have scratched my eyes out." He had seen her temper.

The Tower Theatre had its license suspended, which made other theatres reluctant to hire her.

With a promise to "thrill the men—and make the women green with envy," Faith was back in Boston at the Crawford House for three shows a night. She received "the only real applause" but still would not perform an encore.

Police informed her she must wear more clothes. The next night she danced in a "strapless white bathing suit." The manager complained, called her "dance indecent," and canceled her remaining dates. Faith left Boston in a huff. "I was never treated so severely." She complained that they didn't "know the human form is not indecent. Boston police officers are not gentleman."

Perhaps as payback for her lawsuit against Sally, Faith started her own "Bare Ranch X." It would be short-lived.

Faith and Sir Francis on the streets of Manhattan, 1939

Chapter

THIRTY

SALLY CAME DOWN WITH THE FLU, WORKED THE BROCKTON,
Massachusetts fair, sent her mother one hundred dollars, remained
in debt. She spent six days in Los Angeles shooting *Murder on Sunset
Boulevard* (retitled *Sunset Murder Case*) for Grand National Studio.
She made no secret of reading stacks of plays, wanting to dump her
troublesome fans. She "worried" over how to get into a Broadway
show.

There was no escaping her fan and bubble dance that helped support her mother and brother, paid off a mortgage in Arkansas, and
maintained her orange grove in California. She was on an endless
treadmill.

"I have had some experiences that I wish I never had had, but
that would be true in any business. I cannot say sincerely that I would
have chosen just this road to fortune. Perhaps I might have wished
for another way."

She ended 1938 with a lackluster show in Sacramento at Sweet's

Ballroom. Sally wasn't happy with her lighting, nixed her bubble dance, and offered to refund half the admission to the audience.

When *The Sunset Murder Case* premiered, Sally was given top billing. She performed a peacock dance wearing a sheer body stocking and magnificent tail of white peacock feathers.

"Thin excuse for an hour's screen time" and "routine gangster murder yarn" warned *Variety*. In a year that saw *Gone with the Wind* and *The Wizard of Oz*, her film was a trifling.

Sally beamed from the pages of *Life* magazine. In San Francisco at the 1939 Golden Gate International Exposition, her Nude Ranch had forty-seven girls who "participate vigorously from 1 pm to 2 am daily in various outdoor sports."

To advertise, the beauties on their horses galloped up Market Street on February 17, 1939.

Sally's Nude Ranch attracted more paying customers in the first week than any other attraction, with over 55,000 eager to catch an eyeful of cavorting nudes.

She had incorporated herself as Sally Rand Enterprises, Inc. for the presentation of entertainment and amusements.

Some running the exposition thought Sally's type of dance was out of fashion. She protested, citing all the offers she received weekly.

Before the expo even opened, she was flying back and forth to New York, pitching the inclusion of her Nude Ranch at the coming New York world's fair. The proposition would have to pass two boards that were aware of the income and patronage the name "Sally Rand" brought in. The fair wanted to place stipulations on the nudity. Sally put her foot down: "No clothes or no nude ranch."

Back in San Francisco, she hosted a cocktail party for journalists and editors. She performed three shows a night, and five on Saturdays, to packed houses at her Music Box theatre. The jewel box of a theatre on O'Farrell Street, which she possibly purchased (or more likely leased) in 1935, held about 450 and "did a complete turnover" between shows, due to her continuing popularity. After shows she sat and signed autographs for fans.

The Nude Ranch was situated on "Forty Acres of Fun" on Treasure Island, a man-made island built in San Francisco Bay. The first week the Nude Ranch was "lagging" and had "gone in the red." As the "foreman" Sally played hostess to the crowds watching her girls play games.

By the end of April the police were harassing her to put clothes on the girls. She pulled the show. Only to have it reinstated.

There are a few references to Faith at the Golden Gate Expo. An item in *Variety* noted the concession "Streets of the World" was "dickering" with her. She also danced in the "Greenwich Village" concession. Other than that, there were no headlines.

It seemed to be a troubled fair. Sally took over a concession, renaming it "Gay Paree." She lost all the money she poured into it. She would be in charge of three concessions at the expo.

And there were more lawsuits. She was being sued for an unpaid costume bill by a New York company. Billy Rose sued her to the tune of $100,000, saying she stole his Nude Ranch idea.

Despite fourteen shows a day—every day, without a day off—despite raking in almost $75,000 at the fair, not to mention thousands from her Music Box appearance, by November Sally owed $64,631 and filed for bankruptcy, saying her finances were "a mess." Most of her money went to salaries, costumes, construction of sets. She also admitted to an addiction to hats. It was so severe she would buy them off women's heads if she could. She couldn't afford medical help for her dog. Her Golden Gate Expo feature Gay Paree was closed by creditors.

Sally and her troupe of beauties moved south to perform for strong crowds at N.T.G.'s celebrity-filled Florentine Garden in Los

Angeles. Between the 9 p.m. and midnight shows she again auto-graphed her picture.

Though she had made at least $40,000 the year before, she still had to pawn a watch and a diamond necklace. She "was down to her last fan."

She couldn't afford to pursue her acting; instead she kept her fans firmly in hand and continued on.

THIRTY-ONE

OUR FAN DANCERS HAD PERFORMED IN NEARLY EVERY WORLD'S fair in America since 1933.

Approximately forty-four million pairs of eyes would cast their gaze on "the city of tomorrow." Though the fairs' theme was the future, our beloved fan dancers were decidedly the dance of yesteryear.

Billy Rose was topping even himself with an amphitheatre in New York that sat ten thousand people. His Aquacade featured dozens of synchronized swimmers, Johnny Weissmuller and Eleanor Holm (soon to be Mrs. Billy Rose) included. It was a spectacle of lights, with 8,000 gallons of water per minute pumped into a massive semi-circular pool, with another massive curtain of water. With a seventy-five-foot diving board, it was the number one attraction. It was an absolutely colossal venue loaded with 500 performers.

The only drawback for such a large outdoor venue was that bad weather dictated if the show went on or not. Finally, Rose decided if rain, no costumes. If wind, no big hats, which had previously acted like sails, sending the girls flying.

Opening day it was still too cold for Holm, 250 Aquacade girls, and Faith to appear.

It was reassuringly announced that *this* world's fair would be different, no stooping to vulgar displays of nudity. (Of course, that would not be the case at all.) Anticipating a threatened ban on nudity, crowds booed stripper Rosita Royce when she appeared in clothes. A veteran crowd-pleaser, Royce quickly shed them.

The most in-your-face display of crass chauvinism was the Crystal Lassie, a promised "peep show of tomorrow." Nine women danced topless, or wore sheer open robes, surrounded by mirrors that "multiply the dancing girls a thousand-fold," giving the invasive gaze of the audience access to the girls' every nook and cranny.

N.T.G.'s "Congress of Beauty," with twenty-four dancers and sixteen showgirls, was set to open the twenty-seventh of May, after a week's rain delay. It began with a musical revue. Then Yvette Dare had a parrot peck her clothes off. In the star position, the finale was Faith in Debussy's "Afternoon of a Faun."

In a costume of tulle and a "huntsman's cap, the dance ended in a woodland scene when she loses practically all her costume except the huntsman's arrow which is plunged through her fair body." Faith posed with a "reversible arrow," looking as if she was stabbed through the belly. She wore a g-string with fringe and feathers on her ankles.

Church folk protested Faith's appearance. Proud of her act, she asked, "Do the church people complain about the art galleries?" There should be no "objection to my dance. It's daring, startling, sensuous . . . in the artistic manner."

Dancing four times a day, she would sometimes be plunged into darkness while the fair experienced several power outages.

Working with Faith were Tullah and Miy, "Egyptian harem dancers." They had met years earlier in a club in Arizona. The older sister Tullah would become fascinated by Faith and wanted to write the story of her life.

Faith had been a popular act at Ben Marden's Riviera club in New Jersey, and with the close proximity of the fair he wanted her back. But between four shows at the fair she could not swing an additional three at the Riviera. *Variety* hinted she was let go as she didn't fit into Marden's rule of no nudity.

By July her representative with Fanchon and Marco was negotiating a salary dispute with the fair. Faith was making $450 a week—not indecent when the average yearly income fell well below $2,000—with a guarantee of a graduating scale increase. But the "Congress of Beauty" had started letting other dancers go, wanting to reduce costs.

Variety called Faith "sloppy," something no one had ever accused her of. Perhaps the pills were taking a toll. However, she was still "plenty appealing." Back at Chicago's State-Lake (though she had sued them), she pushed the nudity and critics groused. Faith "manages to be seen occasionally even under the blue lights."

The only hint of a romance was when she was spotted having cocktails with a handsome anonymous man.

In December she was in Detroit, her routine more suggestive than alluring.

She wouldn't allow a photographer's assistant into her dressing room because she was clad only in a kimono. Walter Winchell snidely found that "amusing." The columnist did not understand that nudity on the stage did not equate with nudity in one's personal life.

No one understood.

She closed out the year in Flatbush with the Rita Rio band.

Rita Rio was "known as the Mexican Jumping Bean." It was a "fast paced show" of songs and dances all performed by Rita's all-female band. The former showgirl Rita stood five feet tall with green eyes and reddish hair. The formation of her band had started as an "advertising stunt," but Rita liked it, put together a bigger orchestra, and started touring. After paying the salaries of Faith and the other girls, little was left for Rita. The band would break up by 1940 or '41.

Faith's six-minute dance was derided as awful. "It isn't much of a turn." From behind a curtain Faith reclined on the shadowy stage "slowly squirming around in what's apparently intended to be voluptuous poses." She "prances around the stage" doing ballet steps then, "back on the floor, pokes her head through the curtains for a coy bow." She was reprimanded for possibly wearing tights and not being nude enough! She couldn't win.

Variety said she belonged on the midway. The audience loudly voiced its displeasure, even laughing. Despite this the show did a healthy business.

Faith's work had taken a decided turn. She didn't seem to care, more interested in publicity than what she did on stage. Besides sleeping pills, she could have been taking any number of other pills for pain and injuries.

Known for her delicate health, which included anxiety, insecurity, and nerves, Faith sought relief in her pills and bad decisions, desperate to regain her previous salad days. She was no longer the disciplined dancer.

Faith continued performing throughout the forties though reviewers derided her act, complaining she "scampers about" under a blue light. Her dancing was "anemic," enjoyable but not well choreographed.

She claimed she would head to England to get work as an ambulance driver in the war, even if she had to "pay my own expenses."

She still had plenty of highs to go with her lows. In the spring of 1940 she was back with the Florentine Gardens for an "indefinite stay." In July she checked into a Santa Monica hospital for a "major operation." Some said it was a glandular issue.

She was well enough to be the featured attraction in San Diego for the American Legion State Convention in August and back on stage at the Paramount in downtown Los Angeles.

Ironically, she rode in a parade through the streets of Los Angeles as Lady Godiva, tying up traffic and leaving pedestrians agape. No doubt it was one way she felt she could get back at Sally, by taking on the mantle that had first gotten Sally notice.

In 1942 Faith was the headliner at Los Angeles's Orpheum Theatre on what *Billboard* called a "fast-moving program." Her act was "Death of the Bird of Paradise." The theatre took in $14,000 due to her appearance in one of her best acts.

In the audience sat future burlesque star Lili St. Cyr, who at the time was in the chorus of the Florentine, barely out of her teens and struggling for an identify. She would credit Faith's performance as life-changing. She was struck by Faith's artful dance and how it told a story, which Lili would take to even greater heights. By the time they met a few years later, Faith had "turned bitter and aggressive" and was not receptive to Lili's adoration and compliments.

Lili would partially pattern her own persona on Faith's. Naturally shy like Faith, she would protect herself with an aloof demeanor. Neither dancer mingled with the audience, barely acknowledging them, lost in a world of their own creation, one that overcame troublesome childhoods, mothers who didn't love them, and the sometimes sordid atmosphere of their professions.

In Kansas City, Faith's name drew large audiences. She ended the night with "the Dance of Shame" and a "bra flash."

THIRTY-TWO

FAITH WAS ONLY THIRTY-ONE, TOO YOUNG TO BE TOO OLD. TOO old to start over. She clung to her fans, her swan, and her orchids, touring four shows a day.

In 1940 it was rumored that Faith married Fenton William Perkins, a handsome man with three prior wives (he would have one more after Faith). The son of a reverend, the Michigan-born Perkins was forty-three years old when he allegedly married Faith.

Fenton liked younger girls. There would be pregnancies and marriages with young girls, usually church members. No one knew how many wives Fenton had. It was claimed his marriage to Faith was annulled.

Though Sally appeared to be doing better than Faith, she was bleeding money; she owed taxes, "amazed that they were not paid" by her accountant. She was in "a period of emergency" and would have to wait to even make good her mother's grocery bill. She had purchased a "dilapidated house" in Key West, but lost it to the government most likely due to unpaid bills that overwhelmed her. With so much turmoil in her professional life, she spent a fair amount of time praying, looking for peace of mind. She was a devout Christian Scientist receiving instructions from a practitioner as she worked toward membership in the mother church. Faith would have no such religious or spiritual beliefs to help her through difficult days.

Up to now Sally had conducted a low-key romantic life.

Thurkel "Turk" James Greenough was a Montana cowboy and champion bronco rodeo star who performed with his brother and two sisters. Growing up, his father Benjamin Franklin "Packsaddle Ben" Greenough had lived near Jeremiah Johnson, and Calamity Jane had taken care of him when he was a young runaway. Ben cut wood for Calamity, sold it, and gave her the money to "get drunk on." Turk was one of eight siblings. The kids grew up learning how to break a horse and hunt from their father. Alice, Marge, Bill, and Turk became the "Riding Greenoughs."

The ruggedly handsome Turk towered over Sally at an impressive 6 feet 6.

They met in 1935 at the Cheyenne Frontier Days in Wyoming. Sally was there to dance. Sally "came running up to him to get his autograph" after Turk won a bronco busting contest.

Years later at the Great Falls Rodeo in Montana, Sally was once again an attraction at the rodeo. Usually the aggressor in her relationships, Sally invited Turk to her hotel for an autograph. They spent the night going to nightclubs; she curled up on his lap in the back of her Cadillac. Things blossomed into a fine romance.

He introduced her to his parents at their ranch Red Lodge in Montana.

At the 1939 Golden Gate Expo he taught Sally's Nude Ranch "girls how to twirl their lariats."

Sally would return with Turk to Red Lodge, where she fell in love with the land and him.

She always believed she was that kind of girl, outdoorsy, tough, down to earth. A cowboy was just what she needed. Someone to ground her from feathers and Chopin. He was salt of the earth. She would show her audience she was too.

They announced they would be married in early 1942. She assured her fans she would continue working. She once promised to marry outside show business. Her husband needed to be "busy. I must continue to be busy. I believe in real partnership."

Sally was in for a surprise. In Los Angeles, Helen Greenough called reporters together to inquire how Turk could marry Sally as she, having married Turk in 1933, was still married to him. They had been living together in Red Lodge until June of 1940 when he vanished, leaving her with their three children. The "pretty and frail" Mrs. Greenough had engaged an attorney to look into this puzzling matter.

Turk said it was as if "a horse kicked me." He thought they had a divorce, as Helen had more than once departed for Nevada to seek one.

Turk called his estranged wife to tell her he was in love with Sally. He put Sally on the phone to chat with her. It was a cruel phone call, and Helen would always "hate" Sally. Taking matters into his own hands, Turk filed for divorce.

In Kentucky Turk proudly watched his fiancée entertaining a crowd, not yet realizing the extent of her fame. Sally shopped for furniture, confident Turk would sort out his legal issues and they would soon marry.

They flew to Los Angeles. Applying for their marriage license, a joyous Turk carried Sally on his back into the Marriage License Bureau only to be slapped with a summons. A livid Helen had filed a suit for "maintenance," naming Sally as co-respondent. Claiming she was "poverty stricken," she sought one hundred dollars a week.

By December Turk was divorced, and on January 6, 1942, he walked Sally down the aisle. She was thirty-seven (she would claim thirty-one). They had intended to tie the knot at the Grace Episcopal Church in Glendora, but because of Turk's divorce they could not. Instead, they were married in the adjoining Parish Hall, an arrangement managed by Pastor Rubel (though he himself did not officiate), husband to Sally's best friend Dorothy Rubel, a fellow vaudevillian who had followed her to California and lived nearby.

A nervous Sally showed up half an hour late to her own wedding, stricken with doubts. In theory this was her first marriage, though her son would later claim there was probably one earlier than this. It was late in life for one who had been singularly independent since she was a teen. She had to wonder how a partnership would hamper her lifestyle, touring, performing in the nude for exultant crowds. Not to mention the fact she and Turk were so different.

He was practically inarticulate; she never stopped talking. His world was horses and rodeos; hers was more sophisticated. They had yet to realize the extent to which they had nothing in common.

They also had to wait for the results of their blood test because of a mix-up. And yet a third possible reason to delay the ceremony (according to Turk's bio) claims *he* was having doubts and tried to call it off. When she threw a fit, screaming and crying—there were newsreel photographers outside, for heaven's sake, not to mention a hall full of wedding guests—he relented.

The gorgeous bride wore a long-sleeved, high-necked gown with a bustle of white wool with pink rosebuds embroidered over rare old lace. Turk wore a black cowboy suit and boots.

Sally walked slowly down the aisle, carrying an armload of Cecile Brunner roses. Their day was not without additional drama. Turk was served a subpoena for an unpaid doctor's bill.

He gave her a custom-made maroon 1941 Graham Hollywood supercharged four-door sedan.

Sally said, "I think that so many stage marriages end in divorce because in constantly moving about there is not chance to build up a stock of common interests and activities out of one's work." Which was certainly ironic, as the ink on the marriage license was barely dry and she was gone.

She finished her stint at the Orpheum and then was back on the road, Colorado, Utah, Oklahoma, and Idaho for weeks. Just six days after her nuptials in St. Louis, she had to reprimand the soldiers in her audience who were rambunctious and tried to pop her balloon with pins. She pleaded with them to stop as she only had five balloons. Because of a rubber shortage she had given most of her balloons to the war effort.

In the only way she knew how to be, Sally immediately nosed herself into Turk's career. Turk was offered the role of a villain in the film *Stagecoach Express*, but she forbade him to play a heavy, explaining it was not good for his image. She knew appearances, though she was trapped in hers and resentful she needed the $2,000 a week it brought in. Turk had to be mindful of his reputation, she warned him.

In February a distraught Sally called the State Highway Patrol. Turk was missing. (What was it with Sally and missing men?) They had an airplane flight to catch, and last she had seen him he had been driving her sports car.

Not six weeks after the wedding, she announced she was expecting and hoped for twins. Whether it was wishful thinking, or she later lost the baby, it was not meant to be. One report was she lost the baby after Turk hit her.

When she showed up at his rodeo appearances, audiences gawked. It chafed to have men leering over his pretty little wife. He was used to being the star. Sally wasn't prepared for his jealousy and resentment. Turk would rely on Sally's salary to support the two of them.

Sally decided she would buy Piney Dell, a property on the edge of Rock Creek, next to the family ranch in Montana. At the same time, she was being sued by her booking agent for unpaid commissions. She would finally cough up a check for $825. Then later in the year she would be forced to pay $5,011.11 in unpaid salary to her agent.

Just months after their wedding, Turk was drafted into the army. He went into the cavalry division. Sally performed at a benefit at his training facility at Fort Riley, Kansas, her hair in pigtails, a sombrero on her head.

Sally stayed with Turk's mother Myrtle, who she adored, in Red Lodge, but was soon off to more engagements. In Hollywood the Orpheum took in $16,000 with her headlining. She would never really stop. Ever.

Sally and Turk really did not know each other, as she was discovering, and his people were not her people. She complained that his family was "shockingly insensitive." There were ill feelings amongst the siblings, and Turk's father was "hard" and "difficult," no doubt coolly receptive to a nude dancer as a daughter-in-law. When Sally caught Ben abusing Myrtle, she stopped talking to him.

Sally and Turk had to spend time learning to get along, but now he was gone and she was handling lawsuits and engagements herself. She had a mortgage on Piney Dell and no one to run it. She would write her mother, suggesting she step in.

"Miserable," she poured her "heart sick" feelings out to her mother, explaining in her short time with Turk "we were so happy and learned to [love] each other better and to live together." She promised her mother she would be strong, like Nettie had been when her father had left for war.

Though she had engagements lined up and needed to arrange others, she was waiting to see where Turk would be sent. She helped sell war bonds. Sailors and soldiers poured into the Golden Gate Theatre in San Francisco to see her.

Not long after Sally took her mother into her confidence, "Turk got himself into a jam." He had gone AWOL and had to stand trial and was then thrown in the guardhouse for two months. Sally was shocked by his "willful person, completely lacking in self discipline." She was afraid he would do something "foolhardy." She was "tense" and "unhappy." There was no one else she could confide in.

Sally later told her son that Turk's officer was attempting to give him lessons on how to ride. Turk was "put out"—after all, he was a star on a horse. He just left and showed up back at home. Horrified (she was the son of a military man) Sally asked him what he was doing.

"I quit."

"You quit?"

"No one's teaching me to ride a horse."

Sally knew her husband did not understand the implications of his actions, but she did. She called her father, asking for his help. Beck put in a word for his son-in-law, and Turk went back with his tail between his legs.

They wrote about being together at Christmas, if he was released by then, but Sally was on the road with bills to pay. Boston, Cleveland, Washington, Colorado, Vancouver. She had to work through the holidays and couldn't see him in the prison. She was touring all over.

Her letters hint at the fact he wanted her to change, maybe to quit dancing and revealing her body to others. He now had "complete disapproval" of her work. He didn't trust her and was making life difficult. She said she wouldn't change for a person, or agonize over another relationship. "I agonized ten years over one person and changed the entire course of my life because of it," and she would never do that again. Perhaps she was referring to the mysterious, gone-missing Charles Mahan.

Sally could only "make a home, pay for it, and fix it so that no one can ever take it away from me or Turk or our children." She would always claim a stronger desire for children than she would a mate.

Sally admitted her marriage "will not last." It was a matter of time, hopefully settled agreeably and quickly. She wasn't sure she would be able to keep the ranch, which she so loved because it "suited her."

Turk was officially released from the cavalry, ostensibly because of a leg injury. He probably expected Sally to be waiting for him, to play the adoring wife. But as always she had bills to pay and work booked. They argued when they were briefly together, and then she was on the road.

As was her way, she tried to make him over, suggesting he take speech lessons from a friend of hers, Margaret Prendergast McLean, an author and probably the woman who had helped rid her of the lisp. Sally found Turk limited by his lack of experiences. She sent long self-improvement letters to him. Occasionally she signed them "Daddy's Girl."

Turk was at a loss for how to bring in money. Sally purchased Red Rim Ranch in nearby Wyola, thinking they would make it a working ranch. She was appalled to discover her husband knew nothing about ranching. And though he'd been around livestock all his life, he didn't even "know the gestation period for horses." From the road she needed to find someone to work the ranch, make repairs on the home there, and build a shed. Yet she could not afford any of it.

Though he was harsh with her in person, she toyed with the idea of giving up her dancing to settle on the ranch.

Turk tried to get into the movies to keep up on payments on their ranch, nicknamed "Heaven." He had lost confidence in himself and began to drink heavily.

Frustrated and feeling out of his depth, Turk was ill-tempered and bad-mannered. She felt for him because he did not understand "all that is going on," presumably in her world where he was an outsider. He wouldn't have liked the hoots and hollers from soldiers in her audience.

Coming from "one of the most famous rodeo families of all time," he was used to adoration and accolades. Sally far surpassed him in fame, publicity, and earnings. Sean Rand, Sally's son, would compare it to the trouble Joe DiMaggio had with his sex-symbol wife Marilyn Monroe and how impossible it was for him to deal with her showing her body and sexuality.

Turk suffered a nervous breakdown. Sally alleged that he hit her several times and was being treated for paranoia.

Not wanting to be home with him during most of 1943 and 1944, she remained on the road while he occasionally performed in rodeos.

By June of 1945 she could not take Turk anymore and filed for divorce, claiming desertion in 1943. The decree was granted in June. By July, she charged him with unlawful possession of her automobile. The papers gleefully noted "too much fame for Turk's gal." Sally hightailed it down to Florida, where it was rumored she was seeing a new man.

They would sell both ranches and part amicably.

Sally and Turk in happier times

Side note: The next year Turk and his first wife, Helen, remarried. Without a job and home, they wandered from rodeo to rodeo barely earning a living until he became a security guard and settled in Las Vegas at age forty-five.

Years later Sally would visit, bringing along her young son. Helen Greenough still refused to speak to Sally.

Part

FIVE

THIRTY-THREE

IN 1941, JIMMY DURANTE SHARED THE STAGE WITH FAITH AT A club in San Francisco that was newly refurbished, with all "girl cashiers at the bar, and a fur-lined ladies room." Still ravishingly beautiful with a trim body, Faith promised to do a Lady Godiva dance on horseback.

She played to capacity crowds in the *Hollywood Scandals*, receiving good notices with "laughs aplenty" and "one of the best balanced programs." Jack Benny declared Faith the original fan dancer. The California State Fair featured her picture as part of a "pioneer Sonoma County family."

In Kansas City she refused an encore, preferring to leave the stage when the applause was at its peak.

In the dead of summer she hid out in Tucson visiting Charmion, "a health-seeker."

Faith asked the papers how they found her.

"It said two beautiful women came here in a big car—"

"Yes! One of them is my secretary," she was quick to note.

Charmion was living at the Don Motel, nothing special, typical of the era, modest with an auto court. Faith was leaving as soon as the "theatrical season" began in Philadelphia and New York.

There would be sightings, whisperings and reports of Faith seen with . . . visiting with . . . another woman. It is possible this was Margie Koch, her secretary-chauffer-manager, who was not a girlfriend but an "admirer." Margie "arranged appointments, correspondence with agents, rehearsals, and the sleeping princess slept on." The sleeping princess remained "hooked on barbiturates." She "had lesbian lovers wherever they traveled."

"Obsessed by her beauty" she spent hours in the mirror, worrying over the tiny lines that had begun to appear.

Walter Winchell asked if Faith was "secretly stitched" to an "85th Streeter," meaning an uptown boy.

She returned to Hollywood hopeful for a movie career at least similar to burlesque queen Ann Corio, who starred in several B pictures. However, Ann would never go over big with Hollywood and returned to the stage, creating a burlesque style show entitled *This Was Burlesque* that would run twenty-five years. (Sally would take over a four-week run while Corio was ill.)

Faith signed with producer Sam Coslow for a series of "dance interpretations." In the nearly three-minute *A Lady with Fans* she is beautiful, if not insecure-looking, tentative in expression, beautiful in body as she gradually becomes nude. She was to do her fan dance, "Dance of Shame," and "The Death of the Bird of Paradise." She would only do the first two.

Faith had reason to be hopeful. Coslow would win an Academy Award for the best short film of 1943, *Heavenly Music*. (He also produced Sally's *The Sunset Murder Case*.)

In *A Lady with Fans*, a shapely leg kicks from behind a marble column. A lean arm sweeps out. Faith has lost the bloom of youth, though her body remains perfect. There is strain in her face. The vertebrae down her back are exposed. She is painfully thin.

Faith was in Denver with the "Whirlie Girlie Revue" after "extensive negotiations," and though the week's take was "average," it was no fault of Faith's. Poor box office was instead due to wartime gas rationing.

She played four weeks at Lou Walter's prestigious Latin Quarter in New York then straight into another engagement in Florida. There continued to be plenty of work. Two weeks here, four weeks there.

The press would chronicle Faith's hard times, but not Sally's. Sally hid it better, behind dimples and confidence. It was hard to believe she was actually broke given the sums she brought in.

Fed up with the rumors about herself, Faith wrote the editor of *Variety*:

Noting your many references to Ann Corio and her May 9 engagement at the Oriental, may I ask why you overlooked me? I have an April 18 contract with the Oriental which I am cancelling for the reason that I am to be featured at Joe Tenner's "Stairway to the Stars" theatre-restaurant for which you have mentioned both Gypsy Rose Lee and Sally Rand, neither of whom is appearing there when it opens. I am now in rehearsal for the May 14 opening and have a month's contract with a "climbing scale" of one-third of salary increase with each option taken up.

Also had to cancel May 2 date at Fay's, Philadelphia, where 1 had guarantee and percentage deal. F.B.I. (Faith

Bacon, Inc.) would also like it known that she is not in bankruptcy, but rather insolvent! Thank you. Faith Bacon

Sally smiled and danced through the bills, the arrests, chained
to her fans, waving for her supper. She was cash-poor despite a
$2,500-a-week salary. Money was sent back to Glendora and fil-
tered out to relatives. While the world praised her sold-out shows
and accolades, she struggled with the truth, writing Nettie how
Texas was a "horrible fiasco." She lost all the money earned in the
past year. She was left stranded. In Miami she was stiffed and
could not make payroll. Her car was repossessed. She was down to
seventy-eight dollars and had to borrow money. She was sued by
another woman who claimed she was owed $4,000. That was not
the Sally the world saw.

She was exhausted by the sheer amount of time spent in courtrooms. In June of 1946, Sally and her showgirls performed for a
judge during yet another trial in San Francisco.

She had been playing Club Savoy when she was arrested for
"indecent exposure, corrupting the morals of those viewing the act,
and conducting an obscene show."

Her attorney Jake Ehrlich pled not guilty. "I can ... show ... more
nudity among the classics . . . " he asserted. He also noted, "I could
throw a handful of buckshot out that window and hit twenty-five
fan dancers."

He directed the court's attention to his dimpled client. That face
could not be indecent.

The judge wanted to see for himself and ordered everyone to
the nightclub the following morning (no one is implying an ulterior
motive on the judge's part to be invited to a free show). Ehrlich,
knowing Sally had to dance that night, asked the court to give her a
written order releasing her should she be re-arrested. And she was.

The 9:30 a.m. command performance with orchestra in attendance went on without a hitch.

Normally she came out clothed, bubble in hand. Eventually "her dress slips" and she is "exposed." "Then she hikes the dress back up and starts to climb [stairs] . . . the dress starts slipping again. By the time she gets to the top it's all the way down . . ."

Her bubble was more opaque because of wartime materials, and she purposely failed to turn her back to the judge, as she did at every performance to reveal her bare backside.

The judge found her not guilty.

Tax problems continued to plague her. In 1948, even though her "alcoholic accountant" was not drinking at the moment, she owed money because of his incompetency.

She was booted from the Iowa State Fair because, the fair claimed, "the men would rather look at livestock than a stripteaser." Not likely.

Then Sally found love again. Permanent, earth-shattering love.

THIRTY-FOUR

IT WAS NO PUBLICITY STUNT. SALLY RAND, AT AGE FORTY-FOUR, adopted a son. On tour with a carnival Sally told reporters she "picked up" the "red-headed" boy in Alabama. Sally beamed. For a single woman who danced in the nude, it was no easy thing to adopt a baby, something she had been trying to do for a while. (Her friend Joan Crawford adopted the first of her five children—one would be reclaimed by his birth mother—in 1942.)

A showgirl in Sally's act (or, conversely, *at* her show) ran away from her family so they would not discover she had gotten pregnant by a married man. Sally offered to take the baby when told the young girl was giving it up for adoption.

Shean Orion Rand (the "h" would later be dropped) would tell a different story. His father was a navy man. When a gun tragically backfired, he "disintegrated" because he had not been wearing his asbestos suit on deck. His birth mother decided to give up the baby.

Sally took Sean from a hospital in Key West at birth. When asked where the name Orion came from, Sean explained his mother's love of both astronomy and mythology. She wanted to connect her son with the stars. He would recall many nights sitting under the stars as his mother told him stories about "Orion and his dog." She would point out the Greek hunter's "belt and sword."

Though she claimed she adopted Sean, in reality it would not be legal until Sean turned twenty-one and had to give his consent to the adoption in order to be married. Going before the judge, Sean declared he wanted to be legally adopted by Sally. Finally.

Sally gave her baby the last name of Rand, even though she was still legally Beck.

During Sean's childhood, when asked for his birth certificate for activities such as sports in school, Sally turned evasive and told him she would take care of it, but never did, because she could not. He would have no birth certificate until he was an adult.

By all accounts Sally was a wonderful mother. When she was unable to take him on the road, and she did often, Nettie enjoyed looking after her only grandchild.

Sally would place a sleepy Sean in her huge fan boxes backstage where he was fussed over by the wardrobe mistress, or one or more of her showgirls. After being pushed under a rack of clothing, he would fall asleep to backstage gossip.

Sean's birth mother became a menace. She kept track of Sally and tried for years to take him back.

A scared Sally shoved a wad of cash in her friend Sunny Nivens's hands (Sunny was a showgirl) and told her to take Sean to New York and "under no circumstances to open the door, not even for the police." Sean would recall many times being hidden by various loyal showgirls as Sally dodged his birth mother.

Sally posed with the cute, curly-haired boy with dark blue eyes.

So delighted was she—or at least it made for a good sound bite—she said she would soon adopt a sister for Sean when she found a man who would support her and not "the other way around."

With a payroll of at least fifty on her show, she couldn't afford to support another husband. Traveling with her own tent show, she was responsible for everything. She still made a few weak declarations that she was going to conquer the world with her acting, but no one was listening.

Meanwhile she was having phenomenal success under canvas. Her revue played for thousands, three shows a night, with twelve long-limbed showgirls doing a fan ballet that brought Sally onto the stage. She loved the chaotic, colorful crowds at the fairs and carnivals. The atmosphere was happy and gay. She also liked breaking box office records, even if she did not always break even. Sally preferred carnival work to nightclubs because "when people come to the fair, they come to see you, not drink."

Working in clubs could be difficult on many levels. Catcalls and "the rude stares" from the lecherous crowd made some, like Faith, skittish and even colder. Faith was afraid of the audience (and men in particular). Sally had no such fear.

Sally got into a spat with an owner of a road show after a dispute over their verbal agreement. In a huff, Sally decided to leave and went to reclaim her possessions. The owner had her arrested for burglary.

In court it came to light that it was all a publicity stunt. The judge found the majority of the fault lay with the owner, whom he fined and sent to jail for twenty-four hours.

Sally left the operator of the small-time carnival and signed with the biggest railroad carnival in America, the Royal American Shows.

She planned a "giant flash-act" for thirty backbreaking weeks, in charge of a company of sixty.

In artist Leroy Neiman's biography, he describes being a young boy working for Sally cleaning her dressing room. Sally, now in her mid-forties, was temperamental, a star who expected to be treated like one. Neiman's job was to keep her area clean as she had a "phobia" about everything being clean. He remembered a child's rhyme:

Sally Rand has a fan,
If it drops—oh man!
Sally Rand has lost her fan,
Give it back you nasty man.

Her show for Royal American pulled in record-breaking crowds. It was a hard life, living out of a trailer, with little if any privacy. No relief from casting, directing, performing, and publicizing. Not to mention a minimum sixteen shows a day. Every day.

Never above putting on a pair of baggy pants, climbing a ladder, and wielding a hammer, Sally helped construct sets and sew costumes, whatever it took to get her show up.

She alone pulled in thousands of fair-goers who might not have otherwise attended. Sally appealed to the heartland, to common folks. These people "don't want to stay at home," she said. "So you've got to give them something they don't see at home. They want a good time, not education."

Sally enjoyed appearances in her home state, but got into it with Governor Phil Donnelly, who made it clear she was not "representing" Missouri with her nudie act.

On Royal American she made upwards of $5,000 a week with a percentage of merchandising, programs, and 50 percent of the gross. It was extremely lucrative, which is why she encouraged her friend Gypsy Rose Lee to join Royal American.

Still the money went out: seven thousand on drapery and lighting; in 1948 a fire destroyed her set.

For at least four months of the year Sally roughed it under canvas. In the summer she packed up Sean and took him with her. He

remembered the many times scrambling to get where they were going, dashing across tarmacs late for their flight. Then long rides on
old DC-3s. It was always rush from the theatre, into a pair of warm
pajamas, a ride to the airport, plane ride all night, to land in another
state with barely enough time to make the show. It was understand-
able that Nettie wanted Sean to remain in Glendora with her. Sean
admitted he preferred the "real people" of Glendora to Sally's show
business friends.

Remembering her own childhood, she mused, "There was always enough of everything—except love." She was determined that
would not be the case with her child.

THIRTY-FIVE

FAITH INHERITED A PIECE OF LAND AT "BACON HILLS" IN KERN County in Southern California. She leased it to an oil-drilling company. She probably earned a small income from the oil rights. At some point she might have sold a part of the rights to her Uncle Thomas. She would be named in a suit filed in 1948 that claimed "various oil leases on the property were so negligently made that some defendants were able to gain an advantage over the others."

Digging around family papers, Faith discovered old Henry Douglass Bacon had donated a portion of his art collection to the University of California, Berkeley, said to be valued at $34,750. Faith visited Berkeley to peruse the nude statuary. After all, what better legacy might a nude dancer have than a ton of marble?

She discovered the statues forgotten in the basement of the women's gym, still in their original crates, as they had been for the past sixty-eight years. She didn't think that was right. Her attorney was soon contacting the university, demanding they be put on display or given to Faith.

Her lawyer (she would have many) was Jake "The Master" Ehrlich, a defense attorney in San Francisco. Ehrlich was the real-life model for TV's *Perry Mason*; his slogan "Never Plead Guilty" would be the title of his biography. His clients would include Errol Flynn, Billie Holiday, and, ironically, Sally Rand.

Speaking about Faith years later, the attorney "confirmed that his client had nerves like fiddle strings."

What on earth this nomadic gypsy thought she would do with nine tons of statues we will never know.

The university offered at least a couple of the Carrara marble statutes to Faith. She considered giving them to an "art-lover who will promise to do right by them." No more would be heard about *Adriane, Astride a Panther*, or the other pieces.

Also in 1945 Faith and Sanford Hunt Dickinson applied for a wedding license. Whether they really married or not, they would never live together.

It was a surprising move.

Dickinson was born in May 1887 in Buffalo, New York. He had brown eyes and black hair, standing only an inch taller than Faith. He had been a jeweler in 1916, living with his grandmother, when he enlisted in the cavalry in the Mexican punitive campaign. He also served in the Army during WWII, discharged as a second lieutenant.

He possibly had two marriages prior to his with Faith. He was once a theatrical manager, so it is conceivable that is how they met.

As two odd ducks, perhaps they felt a communion. To whatever degree it was an involvement, they went their separate ways—he to Hollywood, she in search of the next job.

Dickinson would become a musical director for the 1949 film

Devil's Sleep and continued as a musical consultant in B pictures, most notably for director Edward D. Wood, Jr.'s *Glen or Glenda*.

A marriage of convenience? An impulse? Whatever the forces that drew these two together, they would never divorce.

THIRTY-SIX

WORKING A MINIMUM OF FORTY WEEKS OUT OF THE YEAR, PROB-
ably more, Sally couldn't keep her eyes on everything. The IRS filed
a lien because she was delinquent on her taxes for 1947 and '48. She
owed over $21,000 because of an accountant who liked booze better
than numbers.

Much of the correspondence Sally dashed off to her mother and
vice versa was taken up with money troubles. Life should have been
getting easier.

Even as society became more permissive (the bathing suit hit the
beaches in 1946, *Playboy* magazine was a few years from being pub-
lished), Sally continued fighting arrests and was embroiled in lawsuits,
the latest with Carnival Company regarding a shakedown attempt.
She was served with a subpoena. Just one more appearance in court.
Another time she was shut down when she could not produce her em-
ployee ID for the police. Fortunately, a spike in attendance followed
every arrest. "Publicity is like money in the bank," she shrugged.

Her "star-studded review" premiered with Cavalcade of Amusements, a large carnival managed by her lover Harry Finkelstein, another burlesque star's current husband. Brother Hal was part of the "okay talent."

Harry Finkelstein was six years younger and had been managing Sally for several years. He was the owner of several clubs in New York including Mardi Gras (both Sally and Faith would perform there) and the Ringside Club.

With black hair and brilliant blue eyes, Finkelstein stood over six feet tall. He was charming and brash, a womanizer and a liar. He had a tendency to "humiliate little people . . . for the feeling of power," which pained Sally.

His second (and current) wife, Georgia Sothern, was a big burlesque star. She was a hot-style stripper who would "hump" the curtains. Like Sally, Georgia was a fiery, temperamental woman, naughty and wildly popular. Basically born into vaudeville, the uneducated cracker began stripping at the ripe old age of thirteen. She was completely different from wholesome Sally Rand.

Harry had been traveling and carrying on an affair with Sally for years before Georgia finally tossed him out.

Sally and Finkelstein had met sometime in 1947, or at least had become lovers by then. Never a wallflower, Sally hired him to manage her, and Georgia complained she began to see less of her husband. She pursued him to seek a divorce, going "daffy" trying to figure out how to find "evidence." Then she found it.

Georgia must have been broiling mad as she listened behind the locked door. Inside a hotel room she could hear her husband and Sally carrying on, "laughing and talking."

It was a steamy August night as the police removed Sally from the room she shared with Harry, charging her with disorderly conduct.

"I have nothing to hide," Sally yelled.

Sally accused Georgia of manipulating the arrest for publicity. "She could use some."

Sally professed to be merely suffering from heat exhaustion and resting in her room. Finkelstein was "strictly my manager," just there to "give me my medicine."

After months of public feuding and name-calling, Harry and Georgia agreed to a divorce. Georgia said she wouldn't name Sally in the complaint because of her new baby Sean. The charges were dismissed, and after ten years of marriage Georgia and Harry were divorced in February of '49.

By mid-July, Sally was again arrested after nearly a dozen officers caught her show at a fair in Milwaukee.

"You're under arrest," one officer flashed his badge.

Indignant, she said, "You'll have to show me more than that." After all, "badges are a dime a dozen."

Tossing a white mink over her pink net dress, Sally protested all the way to the station. "I've been putting that show on for seventeen years."

Finkelstein too was taken into custody for permitting the offensive performance.

She refused to tell her age. "I'm sorry, I just don't tell my age." They demanded an answer. Finally, she admitted to being "four years away from fifty." Coughing that up was probably more humiliating than the arrest itself.

Exhausted, Sally fell asleep in her cell while brother Harold helped scrounge up $1,000 for her release and $500 for Harry's. The next morning she was back at the fair.

The police ordered her to don panties.

On August 9, 1950, forty-six-year-old Sally married Harry. She wore a royal blue suit and pink gloves. At the time Sally and Sean Orion were living in a "super trailer with a nurse and secretary." Their home away from home on the fair circuit.

After the marriage she took the opportunity to tell reporters she had dreamed up her fan dance because it reminded her of herons flying across her family's farm in Missouri. And she "decided" to wear as little as she could because she had no time to make an outfit.

In January of '51, she was sued by Al Wagner of the Cavalcade of Amusements for $2,000 for allegedly libeling him. On a radio show broadcast from the Chez Paree in Chicago, Sally swore Wagner owed her $23,000 in fees.

Then there was a disorderly conduct charge (ultimately dismissed) regarding a Milwaukee performance. Her lawyers remained busy.

For Sally life was "really tough" and she was still working her "tail off." She appeared carefree and happy. Many assumed wealthy. The truth was she often didn't get paid and was unable to pay her company their salaries. She went through past savings, didn't earn a salary at Florida. Showgirls in her employ were often left high and dry, literally on the roadside without a dime after weeks of work.

She believed *we can only do our best and when that has been accomplished no amount of worrying is going to help . . . I put forth every effort and the result is far from what it ought to be.*

She deserved to be tired. She was forty-six and had been hustling for decades. She was still paying for relatives, adding a son and husband to her responsibilities. All of them worried whether the bills were getting paid. She was delinquent. Harry wasn't much help. Worry. Worry. Worry.

Performing in Calumet City, outside of Chicago, turned out to be "wasted" time. She'd worked vigorously and missed Sean in California. She wrote detailed notes home on how Sean should be cared for. Sally relied on her mid-sixties mother, asking her to send g-strings.

Brother Hal was still proving to be a pain in the ass. His film career had never taken off. He had a bad habit of always "bitching."

He was suspicious, had "fears, worried for tomorrow and today's annoyances." She could only turn "a deaf ear." She had been caring for Hal, who lived in her formidable shadow, for years.

And then her troublesome accountant cleaned her out. In 1952, he left her in "great trouble" and another lien was put on her earnings.

Sally tried to remain upbeat.

Her marriage to Finkelstein would not be an easy one. Harry was no different with her than he had been with Georgia. He continued to lie and cheat. He neglected his new wife and son. She once grew so angry she hit him in the ear, throwing her star sapphire ring at him.

Harry hadn't let his ex-wife go. He became dependent on Georgia for "food, shelter, spending money, and laundry." He went on the road with her.

From Georgia's bed a remorseful Harry confessed and begged Sally for forgiveness. He promised to stop lying.

Hurt, she wrote him a sixteen-page letter meticulously laying out his faults and directing him to what he *had* to do—similar to the improvements she tried on husband Turk Greenough. She wanted to "escape from a situation and a person" that had caused her "pain, grief, humiliation, and loss."

She called him out for playing both sides, or in his case, both women. He was promising Georgia a permanent relationship while he used Sally.

He wrote back admitting that's what Georgia wanted, but he would not oblige, except for the sex.

She called him a "fornicator," vain, lazy.

The only way she would take him back was if he became a "devout" Christian Scientist, changed his name and his nose.

Sally deeply and honestly believed in the doctrine of Christian Science. She accused Harry of not being a devout Jew, giving it only "lip service." Though according to Georgia in her biography, Harry came from an orthodox family.

Sally explained she was not prejudiced about the Jewish religion but by changing his name and nose he would stop carrying "the burden" of his people. She wanted a new nose to be "a symbol of the new man" he would become by devoting himself to *her*.

He was "heartbroken." He promised she would come first. He only cared about her happiness and wanted to smile and have fun. His habits were despicable, "a new cheap broad or broads after the show—eat, drink. Fuck—sleep late. No time for responsibility." It wasn't like she didn't understand men needed sex. She did. But one didn't "make a career out of it."

By October more than 200,000 people had descended on Dallas to see a couple football games and Sally at the fair. One "couldn't get a hotel room for any price."

She made appearances, giving advice on beauty and wardrobe. Sally was still gorgeous. She declared she would live in Houston, as the climate was perfect for raising Sean. She leased a dinner club and planned a television show. She made no mention of Harry.

THIRTY-SEVEN

FAITH WORKED STEADILY THROUGH THE 1940S, TO MOSTLY POSI-tive reviews. With Sally remaining *the* famous fan dancer, Faith did not have the opportunities Sally had nor did she work the large fairs—everyone wanted Sally—but she remained a headliner, draw-ing a generous salary. Her name continued to bring in solid box office at theatres.

She took up more petty fights along the way. Faith got in a tiff with the operator of the Casablanca Club in Solano, California, call-ing him names loud enough for police to be called. Refusing to pay bail (she might not have had it), she spent the night in jail.

She worked at Club Moderne in Oakland, possibly with the Egyptian dancer team Tullah and Miy from N.T.G.'s Congress of Beauty. Bookings dwindled. Then in 1947 she announced she was coming out of retirement.

Tired of "contaminated smoke and liquor air–laden night clubs" she was "thrilled with the prospect of seeing the sun again." She was going to work "outdoor" because nightclub work had taken a toll on not only her health but her spirit.

By 1948, things were not so bad that she didn't sign a thirty-week contract, making $1,800 a week. Faith would head a six-girl troupe. She was promised a big promotion, including a ten-foot poster of her, from the carnival boss John R. Ward.

She was a "stand out," but the show "lacked production qualities." She hated dancing to taped music. In May in Peoria, Illinois, Faith claimed Ward deliberately threw tacks on the stage. He knew she danced barefoot and he was trying to force her to quit, to break their contract, she alleged.

By June, Ward did break her contact, and she sued, claiming he owed her $5,000 in salary and transportation, and for the nonfulfillment of her contract, totaling $44,040.35. She wanted attached two carnival rides and his 1947 Cadillac.

"Faith who keeps her age secret" lost 14 pounds and was down to 110. "I need rest and want to build myself up again." Ward replaced her with another and, humiliated, she decided to enter a sanatorium.

She next showed up in Tijuana, Mexico, at the Midnight Follies. Just across the border from San Diego, the place had been a thriving pleasure town during Prohibition. The Midnight Follies was one of the nightclubs with a floorshow and dancing. Again, it was erroneously printed that she had retired several years ago.

Sad news happened in a flash. In 1948 Earl Carroll and his beloved Beryl were obliterated in a plane crash on their way to New York, the result of a set of unfortunate circumstances involving the DC-6 in which they were traveling. They would be buried next to each other in Los Angeles.

The man who had "brazenly brought to the American stage stark realism in its loveliest, most delicate form . . . displayed only the beautiful side with no strings or garments attached" was gone. And so too was an era.

We start to lose track of Faith. We do know she would use at least one alias, perhaps more, as she tried to make a living doing what she loved. But by now owners were wary of her frivolous lawsuits and feuds. She often showed up late, was usually high on pills.

In '49 Faith was staying with Rose McNavey, a thirty-six-year-old Chicago native, at Rose's small apartment. They shared a bed. Faith's dog Sheppy lay between the two.

Following an argument, Faith bit Rose on the arm. When questioned, all Faith wanted to talk about was an upcoming Miami engagement, perhaps excited she finally had an engagement, and not wanting to explain her sleeping arrangements.

THIRTY-EIGHT

IN 1950 FAITH WAS HELD OVER AT THE MARDI GRAS IN OAKLAND, "really packing in the crowd." She was forty years old, and history would not give her credit for her long career. Her anxiety increased with every passing year, with every fine line discovered on her face.

She claimed to exercise two hours every day. She fought insomnia with pills. She suffered terrible anxiety. Rumors of drugs had followed her for years. Her "nervous system permanently affected" after she fell through the glass drum, she carried hidden scars as well.

She dropped again from the headlines but returned in 1951 when there was a mention that Gilda Gray's comeback was inspiring Faith to return to show business.

Faith performed at the Riptide Club seven nights a week in a "gay and fast moving" show. Calumet City's "sin strip" was three hopping blocks loaded with bars, nightclubs, and striptease joints, just west of the Indiana state line. Always a little naughty, the area had housed brothels at least as far back as 1911. After WWII it was host to big entertainment from Tommy Dorsey to Eartha Kitt. The sidewalks were jammed "shoulder to shoulder" as people spilled in and out of clubs. In a few short years it would be an embarrassment, as the clubs degenerated and prostitution took over.

When Sally performed there she rented an apartment across the street from the club, earning a hefty $2,500 a week.

In May of '51 Sally was performing in Philadelphia with a band when the musicians' union "yanked" them off the stage. Harry owed some musicians $800. She had to perform her fan dance in complete silence, no doubt fuming at her husband.

Sally and Harry would lease a Houston dinner club only to abandon it because they weren't together. Sally obtained her divorce from Harry Finkelstein, who was now planning on remarrying Georgia.

There were more club dates, more lawsuits, an Ohio club's liquor license was being threatened because of her supposed lewd performance. Her performance hadn't changed since 1933, but she was still being charged with the same accusations even as society grew more jaded.

Sally was vulnerable. Maybe she wanted a well-deserved shoulder to rest her weary head on. Perhaps she just needed someone to hold her hand and look at her as a woman, not a meal ticket, not a workhorse, not a mother.

In 1954 she married Fred Lalla. The love letters between the two are beautiful and excruciating.

Fred Lalla was a thirty-one-year-old former bantamweight boxer with a short temper. They met on a plane in Chicago headed to Las Vegas. Sally was frequently the aggressor in her relationships; she made the move and chatted him up.

Soon enough Lalla left his twenty-five-year-old wife and three children, ages two through nine, to be with Sally, age fifty. He would be the only "father" Sean Rand lived with (or remembered living with).

Lalla felt the age difference was the "best thing in the world for us." He didn't feel like most thirty-one-year-old men. She was a woman who knew her mind and accepted the facts. And she "knew how to make a man happy." He was happy. She called him "pops," he called her "mother."

With his wife in California, Fred and Sally set up house in Las Vegas.

At Valentine's he wrote her a poem: "To be my valentine, is what I ask my dear, not for just that day, but always, thru the years . . ." He signed it "Pops."

It was August, hot in the Nevada desert, where Sally was performing at the Silver Slipper, at the semi-leisurely pace of four shows a night. She was also hosting a half-hour television show for a local station, interviewing celebrities, discussing books and the home.

Her face and figure were plastered on huge billboards and posters around Las Vegas. She seemed no less a star than when she was thirty.

The day following Fred's California divorce, they were married at the Last Frontier Chapel between her shows.

They were a handsome couple. Sally looked gorgeous and youthful.

As one paper noted it had been a "busy twenty-four hours." Sally started her marriage when she was served papers for an unpaid loan made in 1940. The original $4,000 judgment had doubled.

That wasn't the only hitch in their happily-ever-after. According to California law, Fred's divorce would not be final for a year. The newlyweds were in a heap of trouble. Mae Lalla promised not to charge bigamy if Fred would continue to send fifty dollars a week in child support. Fred was in apparent agony that his kids liked Mae's new man more than him.

Sally continued touring, and they exchanged thoughtful love letters and carried on long phone conversations (one worth sixty bucks).

Work would once again get in the way. He moved into the Glendora home and missed her. Sally did what she could from the road, calling Mae to pick up the kids, who shuttled between families.

He would discover Sally "wasn't at all like the fan dancer he'd seen on the stage."

Fred would prove to be another husband with a roving eye for younger showgirls. Sally busted him on his "ass-grabbing." They got into arguments, and she swore at him in public.

Sean would say Fred was nice to *him*. Not so much to Sally, who lamented, "I married a man who had no conscience."

Somehow they managed eight years together. It would end in divorce in 1960 (he would have three more marriages). She cited cruelty. A public auction of their household goods was conducted in 1961.

THIRTY-NINE

WHATEVER WORK FAITH COULD FIND IN 1952 GENERATED NO PUB-licity, no mention in the trades besides an attempt to start a line of beauty products. The sound of applause from audiences was now deafening in its silence.

Faith boarded a bus for Bradford, Pennsylvania. She was thin, her clothes shabby, makeup piled on thick. She had recently left a hospital after a nervous breakdown, continuing to be "dogged by nervous incidents."

She was seeking refuge at a former lover's home.

Thomas "Ed" Hanley was a businessman, philanthropist, millionaire. Blonde, blue-eyed, with a large nose and jutting chin, he was a big man, a towering 6 feet 3. Recently divorced, he lived in a two-and-a-half story house in Foster Brook, three miles from downtown Bradford, in a home overtaken with priceless art

Born on August 6, 1893, Ed had a childhood marred by tragedy. An older sister was born mute. A younger brother and sister would die. Another brother would die at twenty-three of pulmonary tuberculosis.

Ed was an arrogant "rich young-man-about-town" with a bad first marriage to a girl who loved to spend his money and loved other men.

In 1945 the most exciting thing waltzed into his life: Tullah Innes. Innes would claim many things, one of which was a Hungarian father and Egyptian mother born into a harem. Born Theresa Erdi (probably in 1910), she had a half-sister, Emma, born in 1915. Their place of birth was Hajdúböszörmény, Hungary.

The sisters arrived in America in 1936. They performed an act billed as "Tullah and Miy" and their paths often crossed with Sally's and Faith's. Tullah and Emma looked almost identical with dark hair, brown eyes. Tullah stood 5 feet 5 and was a 120 voluptuous pounds. She was beautiful, exotic, and *obsessed* with sex.

In May of '39 Tullah married fellow Hungarian Andrew Kiss (formerly Tomcsik).

Tullah and her sister traveled to Europe in 1936 and 1938. In June of 1938 a boy named Istvan would be born in Hungary to Theresa and Andrew Kiss. Most likely a pregnant Tullah had given birth, left the child, and returned to America. In her nearly 500-page autobiography she never mentions a child.

By 1941 Theresa, a dancer, and Andrew were living in North Hollywood.

Papers noted the "colored gals" Tullah and Miy performed what club owners called a "jungle dance," or "African," or an "Egyptian act." They toured many of the same places as Sally and Faith, including Colosimo's and the State-Lake Theatre. Their act was "nothing extraordinary."

The sisters worked a club where, between shows, Sally was teaching herself to type.

Working a Buffalo nightclub in 1945, Tullah met the one thing she had been looking for: a millionaire. Ed Hanley was mesmerized by this exotic, buxom belly dancer.

On March 25, 1946, Theresa Erdi was no more. Tullah became an American citizen with the official new name of Tullah Innes. Sister Emma would become Amy.

After three years of dating, Tullah married Thomas Edward Hanley in 1948 and they set up house in Bradford.

A frequent patron of strip clubs years before he met Tullah, Ed had met and fallen for Faith. He told Tullah he'd met Faith in Arizona, where he had retreated for "sinus trouble." There were many opportunities where the two might have met. He was in Los Angeles in 1934 and 1936 buying books and visiting nightclubs.

Charmion allegedly tried to keep him from Faith. Faith managed to send cards and talk on the phone to advance their romance.

Tullah told Ed she also had met Faith. It had been in San Francisco while Tullah and Miy were engaged at Club Moderne. Though vague about years (she won't quote when she was born), she does say it was the war years, so arguably 1942 or '44. Strangely, she fails to mention working with Faith at the New York World's Fair.

Tullah tried explaining to Ed that Charmion was really Faith's mother and not her sister. He stopped her cold.

"Why should Faith lie to me?"

A year into his marriage he spoke about Faith often.

Faith had been calling the house on Main Street.

Claiming she wanted Ed to rid his mind of Faith, Tullah invited the fan dancer to Bradford.

Faith was working in Syracuse, stripping strictly because her fans and costumes were being held by a hotel that Faith could not pay.

It was September. Faith arrived alone. Ed met her and drove her to his house. Tullah had made up the studio over the three-car garage.

Though she still moved gracefully and retained her muscular

fitness, Faith was wearing out. Tullah plied the pitiful Faith with clothes from her "bulging closets." Tullah arranged to have Ed pay for her confiscated suitcases.

Faith was addicted to barbiturates. Tullah took her to a doctor for a prescription. Faith was "gobbling pills," staying in bed until noon, barely able to get herself together when Ed came home for lunch.

All Faith wanted to do was dance. Her body was that of a teenager. She was terribly thin.

Tullah tried fattening her up with heavy foods. For weeks Faith lay around the house, desperate and emotional.

Tullah felt Faith was "beyond help." Still she phoned her former agent to try and get her work.

Tullah sent her infatuated husband off to Faith's studio alone. Wearing some of Tullah's cast-off "sexy" leotards, Faith practiced dancing while Ed watched.

He asked his wife why she wasn't she jealous.

"She has nothing left for me to be jealous about." She had hit on the truth. Faith was not the radiant creature she had once been.

She was washed up. She lacked confidence, but retained her arrogance.

"Don't you realize that Ed was once very much in love with me?" she asked Tullah. "Suppose I took him away from you?" Faith boasted that if all this was hers she could live like a princess with access to all the pills she wanted.

After several weeks of erratic behavior, more pills, late sleeping, Ed—either out of guilt because they had had sex, or over her sloppy behavior—offered to pay for a hotel room in Buffalo to get her out of his house. He asked Tullah to drive Faith to a gig she had somehow secured.

Tullah claims Faith tried to seduce her in Buffalo. Faith was accustomed to using her powers, and desperate as she was, it isn't a stretch to believe she would go from Ed to Tullah.

Ed Hanley and Faith

It would be a year before the Hanleys saw Faith again. They would have dinner with her in New York around Christmas time. She was inappropriately dressed in a light jacket and sandals, with no stockings even though it was snowing. She "was without jobs, without funds, and on drugs."

A 1954 article in the *Bradford Era* claimed Faith was "active on the middle west nightclub circuit." Possibly the plug was a favor made to Ed. Faith was hardly "active."

Faith's reputation for being drugged and removing too many clothes made management wary of hiring her.

Margie, Faith's faithful manager, left to care for her aging parents in Ohio.

Everyone seemed to be deserting her.

It isn't known how she scraped together the money to start a ballet studio for children, but she next turned up in Hammond, Indiana.

On March 1 a woman called Frances Verdier was discovered unconscious on the cold floor of the studio. She had taken an overdose of sleeping pills. She had been found by a female musician "friend," who called the firemen. They gave the forty-three-year-old woman oxygen and rushed her to St. Margaret's Hospital.

When questioned by police, she told them she suffered from "chronic insomnia."

She was released two days later. A small notice in the paper recalled her glory days. "She appeared under the name of Faith Bacon, as a fan dancer in the Streets of Paris . . . " She would remain teaching in Hammond until at least 1955.

FORTY

AS HARD AS THE 1950S WERE FOR FAITH, THEY WERE NOT EASY for Sally either. Her fan ballet girls deserted her. Because she often did not pay salaries, she was forced by American Guild of Variety Artists to post a bond to ensure her girls would get paid.

Sally was okay with life in a six-by-six dressing room, dipping her "fingers into a jar of inexpensive cold cream." After rubbing the white goop onto the palm of her hand, she patted her relatively un-lined face, then wiped it all clean with a nearby towel. She did sit-ups and gardened when at home. She was finally okay with her life, no more fighting and declaring she was a serious actress. No more dis-carding her fans for other short-lived gimmicks.

The Glendora property was heavily mortgaged. Her last perfor-mance under canvas was in 1958. Because of Sally's many connections reaching back to her vaudeville days, she continued to find work. In the 1960s she worked at Magnum Chateau for a former vaudevillian, Helen Magnum, who also hired Sean to bus tables. He got to meet the ballplayers who came in but was told to stay away from the Mafia who came to see Sally.

Once he overheard two older ladies trying to guess Sally's age.

"Seventy?"

"Forty-five?"

Sally, dancing nearby, paused at their table. "Sixty-two," she said proudly and danced away.

In the '60s she hung around the Rat Pack in Las Vegas, attended Debbie Reynolds's wedding to Eddie Fisher at the Tropicana. Sean sat at a table alone with Frank Sinatra. Sally was an old-school icon. She knew everyone, and everyone knew Sally.

Sally's attitude about aging was the same as her attitude about everything else. You could do anything you want if you put your mind to it. She was fit and healthy. She did her isometrics, though she continued to smoke. She ran around town doing errands "looking like hell." She didn't put on airs.

Though she was no longer as in demand as she had been, she was still popular as a nostalgia act.

She gifted a pair of her (supposed) original fans from the Century of Progress to the Chicago Historical Society.

After the ceremony son Sean asked her, "Those were the fans?"

"No, dummy," she laughed. "These aren't the fans . . . but that's what they wanted to hear." Sally would always choose what someone wanted to hear versus the more mundane truth.

Content with her life with a growing son, her mother still healthy, Sally had many blessings. She was more easily adaptable to the times, flexible with work. Never above performing for a group of ten if that's what was needed. She was making the best of her twilight years.

Faith had once reflected, "Perhaps it was a shame that I got so famous so young." Her name had been around so long "they think I must be about thirty-six or more now, when I'm really only twenty-five." She was forty-six.

By 1956, "the slap happy era was over." Gone were the big girlie musicals. Both Ziegfeld and Carroll were dead. Shows had gone from artistic lineups to "lackluster lovelies" taking off their clothes to canned music.

A different type of performer took center stage. Sally and Faith were competing with younger faces showing bigger bosoms. At the rowdy Sho Bar on Bourbon Street in New Orleans, Sally waved her fans, a decidedly modest act amongst strippers pushing the limits of what was taken off.

Faith found employment in sleazy establishments, probably far more disreputable than we will ever know. No one else wanted to take a chance on a dancer drugged and going nuder than the law allowed. She even tried the nasty places on West Madison Street. Chicago's skid row. Last stop.

Sally was fifty-two, back in Glendora with "plans for a more casual life." Sean was eight years old. She had just completed long engagements in Miami and Las Vegas. She bragged she raked in $14,000 for a day's work in Texas, performing twenty-six times.

As Sean grew older, friends teased him that his mother liked to take her clothes off. Sean was shy, and it embarrassed him. Sally sat him down and explained the dance and what it meant to her (at least one of the versions).

It was Labor Day weekend and Faith was uneasy on stage, argumentative. Her reputation was in tatters. Erratic, drugged. Her thoughts were on obtaining the next job. She had lost touch with Charmion, or Charmion had finally let go.

The memories of those years at the New Amsterdam Theatre, the care and adulation of Mr. Carroll and Mr. Ziegfeld, must have ached.

Did anyone believe she had literally been placed on a pedestal and raised up on the stage for hundreds to admire?

She had been an object of desire, viewed from a distance. Now the audience was too close. She could see into their bored eyes.

Her heart had to be breaking. This was not the tuxedo crowd. Her act was almost thirty years old. Old. She felt old. She had nothing. Nothing to show for those years at the top. Her scrapbooks, her unfinished memoirs, gone. Tossed or left behind. She had only her memories. Burned too brightly and reminding her of what had been and what was no more. There was no love. No family.

She needed to get through that last dance. Yes, she took pills, no doubt drank. She needed to get through. Did she plaster a fake smile to her lips or was even that too much effort?

Calumet City had changed. Known now as "a lawless wasteland a few miles west of Chicago," some called Cal City "cheap and tawdry" with what the girls did there verging on "sex acts." But there were still decent places. Sally herself had been there recently. It wasn't all seedy and prostitution and crime. But it was growing rough. Girls would literally be forced into "bondage."

Still, many places were viable for the greats of burlesque including Fifi D'Orsay, Zorita, Evelyn West, and Jennie Lee.

Faith stayed afloat with the two hundred dollars Ed sent her monthly. He could never really let her go. She rented a pair of fans for a job at a club in Des Plaines, Illinois. The originator of the fan dance was now renting fans like a neophyte.

No other jobs were lined up.

Her "nerves are in shreds. She is always crying. She is a cry-baby. She can't sleep without sleeping pills. She can't eat without reducing pills, she can't digest without bicarbonate and laxatives. She can't relax without tranquillizing drugs. She takes pain killers and headache pills all the time."

She was spotted wandering the streets in the damp, having a conversation with herself.

Faith scratched out a desperate note. *I'll tell you what I did. I wrote my ex-family and told them I was in a spot. I did not have rent for the apartment in Penn. Absolutely nothing, not even an acknowledgement. I'm really scared.*

Desperation clung to her like powder. Panic whipped her eyes.

There was nothing else.

FORTY-ONE

WHAT DOES A SHOWGIRL DO WHEN THE FOOTLIGHTS HAVE BEEN turned off, when no more bouquets are sent?

What happens when seventeen-, eighteen-, nineteen-year-old skin wrinkles?

Earl Carroll's love Dorothy Knapp would say about being labeled the most beautiful: "I have found it isn't a fine thing to be the 'most beautiful,'" warning that if she had had foresight, "I'd have tried to succeed through hard work rather than beauty."

As a young girl Faith had been brought up to believe her importance lay in her beauty. The world was hers if only she remained beautiful.

Perfection had been demanded of Faith for so long. She could no longer live up to Mr. Carroll's principle of "no matter what happens" to carry on "with simulated lightness of heart."

The twentieth century *white* showgirl was a "standard to which the American woman looked." The papers reported on what they wore, who they dated, what they had to say. They were larger than life, taller, thinner, more perfect, in fact, flawless.

More desirable and unobtainable than a movie star, the showgirl existed in a more elite club. Visible yet inaccessible.

The showgirls of the 1920s and '30s had been the goddesses of their day, leading a rarified existence of unimagined fame, adoration, and riches. They had pranced, swished, and enjoyed heights as tall as the elaborate headpieces secured to their anointed heads for a relatively short time on Broadway. But it was all illusion. Behind the smile and the ease of a parade walk it was backbreaking, feet-bleeding, interminable hours of rehearsals. It was pain covered with smiles, no food, no rest, cold, hot, cramped, desire, ambition, hope, escape from otherwise drab reality of sparse childhoods, economic deprivations. A gray world where they wanted color.

Back to the grubby Alan Hotel where she was staying. When Faith had checked in nearly three weeks ago, she registered under her married name, despite the fact she had no idea where Dickinson was.

She had recently returned from Erie, near Buffalo, not far from Bradford. She wanted to stick it out in Chicago.

It was September 26. The day was crisp.

They would call her "friend" her roommate. The friend shared her dismal small room without a bathroom. Most likely Ruth Bishop was more than that. Perhaps she too led a life of disappointments, in a series of dingy rooms. She was forty, worked as a grocery clerk. Her parents, John and Ida, were still alive. She seems never to have strayed far from home, dying in Chicago in 2000.

Faith's costumes, fans, and who knows what else were stored with relatives in Erie; someone mentioned an aunt and uncle. If so, they never stepped forward. Possibly it was Dickinson's relatives. Faith told Ruth, "If I can't do any better here, I'll go back to Erie and get my fans. Maybe they'll use me with my old equipment." Once a fan dancer, always a fan dancer.

Ruth did not want her girlfriend to return to Erie; no dreams of Broadway haunted her. She would not have understood that dancing meant everything to Faith. It was the only thing. It was who she was. Ruth complained Faith was different since she had returned.

They had a lovers' quarrel, arguing, crying, shouting for six hours. They didn't even pause as they ate dinner in their room.

It is probable—we'll never know—Faith was on drugs, because she fell asleep *during* the argument. She had paused to watch the television and fell asleep. When she woke up she was dazed and in pain. Physical? Mental? Pain nonetheless. It was real. Her heart hurt.

Ruth wanted to know. "Are you leaving me, or not?"

Faith's eyes filled with tears. She ran from the depressing little room. She ran from Ruth. She was running from the truth.

Ruth was exhausted. Tired from the marathon hysterics. She didn't look for Faith for nearly thirty minutes; when she did, she found her in the hall bathroom. Perhaps it was in the bathroom that Faith jotted a note on the back of her ID card in her wallet.

I'll tell you what I did. I wrote my ex-family and told them I was in a spot. I did not have rent for the apartment in Penn. Absolutely nothing, not even an acknowledgement. I'm really scared.

Ruth knocked. No answer.

The door was locked.

Ruth heard a loud moan. Did Faith disappear into the bathroom to do her drugs, away from Ruth's prying eyes?

Terrified Ruth broke the door and grabbed Faith by the arm. Faith was in a "stupor."

Ruth led Faith back to their room.

"Faith, if you're determined to go home, finish packing your bag," she told the barely conscious woman.

Did Faith turn and look at Ruth? Did she see a long line of women who had not loved her enough?

Where was Charmion? They seemingly had finally lost touch. There was a rumor Charmion had married a refrigerator salesman in Tucson, fifteen years her junior, though he might not have known of the age difference as she too lied about her age. For a long time Faith had continued to send money to Charm, but visiting would have been painful and expensive, and she wasn't a star any longer, she would not have been welcomed. Or useful.

I'm in a world apart from the people who are looking at me . . . I'm bathed in the soft colored lights. I'm in a world apart. It's something ethereal.

There was nothing to ground Faith except for overwhelming despair.

Again she bolted from the room. This time Ruth chased her down the hall.

There was an open window.

At 1:00 a.m. she leaped.

The striped awning of the tavern next door caught her fall.

"The once beautiful showgirl, who had been the toast of Broadway . . . was broke and forgotten." Her shapely body broken, her skull fractured, lungs punctured, blonde hair spilling across her face. She was only forty-six.

At Grant Hospital the doctors performed surgery, working on Faith for hours trying to revive her.

She remained unconscious then slipped quietly out of life.

"The doctors who tried to save her left in tears."

A nurse cried Faith was "golden and her weight 110." A hospital spokesperson assured reporters "she was really pretty, still slender and not a bit hard looking."

Despite internal hemorrhaging and fractured ribs "her body was still so beautiful."

That would have mattered to Faith.

FORTY-TWO

RUMINATING ON FAITH'S DOWNFALL, JOURNALIST PAUL HARVEY chided readers: "We need not concern ourselves with the morals involved to appreciate the psychological hazard when we magnify and glorify and deify the transient body beautiful."

The audience that had elevated Faith had to accept its share of the responsibility for her end. True, Carroll and Ziegfeld literally placed her on that pedestal (also, strapped her to a cross on stage), elevated and crucified at the same time. Nude for all to see as the "symbol of the cult of glorification." It gave her little control of her destiny. She became a sacrificial lamb with the complicity of a society that clamored to worship her perfect form.

One could ask, did the revues and nudie shows objectify and trivialize women, or did they allow women freedom and more control over their bodies? The answer is both.

It gave incredible opportunity to some, those who did not have

Faith Bacon at her loveliest

the means or education or advice from trustworthy counselors to harness it and keep it and turn it into something past their youth.

Sally, who accidentally picked up a pair of fans, used them to soar to places she never could have imagined. And though she spent a long time trying to discard them, she finally embraced her legacy. With her formidable will and talent, she executed those fans for all they were worth. She made America sit up and take notice and hire her. She held on tightly to her image.

Faith could fly but was rudderless.

Both enjoyed the dance. Perhaps they had no talent for anything else. Perhaps they didn't need to. Both were showgirls who emerged from the chorus line to demand that the audience look at them, confront a woman's sexuality owned wholly by that woman. Both Faith and Sally sought sensationalism. They lived unconventional lives, mostly without the influence of a man or the acceptance of society.

And though Sally would make the lasting mark in history, it was Faith who would profoundly influence a young Sally, searching for something to make her special.

Most of these girls, like Faith, and to a degree Sally, were not well educated. Being beautiful gave them entrée to another world. Both women were unencumbered by relationships. They were not dependent on a husband or father for their livelihood. For a time they were independent birds exploring new heights.

Faith had always been willing to leave people behind and "give up much of her personal life" for her dancing. But ultimately her dancing life would give her up. She had nothing else to hold onto.

As awful as it was, it must have been a relief to finally be free when she made her final dive into oblivion.

"She didn't possess loveliness," said her publicist and friend, "she was loveliness."

EPILOGUE

THE BELONGINGS OF ZIEGFELD'S "LAST VENUS" WERE MEAGER. Perhaps Ruth hid them. All the police logged was a ticket from Erie, a white metal ring, eighty-five cents, and a couple of rented fans. She left behind a few clothes. Nothing significant to mark the remarkable things she'd seen and done. Gone were the furs, the jewels, and the car. Gone.

Ruth ordered a simple wood casket for five bucks, but vanished without paying the bill. Buried in Wunder's Cemetery, her funeral was paid for by the Artists Guild of Variety Artists because no one else stepped forward. The guild was not going to allow one of its own to "go without a decent burial."

There was no word from Charmion, Dickinson, any family. No one was there to see Faith off. It is hard to fathom. Charmion, who lived another twenty years, never went to her daughter's grave. Never came forward. Never acknowledged Faith.

Margie, Faith's old secretary, got word to Ed Hanley. He felt terrible. He paid fifty dollars for a simple gravestone marker and arranged that in death she would receive flowers. His instructions were to have them there in perpetuity. But flowers would only be placed at her graveside for the next ten years, until Ed's death in 1969.

"I had an opportunity and I twisted it to my advantage" was perhaps the closest Sally would admit to appropriating the fan dance from Faith.

Sally would outlive Faith by twenty years. She continued to secure lengthy engagements, like her annual sixteen weeks in Las Vegas.

At age sixty Sally was filling houses for three shows a night at the Colony Club in Gardena. She was asked to host a TV show. She still lived with Nettie, brother Hal (who got into the publicity business), and sixteen-year-old Sean. She was happy to admit her "imitators have faded away." Or killed themselves. Surely she knew about Faith.

She tried keeping age an arm's length away, admitting to more than one face-lift. "It's no more complicated than keeping my hair blonde."

There was "a certain reverence" for Sally that kept her "packing customers in." Her figure was praised for retaining its youthful measurement. "Everything's the same," Sally said, "same music, same fans, and same fanny."

Not quite. Caught by a photographer from behind, she was embarrassed by the revelation of her grandmotherly shape.

Her seven-foot fans shrunk to five feet. She was still posing with her breasts bared at the end of her dance, but made sure the lighting was carefully dim. She taped up her skin, secured wigs, wore miniskirts like the young girls, sprayed on Aliage cologne, and continued to have a ball as the grande dame of the fan dancers. Not slowing down despite her age.

She had a long scar on her thigh from falling on a rickety staircase and impaling her leg in Mexico. She got up and finished the dance with blood everywhere. Echoes of Faith.

She had a wicked cough, still filched cigarettes, smoked incessantly, talked up a storm. Only off stage and up close could you see thin scars from the plastic surgery.

She admitted it was "all illusion," as one reporter witnessed when he knocked on her dressing room door. A little old lady in a neglected robe opened the door. The reporter was shocked. He knew Sally was in her seventies and she looked it, but he had expected the illusion.

They chatted. It becomes time for her to prepare for her show.

On goes a pair of lashes, then another pair. Ten years is knocked off her age.

She pats on foundation and blue eye shadow and knocks off another decade.

Body makeup, wig, and another hairpiece on top. On stage under the blue lights "time has stood still." She was twenty-nine-year-old Sally, frozen in 1933.

She said she'd "be devastated" if she couldn't wave her pink fans anymore. Even though the days when thousands poured in to see her were over. She admitted she kept dancing because of tax problems. She was never unemployed. But truthfully, Sally loved it. She would show up at a grocery store if asked. She played a bowling alley, a living room for ten people, outright strip clubs, the Body Shop in Los Angeles, with women decades younger who were more beautiful and more nude.

Nettie said, "She'll probably never retire." No matter the venue, Sally performed with her head held high.

Sally remained engaged, curious, and interested in the world around her, enrolling in psychology and science courses. She took up painting and won prizes; she worked tirelessly in her garden. She was still cursing out anyone who crossed her. She was utterly herself, with no airs about her. She donated her time to local performances in Glendora. She helped at local shows and charities. She built eight apartments and rented them for the income. Generous to a fault, she had given and spent much of her money and now lived modestly. Sally and her friend Dorothy Rubel would pull out old vaudeville props and clothes for parties and entertained. She threatened to take up hang gliding at seventy. Fearless always. Sally's beloved Nettie died in 1970.

Growing up, Sean only gradually developed a sense of his mother's enormous fame. It only really impressed him when it involved a sports figure, like the time she took him to a ball game and introduced him to the manager of the New York Mets, Casey Stengel.

Sean was extremely proud of his mother. They were so close that in 1978 she would abandon Christian Science for his religion of choice, the Church of Latter-Day Saints.

Her last arrest had been in Omaha, Nebraska, in 1964. When accused by the police of going too far, she noted it was the same act she had been doing since 1933. She got off. She became a grandmother in 1974 and loved it. She famously said, "What in heaven's name is strange about a grandmother dancing nude? I'll bet lots of grandmothers do it."

She found a whole new audience to talk to with seniors, giving inspiration and talks and performances, motivating them that life wasn't over. "I'm not the type to sit on the porch and watch life go by." She didn't want others her age to stop participating. She took classes at a local college to keep her mind sharp.

She never lost her sense of humor. When she went to the hospital for an operation after a breast cancer scare, she pinned a note to her gown: "If you have to remove one, put one in the center, at least I'll be a novelty."

In 1977 she suffered a heart attack that damaged 75 percent of her heart. She told no one, not even Sean. She kept on trooping wherever someone would have her.

Sally at age seventy

She was ill and performed without complaint. "Once she got in the spotlight, you'd never know" she was dying. Her last performance was in 1979 in New Mexico for a home show.

"God knows, I like doing this," she said. "It's better than doing needlepoint on the patio."

In 1979, Sally, still fiercely independent, checked herself into the local Glendora hospital. After a lifetime of smoking, a Benzedrine habit, all the things that had kept her going, her heart and lungs were in terrible shape. For years she suffered from terrible asthma. She spent eight days in the hospital, too ill to receive visitors. She wanted to pass at home. Sean consulted the doctors, who said she wouldn't survive the two-mile drive.

My interpretation of a white bird flying in the moonlight at dusk. It flies up into the moonlight. It is dusk. It flies low. It flutters. Then it begins to climb into the moonlight.

Sally Rand died of congestive heart failure on August 31, 1979, at age seventy-five.

Sally's appeal had always been that she was considered "the apotheosis and the epitome of the American success story." From nothing she made herself the icon of the Great Depression, the symbol of the future at the Chicago World's Fair. A beacon of hope for a nation struggling. Throughout her decades of dancing she seemed to defy not only gravity and age but others' expectations of her as a woman, a single woman, a mother, and a senior. She proved time and again she could live her life as she wanted.

Those lucky enough to have seen her at the fair in 1933 witnessed "a woman determined to succeed despite obstacles." Folks with troubles themselves, with doubts and worries about the future, "wanted to reclaim that determination for themselves."

By the end of her life she estimated that she had performed for seven million people, even Queen Elizabeth. She had performed in every state, England, Mexico, Singapore, and Australia.

Shaped by strong women, Sally was formidable. Her story isn't a love story. It's not about a romance, or a man. It's about Sally Rand. She was outspoken, fearless, and daring, and that endeared her to many.

"We shall not look upon her like again." She had done her part for history. "Sally Rand served to make America sex-conscious."

ACKNOWLEDGMENTS

I BECAME BY FASCINATED BY FAITH BACON WHEN WRITING ABOUT her for my book *Behind the Burly Q.* I was haunted by the image of her jumping out of a window. How had she come to that end?

I knew much more about the publicity-loving Sally Rand. Still there had only been one uncited biography about Sally, written by a supposed "friend," a good ten years after Sally's death. The book, quoted by innumerable sources, does much to perpetuate Sally's myth.

I had numerous times interviewed her son, Sean. Sean was generous with his stories and Sally's scrapbooks.

I assumed like the rest of the world that Sally had originated the fan dance. What fascinated me about these two very different women was their struggle for artistic expression.

I enjoyed the archeological dig into their pasts and wish to acknowledge those who helped. If I have forgotten anyone, do forgive me as this has been a many-years-long process.

Of course the gracious Sean Rand was invaluable answering numerous questions, especially difficult during his wife's long illness.

I was thrilled to stumble upon Ruth and Lance Frederiksen. Lance's mother was Faith's first cousin. I'm sorry Ruth is no longer here to read this.

On my knees to all the librarians who diligently searched, answered questions, and answered emails over and over again. Thank you to Dennis Frank at the Bradford Historical Society for insight into Tullah and Ed Hanley. Thank you Renato Rodriguez, archivist at the San Diego History Center, for information on Sally's San Diego visits. I am most grateful to Milt Larsen, who shared his memories and Earl Carroll's scrapbooks, which gave me invaluable insight into this much-misunderstood impresario.

I most certainly appreciated a lovely visit to Wunder's Cemetery to pay my respects to Faith, guided by Valerie Stodden, which yielded much information about Faith.

Thank you to my pal Liz Garibay, an extraordinary researcher herself who encourages and likes to dive into the dusty past. Without the encouragement and hilarious emails from Sara Gruen and David Verzello the process would have been a lonelier one.

Eileen Cope, literary agent and friend, I cannot express my gratitude enough. There would be no book without your belief.

To Counterpoint Press for diving in again with me on another book, I am so blessed. Dan Smetanka, you're the bomb of editors. You keep my side trips to a minimum. You are the biggest pleasure to work with, and I always look forward to your notes.

Huge thank you to the rest of Team Counterpoint, from the publicity mavens Megan Fishmann, Katie Boland, and Alisha Gorder to everyone else making this dream a reality, much love.

Monique Perez, Matthew Richmond, and Morgan William McDonald, I would have no hope of getting from A to Z without you. Thank you for doing the impossible.

To my family I owe everything. Thank you to Zsa Zsa, Zane, Rhys, and Bob. I hope they write stories about all of you one day.

PHOTOS

NOTES

PROLOGUE

4   "stepped out of line and offered a suggestion": *Port Arthur News*, July 19, 1936.

4   "bag lady": Author interview with Lee Stuart.

4   "to the inhaling and exhaling of the audience": *Chicago Daily Tribune*, July 14, 1934.

4   "palpitating audience": *The Button Box*, Ruth Ellen Patton Totten.

5   "Try to get yourself arrested as much as possible": *Behind the Burly Q*, Leslie Zemeckis.

6   "The Marilyn Monroe of her day": *New York Confidential*, Jack Lait and Lee Mortimer, 1956.

CHAPTER ONE

12   "was an ugly, overgrown town": *Chicago and the World's Fair 1933*, Fred Husum (Internet Archive, www.archive.org/details /chicagoworldsfaioohusu).

13   "promised abundance in a world of tomorrow": *World of Fairs*, Robert W. Rydell.

14   "From a shabby little outpost on the shores": *San Antonio Light*, May 28, 1933.

14   "miniature world in itself": *Xenia Evening Gazette*, May 27, 1933.

15   "symbol of hope": *San Antonio Light*, May 28, 1933.

15   "their dreams of a more carefree way of life": *Xenia Evening Gazette*, May 27, 1933.

15   "specimen of mankind": Ibid.

16   "savages": *World of Fairs*, Robert Rydell.

16   "Amid pomp and ceremony": *San Antonio Light*, May 27, 1933.

16   "they planned this Fair": *Hard Times*, Studs Terkel.

17   "People come to see a show": Ibid.

17   "Of course many sins are committed in the name of art": *World of Fairs*, Rydell.

17   "graying," "turkish trousers," and "I'd never go before an audience like that": *Nevada State Journal*, July 31, 1933.

18   "a great secret": *Belton Journal*, June 29, 1933.

18   "American way of life": *World of Fairs*, Rydell.

18   "Laughter and fun": Ibid.

18   "name on the lips of thousands" and "nothing but a pair of fans and a smile": *Nocona News*, August 11, 1933.

19   "hick": Sally letter to her mother.

19   "became the fair's enduring icon of optimism and hope": *The 1933 Chicago World's Fair*, Cheryl Ganz.

19   "Ladies and Gentlemen, I give you the one and only Miss Sally Rand": *Cadet Gray*, James M. Vesley.

19   "hillbilly": "Mozark Movements: Sally Rand: FAN-tastic MOzarks Dancer", Paul Johns January 3, 2010.

CHAPTER TWO

21   "so small they had to catch": *Syracuse Post Standard*, September 1, 1979.

21   "flowers for General Lafayette" and "god quilts": Sally letter to her mother.

21   "a higher percentage of participants": *Insiders' Guide to Branson*, Fred Pfister.

22   "order in life": *Oakland Tribune*, June 14, 1928.

22   "arrived at the age to be giggly": *Hard Times*, Terkel.

23   ". . . there is probably no county in the state": *A Preliminary Catalogue of the Birds of Missouri*, Otto Widmann.

23   "would tell the story of a dying swan": *Dance Magazine*, August 1931.

23   "It was a combination": Ibid.

23   "every inch of her being": *Dance of the Swan, A Story about Anna Pavlova*, Barbara Allman.

23   "sat up and wept": *Oakland Tribune*, June 14, 1928.

23   Some accounts place Sally running away from Elkton. One story claims Nettie knew she was leaving and gave her blessing—not an unlikely scenario as Nettie would seem to implicitly trust her mature daughter's judgment and never once question her career choice or try to deter her.

24   "bird-like movements": *Dance of the Swan*, Allman.

24   "starved for affection": Author interview with Sean Rand.

24   Note: Though called "Colonel" by the Rand family and the papers, records at his death show he was discharged as lieutenant colonel, with his former rank being captain.

24   "I wanted to fly—to leave the earth, soar . . . to the sky": *Albuquerque Journal*, April 21, 1935.

25   "instant gratification": unknown newspaper.

26   "living statuary": *Kansas City Times*, 1982.

26   "emerging from a fountain": PdxHistory.com, "Electric Park—Kansas City's Coney Island."

26   "I found many unscrupulous men in my path": *Fort Madison Evening Democrat*, October 11, 1933.

CHAPTER THREE

31   Regarding Roy Albert Rice and Charmion's marriage, Charmion listed her father as T. J. Butts, so possibly her mother had remarried.

32   "dance orgies of the natives": *Love of Art & Art of Love*, Tullah Hanley.

32   "frustrated ballet dancer": Ibid.

CHAPTER FOUR

33   "bring culture": *Hard Times*, Terkel.

33   "toe dancer": *Butte Montana Standard*, September 8, 1957.

33   "net girl and trapesist": *Pacific Stars and Stripes*, May 12, 1979.

34   "one of the fastest and most sensational trapeze acts": "The Flying Wards Circus Act," www.texashistory.unt.edu.

35   Years later Mayme Ward, Eddie's wife and former catcher, cre-
     ated wardrobe for Sally's Nude Ranch. "I did go broke, but I didn't
     care": *Huron Evening Huronite*, South Dakota, October 12, 1933.

CHAPTER FIVE

37   "simple": *Encyclopedia Britannica*, www.britannica.com/biography
     /Albertina-Rasch.

37   "terror who would hit a student with a stick": *Life as a Tarantella*, Jill
     D. Sweet.

37   "high and low": *Agnes De Mille Telling Stories in Broadway Dance*,
     Kara Anne Gardner.

CHAPTER SIX

38   Today the former New Amsterdam Theatre houses Disney specta-
     cles and the rooftop theatre no longer exits.

39   "It's the quickest, cleanest": *Flying Magazine*, vol. 5, no. 3, Septem-
     ber 1934.

39   "The time will come . . .": Ibid.

40   Neither "Billie" nor "Helen" appears in the credits. She claimed it
     was before 1927. The Blackbirds started in 1926. In one interview
     Sally gave in 1934 she claimed it was definitely before 1927. In 1934
     she did dance with the revue for a charity benefit, but by then Sally
     Rand was a huge draw.

41   "artistic feet": *Madison Capital Times*, September 27, 1923.

41   "sorta protégé": *Variety*, March 16, 1927.

41   "charged with domestic indiscretion": *Hamilton Evening Journal*,
     January 27, 1923.

41   "aviation fanettes": *Los Angeles Times*, January, 1924.

41   "hard luck": *Variety*, March 16, 1927.

CHAPTER SEVEN

44   "salary, and she never got money of her own": *Love of Art & Art of
     Love*, Hanley.

45   "The Revue is one Broadway tradition that was great": *Revue*, Rob-
     ert Baral.

45 "variety, vaudeville, minstrelsy and burlesque": Ibid.

45 "carried a renown": Ibid.

46 "Scions of New York's most distinguished families": *Midnight Frolic*, Marcelle Earle and Arthur C. Homme.

CHAPTER EIGHT

49 "adorned with collars": Winter Garden Program, author's collection.

49 "The girls started getting slimmer": *The Brothers Shubert*, Jerry Stagg.

49 "Bridge of Thighs": *The Ziegfeld Follies*, Marjorie Farnsworth.

50 "more daring and vulgar": *Variety*, July 1, 1925.

50 "sophisticated revue" and "One of the best": *Variety*, July 1, 1925.

50 "weak on content but lavish": *Broadway Plays and Musicals*, Thomas S. Hischak.

51 "breakfast in some chain rest or cafeteria" and "Inside a 1920s chorus girls dressing room": *The Competitors Journal* (c. 1920s) www .glamourdaze.com, January 6, 2013.

52 "My time does not belong": *Hammond Lake County Times*, March 21, 1925.

52 "make hay while the sun shines": *The Competitors Journal*.

52 "A girl had to train for weeks": Ibid.

52 "Many of the girls had to buy the clothes they wore on the stage": Ibid.

52 "pleasant to kiss": Ibid.

52 "Not very hygienic": Ibid.

CHAPTER NINE

54 "a girl trying to break into pictures has to think of everything": Sally Rand scrapbooks, unknown magazine article "Sally Rand Sets the Pace" by Charles West.

54 "extra in Hollywood is like a man on a raft in mid-ocean": Ibid.

55 "art of self-defense": *Los Angeles Daily Times*, unknown date.

55 "picked from the surf": *Madera Tribune*, August 18, 1925.

55 "school where they rode directly to stardom": Unknown newspaper.

56 "the most beautiful girl in America" and "Sally Dove into the Movies": Unknown magazine.

56 "That's it!": *Sally Rand: From Film to Fans*, Holly Knox. The other story regarding the origins of Sally's name was told to the author by SR.

57 "the luxuriant semi-tropical growth": *Stories of Old Glendora*, Ryan Lee Price.

57 "blonde kid trimmed": *Picture Play*, June 1926.

57 "to occupy positions in the spotlight of beauty": Unknown newspaper, Sally Rand scrapbooks.

58 "greatest exponent of the Charleston in America": Ibid.

58 "Study of Sally Rand": Ibid.

58 "Sweet Sally Rand, the mischief in your eye": Ibid.

58 "Nell Brinkley curls": Unknown newspaper. Nell Brinkley was a comic illustrator who created female characters that were cheery and lighthearted.

59 "I know for a fact he wasn't impotent": Author interview with SR.

59 "butter-and-egg": *Stockton Cal. Eve. Record*, January 8, 1926.

59 "one-piece costume": Ibid.

59 "claim she compromised the moral standing": *Stockton Evening Record*, January 8, 1926.

60 "The finger of destiny points": *Helena Independent*, July 5, 1927.

61 "varied, colored striped": *New York City News*, February 27, 1927.

61 "mirror-faceted sphere": Ibid.

62 "baby blue evening wrap": *Amarillo Sunday News Globe*, March 6, 1927.

62 "over dressed": Ibid.

62 "striking beauty": Ibid.

62 "flying from town to town": *Oakland Tribune*, June 14, 1928.

62 "short and smooth": Ibid.

63 "Miss Rand, leave my Jesus Christ alone!": *Movie Stars Do the Dumbest Things*, Margaret Moser.

63 "golf widows": *Hammond Lake Times*, July 9, 1929.

64 "another mere dancing girl in the divertissement": *Laredo Times*, June 29, 1930.

64 "one of the most popular of the screen's ingénues": *Salt Lake Tribune*, December 14, 1928.

CHAPTER TEN

66   "the edgy, the queer, and the sexy": Website broadway.cas.se.edu /content/Gertrude-hoffman.

66   "frequently stopped the show with their aerial feats and stunts": (walery, aicis collection).

66   "You have nothing to be ashamed about": *Bird's Eye View*, Dorothy Bird.

66   "make the show": *Variety*, 4, 1926

66   "bacchanale which is far more thrilling": *Jazz in Print*, Karl Koenig.

67   "comely, agile, tireless . . .": *Variety*, July 1, 1925.

67   "Please don't ask to take us out": *Port Arthur News*, August 2, 1925.

67   "I never thought of my body when I was dancing": *Bakersfield Californian*, July 14, 1925.

67   "nudes, nudes, nudes, and more nudes": *Variety*, August 4, 1926.

CHAPTER ELEVEN

70   "of her ability to do all kinds of dances and athletic stunts": *Los Angeles Cross Tribune and Leader Press*, July 26, 1928.

71   "wonderful personality": Unknown newspaper.

71   "a toe dance, and adagio fantasie": *Ogden Standard Examiner*, July 9, 1928.

71   "diminutive and attractive": *Salt Lake Tribune*, August 9, 1928.

71   "good singing voice": *Variety*, December 19, 1928.

71   "for all of her shapeliness": *Variety*, September 26, 1928.

71   It is noted in Sally's scrapbooks that her mother moved to Los Angeles in 1929.

72   "didn't say two words": Author interview with SR.

CHAPTER TWELVE

73   "monumental sets and spectacular transformation scenes": *Frederic Franklin: A Biography of the Ballet Star*, Leslie Norton with Frederic Franklin.

73   "majestic and sublime": *History and Anthology of French Song*, Maximillien de Lafayette.

74   "There is a great deal of splendor": *Port Arthur News*, May 15, 1927.

75 "brilliant show": *Variety*, August 31, 1927.

75 "showed herself naked": *New York Confidential*, Lee Mortimer, 1956.

CHAPTER THIRTEEN

83 "flesh peddler": *Gentleman Jim Mooney*, Daniel Best.

83 "Carroll gyped me out of": *Sarasota Herald Tribune*, June 24, 1976.

83 "tawdry": *Scandals and Follies*, Lee Davis.

83 "disreputable": Ibid.

84 "tipsy": *The Body Merchant*, Ken Murray.

84 "fifteen nearly-empty liquor cases": *Kingston Gleaner*, March 8, 1926.

84 "obstinate grittiness": *Brownsville Herald*, January 18, 1940.

85 "at least ten times before he divides them into three classes": Unknown newspaper.

85 "100 nearly perfect girls": Unknown newspaper.

85 "a real knockout": *The Body Merchant*, Murray.

85 "seven numbers" *Man on the Flying Trapeze*, Louvish.

85 "greatest sketch of all time": Ibid.

86 "eleven in the morning until five the next morning": *The Body Merchant*, Murray.

86 "lemon yellow": Ibid.

86 "the best *Vanities* of them all": Ibid.

86 "placing opportunity in the girl's way": *Vanities* program, author's collection.

86 "abundant opportunities": Ibid.

87 "seen from the audience": Unknown newspaper.

87 "took seven railroad cars": *Hanover Evening Sun*, December 29, 1928.

87 "fifty-six chorus girls," "fifteen mothers," "beautiful buildings," and "gorgeous scenic": Ibid.

88 "highest paid chorus girls in the history": Ibid.

88 "remove all clothing": *Bakersfield Californian*, December 14, 1929.

88 "eight hours a day and returned for night": *Daily News*, December 14, 1928.

88 "raiding the Ziegfeld, White, and Shubert": *Sandusky Register*, January 15, 1929.

88 "which isn't bad for Baltimore": *New Castle News*, January 17, 1929.

88   "outstripped his rivals in point of lavish display": *Hanover Evening Sun*, February 16, 1929.

88   "the handsomest production": *Brownsville Herald*, February 13, 1929.

89   "a hit": *Burlington Hawk Eye*, March 3, 1929.

89   "pretension": *Variety*, February 6, 1929.

89   "neglected": *Variety*, February 13, 1929.

89   "no action and hardly a laugh": Ibid.

89   "acres . . . of girls": *Variety*, February 2, 1929.

89   "no vitality," "faltering," "queen," and "beautiful but dumb": *Variety*, May 8, 1929.

89   "engaging talent": *Variety*, February 12, 1929.

89   "long life ahead of it": *Hanover Evening Sun*, February 16, 1929.

89   "tired of paying": *Wichita Daily Times*, April 19, 1929.

89   "with a songbird": Ibid.

90   "swashbuckling young": *Variety*, February 12, 1929.

90   "had no voice": *Hamilton Evening Journal*, February 1, 1930.

90   "six cents": *The Body Merchant*, Murray.

90   "close companion": Ibid.

90   "out of obscurity into the lime lights": *Variety*, July 31, 1929.

90   "all the nudes": Ibid.

91   "fiend": *Variety*, July 31, 1929.

91   "I can't cook": Ibid.

91   "I'd be the boss": Ibid.

91   "illusion that brought millionaires": *The Ziegfeld Follies*, Farnsworth.

CHAPTER FOURTEEN

92   "star of screen": *New York Times*, November 1, 1929.

92   "a very young girl": *Variety*, February 13, 1929.

92   "average dance floor": *Variety*, June 11, 1930.

93   "disturbance," "prima donna," and "pest": *San Antonio Light*, November 27, 1928.

93   "epidermis from his elbow": *New York Times*.

94   "film star": *Variety*, August 6, 1930.

94   "chorus boy": *Variety*, September 24, 1930.

94   "tell of certain orgies": *Love of Art & Art of Love*, Hanley.

94   "the spray of chilled air": *Variety*, September 24, 1930.

94   "I can't do this anymore": *The Ziegfeld Touch*, Richard and Paulette Ziegfeld.

95   "The 1927 crowd": *Madison Capital Times*, April 12, 1931.

95   "will be remembered for her work with Cecil B. De Mille": *Lowell Sun*, October 10, 1931.

95   "Freelancing in films": *Variety*, June 2, 1931.

CHAPTER FIFTEEN

96   "the hottest place on the planet": *Gangsters and Gold Diggers*, Jerome Charyn.

96   "were intensely loyal to him": *New York Sun*, unknown date.

97   "Girls are a commodity": *The Body Merchant*, Murray.

98   "Everything is coming along lovely": Unknown newspaper, "Times Square Tintype" by Skolsky.

98   "Meticulous": *Canton Daily News*, March 17, 1929.

98   "I must be constantly preaching, pleading, ordering and threatening": *The Body Merchant*, Murray.

98   "sensitive face": *Canton Daily News*, March 17, 1929.

98   "one piece bathing suits": Ibid.

98   "brutally thorough": Ibid.

98   "beauty and charm": Ibid.

98   "is not an easy one": Ibid.

98   "bright, happy vivacious": Ibid.

98   "is free to make": Ibid.

99   "Beauty is a woman's": Ibid.

99   "ideal of beauty": *Canton Daily News*, March 17, 1929.

99   "it a point": Ibid.

99   "Women of the theatre": Ibid.

99   "I don't care about character": Unknown newspaper. "Overseer of the Pure" by Michel Mok, October 25, 1939.

99   "Only the most fortunate": *Canton Daily News*, March 17, 1929.

99   "no matter what happens": Ibid.

99   "Mr. Carroll, why can't we do a number": *Bakersfield Californian*, October 12, 1938.

100   "I think of my body only as a thing of beauty": *Variety*, July 31, 1929.

100   "the heroine": Wikipedia.

100   "Call it daring or bold": Ibid.

100   "I'd cover myself with fans": *Bakersfield Californian*, October 12, 1938.

101   "green, mother of pearl, and mauve": *Lost Broadway Theatres*, Nicholas Van Hoogstraten.

101   "super-spectacle of sixty-eight scenes": *Vanities* program.

101   "Here NOW": *Chicago Daily Tribune*, July 10, 1930.

101   "A Field of Daisies": *The Body Merchant*, Murray.

101   "two white" and "fans, revealing": Ibid.

102   "simple": *Bolero: The Life of Maurice Ravel*, Madeleine Goss.

102   "simple": Unknown newspaper, New York Performing Arts Library.

102   "dangled between": *The Body Merchant*.

103   "no action would be taken until the matinee was over": *The Body Merchant*, Murray.

103   "unfastening their garter belts": *Chicago Daily Tribune*, July 10, 1930.

103   "come quietly": *New York Times*, July 10, 1930.

104   "a show so bad that it had to be raided": *The Body Merchant*, Murray.

104   "it was one of the filthiest": *Ziegfeld and His Follies*, Cynthia Brideson.

104   "was in no position to talk": *New York Times*, July 13, 1930.

105   "double white fox fur reached": *Hamilton Daily News*, July 1, 1930.

105   "to hurt him": *Madison Capital Times*, July 13, 1930.

105   "in the gloomy interior of Jefferson Market court room": Ibid.

105   "we have an artistic show": Ibid.

105   "excites much comment even with her clothes on": *Charleston Gazette* July 11, 1930.

105   "maharajah of Baluchistan": *Charleston Gazette*, July 16, 1930.

105   "That's her": *Bluefield Daily Telegraph*, July 12, 1930.

106   "came down a long ensemble of girls": *San Francisco Examiner*, July 12, 1930.

106   "While she was doing the dance facing the audience": *The News* (Frederick, MD), July 11, 1930.

107   "the question whether a play": *Chicago Hearld*, July 12, 1930.

107   "judges' opinions are the result": Ibid.

107   "fanny dancer": *Variety*, August 4, 1930.

107   "some religious picture": *Port Arthur News*, August 11, 1930.

107   "starry-eyed": Ibid.

107   "nervous breakdown": *Variety*, August 4, 1930.

108   "I am a natural dancer": *Low Man on a Totem Pole*, H. Allen Smith.

108   "presenting an obscene and indecent theatrical production": *Dubuque Telegraph Herald*, August 12, 1930.

108   "the top glamour gal on the most glamorous street": Unknown newspaper.

109   "I will not permit a man to spoil the beauty of my perfect body": Unknown newspaper.

109   "Many were called but few were chosen": *Herald Journal*, October 30, 1937.

109   "looking forward to a life of fame": *Ogden Standard Examiner*, August 9, 1936.

109   "thousand-dollar bills tucked": *The Ziegfeld Follies*, Farnsworth.

109   "No chorine, however": Unknown newspaper, 1949.

110   "You don't have anything": *Ocala Star Banner*, May 1, 1975.

CHAPTER SIXTEEN

111   "extra large sums": *High Point Enterprise*, September 18, 1930.

111   "unlimited wealth": *Pittsburgh Press-Gazette*, July 28, 1935.

111   "sea gulls": *Atchison Daily Globe*, September 23, 1930.

111   "most risqué": Ibid.

112   "multi-colored": Ibid.

112   "angelic looking": *Atchison Daily Globe*, September 23, 1930.

112   "Faith Baker": Ibid.

112   "elegant dowagers": Ibid.

113   "She's gonna do the same": *Queen of the Nightclubs*, Historic Films Stock Footage Archive. The fan dancer is mistakenly identified as Sally, when it is clearly Faith, especially as Texas references her appearance at Earl Carroll's the year before.

114   "choreographed to convey desire": *Ziegfeld Girl*, Linda Mizejewski.

114   "With the position as a Follies girl, came a promise": Ibid.

114   "unattainable and irresistible": Ibid.

115   "symbol of liberty and independence": Ibid.

115   "grueling": *Midnight Frolic*, Earle.

115 "demanded ermine, chinchilla, ermine, and pearls from Tiffany and Cartier": Ibid.

115 "You see, getting a job" and "Inside a 1920s chorus girls dressing room": *The Competitors Journal.*

115 "immaculate": Unknown newspaper.

115 "A girl is only beautiful when everyone says she is beautiful": Unknown newspaper.

116 "entrepreneur of sensual desire": *The Ziegfeld Follies*, Farnsworth.

116 "selective enforcement": *Revue*, Baral.

116 "who shaped the American": *Ziegfeld Girl*, Mizejewski.

116 "prized beauty": *Beckley-Raleigh Register*, July 14, 1931 .

116 "perfect": *Kittanning-Simpson Leader Times*, March 5, 1931.

117 "the most humorous" interviews that were "shockingly frank": *Sandusky Register*, March 28, 1931.

117 "The baby faced": *Twin Falls Daily News*, April 9, 1931.

117 "due to a tummy ache, sore ankle, or something": *Alton Evening Telegraph*, July 14, 1931.

117 "Posed as a kind of water carrier without a jug . . .": *Chicago Daily Tribune*, July 12, 1931.

117 "herd of elephants, their trunks carrying scantily clad women": *The Ziegfeld Touch.*

118 "good fun to tear a herring with after the show": Unknown newspaper.

118 "awe-inspiring undress": *Alton Evening Telegraph*, July 1, 1931.

118 "silence" and "disarming": *Port Arthur News*, "On Broadway" by Walter Winchell, July 17, 1931.

CHAPTER SEVENTEEN

120 "Movie Actor Quits Wife Because Parents Object": *El Paso Herald Post*, August 23, 1932.

121 "financial failure": *Burlington Daily Times News*, October 19, 1933.

121 "coldest October day": *Moorhead Daily News*, October 18, 1932.

121 "desperate": *Burlington Daily Times News*, October 19, 1933.

122 "heavy coat of cream": *Murphysboro Daily Independent*, October 17, 1932.

122 "I haven't been out of work since the day": *San Antonio Light*, September 24, 1933.

123 "My interpretation": *Stories of Old Glendora*, Price.

123 "It flies up into the moonlight": Ibid.

123 "I searched my mind": *Burlington Daily Times News*, October 19, 1933.

123 "created in 1929": Ibid.

123 "I have done this dance to get money to get back to Hollywood": *Murphysboro Daily Independent*, October 17, 1933.

123 "I know I'm no Ethel": *Butte Montana Standard*, September 8, 1957.

124 "Some hoodlum admirers": *Indiana Evening Gazette*, September 1, 1967.

124 "disturbing culture of crime churned insidiously around most nightclubs": *The 1933 Chicago World's Fair*, Ganz.

124 "not a nice guy": Author interview with SR.

CHAPTER EIGHTEEN

127 "Fighting went on in the dressing room every performance": *Midnight Frolic*, Earle.

127 "famous fan stepper": *Variety*, December 13, 1932.

127 "standing stark naked backstage": *New York Confidential*, Lait and Mortimer, 1948.

127 "My body is a work of art": Unknown newspaper, New York Performing Arts Library.

128 "takes particular joy in just being beautiful": *Hagerstown Daily Mail*, July 1, 1932.

128 "$2,000 worth of new jewels": *Sandusky Register*, April 9, 1932.

128 "jewels for safekeeping": *Love of Art & Art of Love*, Hanley.

128 "playboy broker": *Albuquerque Journal*, April 21, 1935.

128 "I have always loved Faith": *Fort Madison Evening Democrat*, December 1, 1933.

128 "romance has no place in the life of a classic statue": Unknown newspaper.

128 "are often as detached and cold in their devotion": *Blondes, Brunettes and Bullets*, Nils T. Granlund.

129 "Remembrances of a Nude": *Pittsburgh Post-Gazette*, February 26, 1934. After her death, it was claimed her PR man, Marc Chlemens, a friend of over twenty-five years, was going to publish her memoirs.

129   "ordered to Arizona" and "due to the cold": *New York Herald Tribune*, November 7, 1933.

129   "roughed it": *Fevered Lives*, Katherine Ott.

130   "I have to have the money": *New York Herald Tribune*, November 7, 1932.

CHAPTER NINETEEN

132   "for the next five months": *San Antonio Light*, May 28, 1933.

132   "Atlantic," "in spirit," and "the wicked city": *Liberty Express*, July 20, 1933.

132   "Direct from Montmarte!": Ibid.

132   "bar every minute": Ibid.

132   "typical of Paris": Ibid.

132   "Merriment": Ibid.

133   "Gigolos": *Blytheville Courier News*, June 28, 1933.

133   "Harvard, Broadway": *Scranton Republican*, June 29, 1933.

133   "brain whirling": *Austin Daily Texan*, September 17, 1933.

133   "lady with eight feet of red": Ibid.

134   "trained fans": Ibid.

134   "lively red head": *Austin Daily Texan*, September 17, 1933.

134   "strategically located patch": *Never Plead Guilty*, Noble.

134   "I never expected to make a living": *Oakland Tribune*, June 14, 1928.

135   "harassing": *Hard Times*, Terkel.

135   "insulted" and "put down": Author interview with SR.

135   "Ed, I can't get into the fair": *Sally Rand from A to Fans*; Knox fails to mention her stint the year before as Lady Godiva that had made all the papers.

135   "The Chicago Artists Ball": *El Paso Herald*, December 15, 1932.

136   "rehearsing": *Iola Register*, December 5, 1932.

136   "Bring me a table and four bus boys": *El Paso Herald Post*, December 15, 1932.

136   "little man": Classic Chicago Magazine.

136   "Lady Godiva will take": *Hard Times*, Terkel.

136   "clippity clop" and "on every newspaper": *Behind the Burly Q* (film), Zemeckis.

137   "I'm the lady": Classic Chicago Magazine.

137   "knew she had arrived": *Sally Rand: From Film to Fans*, Knox.

137   "lewd": *Chicago Daily Tribune*, Oct 27, 1937.

138   "either you put on some of this": *San Antonio Light*, September 24, 1933.

138   "My technique": *Never Plead Guilty*, Noble.

138   "beautiful artistic dancer": *Moorhead Daily News*, August 9, 1933.

139   "sensational publicity": *Riverdale Pointer*, October 20, 1933.

139   "got a completely": *That Toddlin' Town*, Sengstock Jr..

139   "Everyone adored Sally": *Not Pretty Enough*, Hirshey.

139   "metaphor for hope": *The 1933 Chicago World's Fair*, Ganz.

139   "lewd and lascivious": *Chicago Daily Tribune*, July 19, 1933.

140   "huge amphitheatre": *Delphi Citizen*, July 13, 1933.

140   "separate banking facility": *Not Pretty Enough*, Hirshey.

140   "People go to 'Paris'": *Wisconsin State Journal*, July 19, 1933.

140   "Sally Rand is well known around" and "a lot of boobs": Ibid.

141   "the aesthetic and financial": *Wisconsin State Journal*, July 26, 1933.

141   "I have not been put out of work": *Winnipeg Free Press*, December 16, 1967.

141   "hours of practice": *Wisconsin State Journal*, July 26, 1933.

141   "The Rand is quicker": *Sally Rand: From Film to Fans*, Knox, and multiple other sources.

141   "evolved after I": *Wisconsin State Journal*, July 26, 1933.

141   "sickly child": Ibid.

CHAPTER TWENTY

142   "the originator" and "inventor of the skin displaying act": *Chicago Tribune*, September 8, 1933.

142   "underfed ostriches": *Albuquerque Journal*, July 19, 1936.

142   "war": *Port Arthur News*, September 10, 1933.

143   "the best show on the grounds": *Wisconsin State Journal*, September 1, 1933.

143   "the best nude in the business": *Ironwood Daily Globe*, March 31, 1933.

143   "Sally has asked her to take over the nude spot": *San Francisco Examiner*, mid-to-late 1930s.

143   "hiding behind a few beads": *Ironwood Daily Globe*, March 31, 1933.

143   "flooded the nation with publicity releases": *World of Fairs*, Rydell.

143   "staggering proportions": *Chicago Tribune*, August 7, 1933.

143   "belles being staged to see who can wear the least": *Nevada State Journal*, September 10, 1922.

144   "single dimension": *El Paso Herald Post*, June 13, 1934.

144   "an impression of aloofness": *Indiana Evening Gazette*, March 28, 1933.

144   "Sure I'm an Ozark": "Mozark Movements: Sally Rand: FANtastic MOzarks Dancer," Paul Johns January 3, 2010 (ccheadliner .news).

144   "nude and free on the stage, but timid and shy": *Love of Art & Art of Love*, Hanley.

144   "In a night club, when I'm on the floor": *Low Man on a Totem Pole*, Smith.

145   "Rumors of a rift": *Valparaiso Vidette Messenger*, August 10, 1934.

145   "billowing skirts": *Racine Journal Times*, August 5, 1933.

145   "strain": *Charleston Daily Mail*, August 12, 1933.

145   "I took the opportunity that came to me," Sally said. "Certainly I am an opportunist": IMDb.com.

146   "repulsive to public decency": *Morning Call* (Allentown, PA), October 11, 1933.

146   "indecent and immoral and cannot be tolerated by": Unknown newspaper.

146   "Look! She bites the hand that feeds her": *San Antonio Light*, November 27, 1938.

147   "The fan dance was a means to an end": *Ludington Daily News*, November 4, 1933.

147   "With every other dancer": *Port Arthur News*, August 27, 1933.

147   "I'll never do the fan dance": *Muscatine Journal*, November 4, 1933.

147   "in a blaze of glory": *Jefferson City News*, November Tribune 19, 1933.

147   "It was a great splash": Ibid.

148   "hundreds of thousands of visitors": *Murphysboro Daily Independent*, October 17, 1933.

148   "had made the world a better place": *Al Capone and the 1933 World's Fair*, William Hazelgrove.

148   "increased liberation": *World of Fairs*, Rydell.

148   "was an inconspicuous figure": *Avalanche Journal*, August 28, 1960.

149 "will be able to walk all right in a few days": *Beckley Post Herald*, November 10, 1933.

CHAPTER TWENTY-ONE

153 "one of the world's finest exponents of the dance": *Evening Independent* (Massillon, Ohio), February 19, 1934.

153 "louder and more blatant": *Wisconsin State Journal*, July 1, 1934.

153 "They have beautiful paintings of nude": *Brookfield Suburban Magnet,* December 28, 1933.

153 "fan dancers and peep shows": Ibid.

153 "vulgarity" and "freaks": Ibid.

154 "rickshaw boys": *Ironwood Daily Globe*, July 13, 1934.

154 "about face": Ibid.

154 "practically every café, beer garden": *Evening Independent*, July 2, 1934.

154 "very cool": Ibid.

154 "$1,500 announcing her appearance": *Chicago Ins*, July 23, 1934.

154 "I'm not nude. I've got tape": *Dubois Courier*, September 8, 1934.

154 "tintillated" and "stood in the spotlight": Ibid.

155 "black wagon wheel hat": *Chicago Daily Tribune*, July 8, 1934.

156 "with all the grace": *The 1933 World's Fair*, Ganz.

156 "former bubble dancer": *Displaying the Marvelous*, Lewis Kachur.

156 "It takes a lot of work to fill the balloon": *My Ears Are Bent*, Joseph Mitchell.

157 "It's just a dance, and they can take it or leave it": *Variety*, May 15, 1935.

157 "forced to put on pants": *Clovis Evening News Journal*, August 3, 1934.

158 "the spirit" and "changing notions": *The 1933 World's Fair*, Ganz.

158 "as the bubble": A Tru-Vue film, *Sally Rand in her Fan Dance*, author's collection.

CHAPTER TWENTY-TWO

159 "in closing the Fair": Sally letter to her mother.

160 "I think it was delightful": Author interview with SR.

160 "I am the one who must": Sally letter to her mother, November 5, 1934, New York Performing Arts Library.

160 "spiritual solitude": *Variety*, July 14, 1937.

160   "marquee draw": *Variety,* February 2, 1934.

160   "succession of alluring women": Ibid.

161   "she had been promised a chance": *Variety,* December 16, 1933.

161   "were about to lose": *Sally Rand: From Film to Fans,* Knox.

161   "no security": Sally letter to her mother, April 1942, Chicago History Museum.

162   "consumptive" and "build up her frail body": *Pittsburgh Press,* October 3, 1956.

163   "*Moonlight Sonata* and a Brahms waltz": *Never Plead Guilty,* John Wesley Noble.

163   "strip bubble dance": *Variety,* January 15, 1935.

163   "abandon fans": *Chicago Tribune,* March 13, 1935.

163   "When this time of earning": *Hattiesburg American,* March 7, 1935.

163   "the bare facts of beauty": *Dubois Courier,* August 14, 1935.

163   "the economic dangers of communism in America": *Sandusky Register,* May 4, 1935.

163   "Dancing is a more normal form of expression": *Oakland Tribune,* June 14, 1928.

164   "I had . . . the ability": *Hammond Times,* June 20, 1935.

164   "mystery": *Variety,* May 15, 1935.

164   "ungraceful picture": *Chicago Tribune,* August 13, 1935.

164   "Brief and uninteresting": *Variety,* August 14, 1935.

164   "I haven't time to think": *Hammond Times,* June 20, 1935.

164   "She would get in your face": Author interview with SR.

164   "She was a great lady, but a bitch-on-wheels": *Sally Rand: From Film to Fans,* Knox.

165   "even if she came on the stage" *Variety,* October 23, 1935

165   "He was cruel": Ibid.

165   "It's just a shame that there are narrow-minded persons": *Victoria Advocate,* April 9, 1936.

165   "jewel of America's": Website www.lakewoodtheater.org.

165   "her voice as clear": *Berkeley Daily Gazette,* August 27, 1935.

165   According to Holly Knox (to be repeated by many others) this performance was in 1925. But playbills clearly prove it to be 1935. In 1925 she wasn't yet Sally Rand. Another biographer claimed Bogart took the job, curious about working with the notorious Sally Rand. His

star wasn't so ascended. He would have been grateful for the work with a bigger name.

165   "red-headed sweetheart": *Fort Madison Evening Democrat*, August 10, 1935.

166   "in debt": *Sally Rand: From Film to Fans*, Knox.

166   "I put forth every effort": Sally letter to her mother, New York Performing Arts Library.

166   "I want to change the public's conception": *Hattiesburg American*, March 7, 1935.

166   "two minds": *Greenville Evening Banner*, March 9, 1935.

166   "very understanding": Ibid.

166   "Does he want me to carry fans in my toes?": *Lowell Sun*, September 27, 1935.

CHAPTER TWENTY-THREE

168   "Aren't you sorry you tried to do this?" *Athens Messenger*, February 13, 1936.

169   "stubby": www.sandiegohistory.org archives.

169   "I like to be as naked as possible," "I'm against organized nudism" and "all the nudists": *My Ears Are Bent*, Mitchell.

169   "rowdies peppered her": *Biloxi Daily Herald*, April 16, 1936.

170   "Don't you recognize me dressed": *Oakland Tribune*, May 21, 1936.

170   "quite a flop," "new publicity impetus," and "under 'canvas'": Sally letter to her mother, August 2, 1935, Chicago History Museum.

170   "Six ministers in Cheyenne and the Bishop": Ibid.

170   "freak western wind": Ibid.

171   "He that is first": *Bluefield Daily Telegraph*, January 14, 1936.

171   "sheer volume of publicity": *Valley Morning Star*, November 29, 1936.

171   "one of the sharpest": *San Antonio Light*, July 6, 1936.

171   "urchin": *D Magazine*, "Makin' Whoopee," Jerry Flemmons, April 1978.

172   "put on a show the like of which has never been seen by the human eye": Ibid.

173   "America's No. 1 stripper": *San Antonio Light*, August 9, 1936.

173   "dated": *Renegades, Showmen, and Angels*, Jan Jones.

173 "carefully applied by her 'male maid'": *Forth Worth Entertainment Journal,* vol. 44, no. 1, Annie O. Cleveland.

173 "cavort behind glass wearing as little as the law allowed": *Variety,* June 25, 1936.

173 "athletic gyrations": *Variety,* June 25, 1936.

174 "looked to me as though a bath wouldn't hurt": *Ardmore Daily Ardmoreite,* October 9, 1936.

174 "best dancers": *Renegades, Showmen, and Angels,* 1873–2001, Jan Jones.

174 "immoral" and an "insult to the decency of . . . womanhood": *Brownsville Herald,* November 22, 1936.

CHAPTER TWENTY-FOUR

175 "high priced": *New York Herald Tribune,* November 7, 1932.

175 "artistic": Unknown newspaper, Temple University collection.

175 "I've achieved success": *Port Arthur News,* July 9, 1936.

176 "I am a native": *Love of Art & Art of Love,* Hanley.

176 "The Show was called 'Temptations'": *Chicago Tribune,* December 6, 1937.

176 "deep and ugly scars": *Hammond Times,* February 25, 1937.

177 "gigantic ambulance-chasing": *San Antonio Light,* December 12, 1936.

177 Elizabeth Dickinson—probably only a coincidence and no relation to Faith's future husband Sanford Hunt Dickinson.

177 "extensive filing cabinets": *Wisconsin State Journal,* December 18, 1936.

CHAPTER TWENTY-FIVE

178 "used to hold my fans": *Hammond Times,* February 25, 1937.

178 "I'm an artist": Unknown newspaper, Temple University collection.

178 "chunky": *Lincoln Sunday Journal and Star* (Lincoln, Nebraska) October 3, 1937.

179 "most daring of all nudes": *Cumberland Evening Times,* October 7, 1937.

179 "she comes on the stage wearing three orchids": Ibid.

179 "dance le nudite": *Valparaiso Vidette Messenger,* February 1, 1937.

179   "wine red velvet negligee": *Murphysboro Daily Independent*, February 25, 1937.

179   "beauty is my livelihood": *Madison Evening Democrat*, February 24, 1937.

179   "more interested in the artistic side": *Hattiesburg American*, September 17, 1937.

179   "strictly ethereal atmosphere": *Low Man on a Totem Pole*, Smith.

180   "sober conservative street suit": *Oakland Tribune*, February 24, 1937.

180   "I really dance": *Joplin Globe*, May 21, 1937.

180   "as long as you keep that violet-blue spot on her": *Variety*, August 25, 1937.

181   Faith, "one of the brightest stars": *Evening Democrat*, September 15, 1937.

181   If it's the same Lew Parker, and there is no reason to believe it isn't, he would find some fame as Marlo Thomas's father on the TV show *That Girl*.

181   "two armed white men": *Hattiesburg American*, November 17, 1937.

181   "naked she-male": *Biloxi Daily Herald*, November 29, 1937.

CHAPTER TWENTY-SIX

182   "must at all times look pleasing to the eye": *Daily News Standard*, June 14, 1937.

182   "free of risqué entertainment": *Van Wert Times Bulletin*, March 24, 1937.

183   "humiliated": *Elyria Chronicle Telegram*, March 19, 1937.

183   "got in his face": Author interview with SR.

184   "retire a rich old maid": *Big Spring Herald*, March 8.

184   "super-perfect form": *Port Arthur News*, March 22, 1936.

184   "you're so afraid of men": *Port Arthur News*, July 19, 1936.

184   "out of necessity": *Art of Love & Love of Art*, Hanley.

184   "I want a man—a man to love!": *Albuquerque Journal*, July 19, 1936.

184   "Faith on sleeping pills": *Art of Love & Love of Art*, Hanley.

184   "wanted delicate flower treatment": Ibid.

CHAPTER TWENTY-SEVEN

185   "I am not through": *Low Man on a Totem Pole*, Smith.

186   "stunning line of show": *Dunkirk Evening Observer*, January 24, 1938.

186   "matronly": *Corsicana Daily Sun*, February 2, 1938.

186   "Oh dear": Unknown newspaper.

186   "best undressed list": *Nevada State Journal*, May 9, 1938.

187   "hobbled": *Variety*, May 20, 1938.

187   "How to be intelligent": *Santa Fe New Mexican*, May 6, 1938.

187   "doesn't fit into our picture": *Variety*, June 30, 1938.

187   "screams like a banshee": *Blytheville Courier News*, May 3, 1938.

187   "headed for a nervous breakdown": *Coshocton Tribune*, March 10, 1938.

188   "to be a real actress": *Racine Journal Times*, May 8, 1938.

188   "tilled by a Rand relative": *Blytheville Courier News*, May 3, 1938.

188   "I keep right on doing the same thing, touring is very repetitive": Sally letters to her mother.

189   "number thirty-seven, or midnight blue": *Never Plead Guilty*, Noble.

189   "My work represents": *Sault Sainte Marie Evening News*, November 3, 1938.

189   "took Stanford": *Moorhead Daily News*, July 23, 1938.

189   "This will cost you plenty": *Oakland Tribune*, November 2, 1938.

189   "nude dancer": *San Antonio Light*, November 27, 1938.

190   "I won't have my picture taken with a policewoman": *Amarillo Daily News*, October 18, 1938.

190   "Whatta Surprise!": *Oakland Tribune*, November 2, 1938.

190   "modest blue wool dress": *Oakland Tribune*, October 31, 1938.

191   "I fail to see what purpose could be served": *Wisconsin State Journal*, November 2, 1938.

191   "nine gray-haired women": *Biddeford Daily Journal*, November 4, 1938.

191   "I was defenseless": *Cumberland Times* (Cumberland, Maryland) November 4, 1938.

191   "glum looking": *Oakland Tribune*, November 3, 1938.

191   "Apparently I'm to have no such thing as privacy": *Burlington Hawk Eye Gazette*, November 8, 1938.

191   "Everything I say just seems to result": *Oakland Tribune*, October 18, 1938.

192   "It sears my soul, all this is bad publicity": *Wisconsin State Journal*, November 2, 1938.

192   "Sally has so many": *San Antonio Light*, November 27, 1938.

CHAPTER TWENTY-EIGHT

193   "Sally always admits I originated it when I'm around": *Oakland Tribune*, February 6, 1938.

194   "the kindness of her heart": *San Antonio Light*, November 27, 1938.

194   "All she does": *Wisconsin State Journal*, October 11, 1938.

194   "The fan idea is as old as Cleopatra": Unknown newspaper, Temple University collection.

194   "Ostrich feathers!": Unknown newspaper, New York Performing Arts Library.

194   "Webster suing": *San Antonio Light*, November 27, 1938.

194   "one of ethereal beauty": Ibid.

194   "A little talcum": Ibid.

195   "Fan dancing is my baby": "Fan Dancing's Her Baby," H. Allen Smith, unknown newspaper.

195   "champagne blonde": Ibid.

195   "It's always requested": Ibid.

195   "I do my dancing in bare feet": *Billboard*, May 29, 1943.

195   "I figure her use of my dances": *Galveston Tribune*, October 11, 1938.

195   "Once Broadway's": *Amarillo Globe*, October 11, 1938..

195   "I am going to see if the authorities": Unknown newspaper, Temple University collection.

195   "dance concerts": *Low Man on a Totem Pole*, Smith.

196   "How long have you performed as a nudist?": *Twin Falls News*, November 22, 1938.

196   "charges were never pressed": *Valparaiso Videte Messenger*, February 1, 1937.

CHAPTER TWENTY-NINE

197   "silver fox cape": *Arcadia Tribune*, December 3, 1938.

197   "Flying is like dancing": "Faith Bacon, Fan and Orchid Dancer,

Would Like To Perform 'Apres-Midi d'un Faune,'" unknown newspaper, February 25, 1939.

197 She would also appear in two shorts in 1942, *The Dance of Shame* and *A Lady with Fans*.

198 "eight autumn leaves": *Daily News*, unknown date.

198 "Grecian type dress": *Life*, May 8, 1939.

198 "This tiny deer was a freak, never grew much more than two feet": *Evening Journal*, April 25, 1952.

198 "taking my fawn for a walk": Unknown newspaper, Temple University collection.

199 "mean" and "running away from a fire": *Wisconsin State Journal*, April 24, 1939.

199 "with causing a crowd to collect": Ibid.

199 "you'll be leaving the rest of your jewelry here": Unknown newspaper.

199 "several hundred": Unknown newspaper.

199 "You probably": Unknown newspaper.

199 "hungry for publicity" and "scratch eyes out": *Lowell Sun*, April 26, 1939.

200 "thrill the men—and make the women green with envy": Unknown newspaper.

200 "the only real applause": *Variety*, February 22, 1939.

200 "strapless white bathing suit": Unknown newspaper, Temple University collection.

CHAPTER THIRTY

202 "I have had some experiences": *Stories of Old Glendora*, Price.

203 "Thin excuse": *Variety*, September 3, 1941.

203 "participate vigorously": *Life*, March 6, 1939.

203 "No clothes or no nude ranch": *Monroe News Star*, February 1938.

204 "did a complete turnover": *Variety*, February 22, 1939.

204 "lagging" and "gone in the red": *Variety*, April 12, 1939.

204 "dickering": *Variety*, August 23, 1939.

204 "a mess": *Racine Journal Times*, October 16, 1939.

205 "was down to her last fan": *Variety*, October 17, 1939.

CHAPTER THIRTY-ONE

207   "peep show of tomorrow": *World of Fairs*, Rydell.

207   "multiply the dancing girls a thousand-fold": *Variety*, May 31, 1939.

207   "huntsman's cap": *Galveston Daily News*, June 11, 1939.

207   "Do the church people": Unknown newspaper.

208   "sloppy": *Variety*, November 3, 1939.

208   "amusing": *San Antonio Light*, April 9, 1939.

208   "fast paced show": *East Liverpool Review*, December 15, 1939.

209   "It isn't much of a turn": Unknown newspaper.

209   "scampers about": *Variety*, January 1, 1940.

209   "pay my own expenses": *Butte Montana Standard*, July 3, 1940.

209   "indefinite stay": *Goddess of Love Incarnate*, Zemeckis.

209   "major operation": *Variety*, July 22, 1940.

209   Information regarding Faith's possible glandular surgery was posted on www.IMDb.com by Gary Brumburgh.

210   "fast-moving program": *Billboard*, November 21, 1942.

210   "turned bitter and aggressive": *Ma Vie de Stripteaseuse*, St. Cyr.

210   "bra flash": *Variety*, November 13, 1940.

CHAPTER THIRTY-TWO

211   Fenton Perkins story relayed to author by a relative who wishes to remain anonymous.

211   "amazed that they were not paid": Sally letter to her mother, Chicago History Museum.

212   "dilapidated house": *Grits & Grunts*, Stetson Kennedy

212   "Packsaddle Ben": *When the Whistle Blows*, Tom Ringley.

212   "get drunk on": *Cowgirls, Women of the American West*, Teresa Jordan.

212   "Riding Greenoughs": *Notable American Women*, vol. 5.

212   "came running up to him to get his autograph": *Oakland Tribune*, October 3, 1941.

213   "girls how to twirl their lariats": *Sally Rand: From Film to Fans*, Knox.

213   "busy. I must continue to be busy. I believe in real partnership": *Oakland Tribune*, June 14, 1928.

213   "pretty and frail": *Victoria Advocate*, October 3, 1941.

213   "a horse kicked me": *Racine Journal Times*, October 4, 1941.

213   "hate": *When the Whistle Blows*, Ringley.

214 "maintenance": *Lowell Sun*, November 1, 1941.

215 "I think that so many stage marriages": *Oakland Tribune*, June 14, 1928.

216 "shockingly insensitive": Sally letter to her mother, April 18, 1942.

216 "Miserable," "heart sick," and "we were so happy": Ibid.

217 "Turk got himself": Ibid.

217 "put out" and "I quit": Author interview with SR.

217 "complete disapproval": Sally letter to her mother.

218 "Daddy's Girl": *When the Whistle Blows*, Ringley.

218 "know the gestation period for horses": Ibid.

218 "all that is going on": Sally letters.

218 "one of the most famous rodeo families of all time": *Cowgirls, Women of the American West*, Jordan.

219 "too much fame for Turk's gal": *San Antonio Light*, February 11, 1945.

CHAPTER THIRTY-THREE

223 "girl cashiers at the bar": *Variety*, May 7, 1941.

223 "laughs aplenty": *Ogden Standard Examiner*, April 5, 1941.

223 "pioneer Sonoma County family": *Berkeley Daily Gazette*, July 31, 1941.

223 "a health-seeker": *Tucson Daily Citizen*, August 29, 1941.

224 "admirer": *Love of Art & Art of Love*, Hanley.

224 "secretly stitched": *Blytheville Courier News*, September 11, 1941.

224 "dance interpretations": *Billboard*, July 25, 1942.

225 "extensive negotiations": *Billboard*, June 20, 1942.

225 "Noting your many references": *Variety*, April 30, 1941.

226 "horrible fiasco": Sally letter to her mother.

226 "indecent exposure:" *Never Plead Guilty*, Noble.

226 "I could throw a handful": Ibid.

227 "alcoholic accountant": Sally letter to her mother, Chicago History Museum.

227 "the men would rather": *Fairfield Daily Ledger*, April 26, 1948.

CHAPTER THIRTY-FOUR

228 "picked up": *Kingsport News*, October 18, 1948.

228 "disintegrated": Author interview with SR.

229   "under no circumstances": Ibid.

230   "the other way around": *Alice Daily Echo*, November 13, 1949.

230   "when people come": *Fairbanks Daily News Miner*, September 27, 1957.

230   "the rude stares": *Albuquerque Journal*, July 19, 1936.

230   "giant flash-act": *Variety*, February 13, 1948.

231   "phobia": *All Told*, Leroy Neiman.

231   "don't want to stay at home": *Fairbanks Daily News Miner*, September 27, 1957.

231   "representing": *Variety*, September 2, 1953.

232   "real people": Author interview with SR.

232   "There was always enough": *Hard Times*, Terkel.

CHAPTER THIRTY-FIVE

233   "various oil leases": *Bakersfield Californian*, October 13, 1948.

234   "confirmed that his client": *Reno Evening Gazette*, April 24, 1961.

234   "art-lover": *San Antonio Light*, July 8, 1945. The statutes have since vanished. Berkeley no longer has a record of them, and Bacon hall was razed in 1961.

CHAPTER THIRTY-SIX

236   "Publicity is like money": *Wisconsin State Journal*, May 14, 1947.

237   "okay talent": *Billboard*, June 24, 1950.

237   "humiliate little people": Sally letter to her mother.

237   "hump": *Behind the Burly Q*, Zemeckis.

237   "daffy": *Lowell Sun*, November 20, 1947.

237   "laughing and talking": *Ardmore Daily Ardmoreite*, August 17, 1947.

237   "I have nothing to hide": *Corpus Christi Caller-Times*, August 17, 1947.

238   "strictly my manager": *Ogden Standard*, unknown date.

238   "You're under arrest": *Dunkirk Evening Observer*, July 14, 1950.

238   "I'm sorry, I just don't tell": *Ames Daily Tribune*, July 14, 1950.

238   "super trailer": *Toledo Blade*, August 22, 1950.

239   "decided": *Toledo Blade*, August 24, 1950.

239   "really tough": Sally letter to her mother, Chicago History Museum.

239   "we can only do our best": Ibid.

239 "bitching": Ibid.

240 "great trouble": Ibid.

240 "food, shelter" and remaining quotes regarding Sally and Harry are from her letters, Chicago History Museum.

241 "couldn't get a hotel room for any price": *Centralia Evening Sentinel*, October 14, 1950.

CHAPTER THIRTY-SEVEN

242 "contaminated smoke and": *Billboard*, December 27, 1947.

243 "stand out" but the show "lacked production qualities": *Billboard*, May 9, 1948.

243 "Faith who keeps her age secret": *Sheboygan Press*, June 8, 1948.

243 "brazenly brought to the American stage": Unknown magazine, New York Performing Arts Library.

CHAPTER THIRTY-EIGHT

245 "really packing in the crowd": *Oakland Tribune*, September 9, 1950.

245 "nervous system": Unknown newspaper.

245 "gay and fast moving": *Southeast Economist*, May 3, 1951.

246 "shoulder to shoulder": "Calumet City Centennial. 'Sin Strip' Only a Shadow of Its," *New York Times*, Kym Lieber, January 29, 1993.

246 "yanked": *Variety*, May 2, 1951.

247 "best thing in the world for us": Sally letter.

247 "busy twenty-four hours": *Waterloo Daily Courier*, August 12, 1954.

248 "wasn't at all like the fan dancer he'd seen on the stage": Sally letter.

248 "I married a man who had no conscience": Author interview with SR.

CHAPTER THIRTY-NINE

249 "dogged by nervous incidents": *Ogden Standard Examiner*, April 24, 1961.

250 "rich young-man-about-town": *New York Times*, October 11, 1987.

250 "colored gals": *Variety*, May 25, 1938.

251 "Why should Faith lie to me?" *Love of Art & Art of Love*, Hanley.

252 "bulging closets," "gobbling pills," and "beyond help": Ibid.

254   "was without jobs, without funds, and on drugs": Ibid.

254   "active on the middle west nightclub circuit": *Bradford Era*, May 25, 1954.

254   "friend": *Anderson Herald*, March 4, 1954.

254   "chronic insomnia": Ibid.

254   "She appeared under the name of Faith Bacon": *Logansport Pharos Tribune*, March 3, 1954.

CHAPTER FORTY

255   "fingers into a jar of inexpensive cold cream": *The Sheboygan Press*, Wisconsin, March 2, 1955.

256   "Seventy?": Author interview with SR.

256   "looking like hell": Ibid.

256   "Those were the fans?": This conversation was an author interview with SR.

256   "Perhaps it was a shame that I got so famous so young": Unknown newspaper, 1938.

257   "the slap happy era was over": *Brownsville Herald*, 1940.

257   "lackluster lovelies": Ibid.

257   "plans for a more casual life": *Star News*, September 10, 1956.

258   "a lawless wasteland": *The G-String Murders*, Elaine Hatfield.

258   "bondage": *Madison-Wisconsin State Journal*, June 20, 1962.

258   "nerves are in shreds": "Beauty Through Health and Culture," Lecture at the YWCA, Tullah Hanley, October 1959.

259   "I'll tell you what I did": *Chicago Tribune*, September 29, 1956.

CHAPTER FORTY-ONE

260   "I have found it isn't a fine thing to be the 'most beautiful'": *Helena Independent*, August 14, 1929.

260   "no matter what happens" to carry on "with simulated lightness of heart": *Canton-Daily News*, March 17, 1929.

260   "standard to which the American woman looked": *Ziegfeld Girl*, Mizejewski.

261   The Alan Hotel was located at 204 Lincoln Park West.

261   "If I can't do any better": *Dunkirk Evening Observer*, September 27, 1956.

262   "Are you leaving me, or not?": *Hammond Times*, September 26, 1956.

262   "stupor": Ibid.

263   "Faith, if you're determined": Ibid.

263   "I'm in a world apart": Faith Bacon quote, unknown newspaper.

263   "the once beautiful showgirl": Unknown newspaper, Temple University collection.

263   "The doctors who tried to save her": *New York Confidential Mirror*, Lee Mortimer, 1956.

263   "golden and her weight": (1956) maybe above.

264   "her body was still so beautiful": Unknown newspaper, New York Performing Arts Library.

CHAPTER FORTY-TWO

265   "We need not concern ourselves": *Denton Record Chronicle*, "Faith Bacon: Post-Mortem On Once-Beautiful Woman," Paul Harvey October 8, 1956,

265   "symbol of the cult of glorification": *Chicago Daily Tribune*, January 19, 1932.

267   "give up much of her personal life": *Lubbock Avalanche Journal*, September 30, 1956.

267   "She didn't possess loveliness": *Oakland Tribune*, October 15, 1956.

EPILOGUE

268   "last Venus": *Lowell Sun*, September 27, 1956.

268   "go without a decent burial": *Corpus Christi Caller-Times*, September 27, 1956.

269   "I had an opportunity and I twisted it to my advantage": *Avalanche Journal*, August 28, 1960.

269   "imitators have faded": *Coshocton Tribune*, February 6, 1964.

269   "It's no more complicated than keeping my hair blonde": *Panama City News Herald*, August 1, 1979.

269   "a certain reverence": *Playground Daily News*, August 31, 1967.

270   "all illusion": *Republic* (Phoenix, Arizona) July 8, 1973.

270   "time has stood still": *Avalanche Journal*, August 28, 1960.

270   "be devastated": *Pacific Stars and Stripes*, May 12, 1979.

270   "She'll probably never retire": Author interview with SR.

271   "What in heaven's name is strange about a grandmother dancing
       nude?": *Stories of Old Glendora*, Price.

271   "I'm not the type to sit": Ibid.

271   "If you have to remove one": Author interview with SR.

272   "Once she got in the spotlight, you'd never know": *Leatherman*,
       Tracy Baim and Owen Keehnen.

272   "God knows, I like doing this": *Kenosha News*, August 31, 1979.

273   "My interpretation": *Stories of Old Glendora*, Price.

273   "make America sex-conscious": *Athens Messenger*, June 12, 1934.

BIBLIOGRAPHY

Allman, Barbara, and Shelly O. Haas. *Dance of the Swan: A Story about Anna Pavlova*. Carolrhoda Books, 2001.

Baral, Robert. *Revue: The Great Broadway Period*. Introduction by Robert J. Landry. Fleet Press, 1962.

Bergreen, Laurence. *Capone: The Man and the Era*. Simon and Schuster, 1994.

Bilek, Arthur J. *The First Vice Lord: Big Jim Colosimo and the Ladies of the Levee*. Cumberland House, 2008.

Bordman, Gerald Martin, and Richard C. Norton. *American Musical Theatre: A Chronicle*. Oxford University Press, 2014.

Brideson, Cynthia. *Ziegfeld and His Follies: A Biography of Broadway's Greatest Producer*. University Press of Kentucky, 2018.

Charyn, Jerome. *Gangsters and Gold Diggers: Old New York, The Jazz Age, and the Birth of Broadway*. Four Walls, Eight Windows, 2003.

Clar, Reva Howitt, and Mimi Melnick. *Lollipop: Vaudeville Turns with a Fanchon and Marco Dancer*. Scarecrow Press, 2002.

Cullen, Frank, et al. *Vaudeville, Old & New: An Encyclopedia of Variety Performers in America*. Routledge, Taylor & Francis Group, 2007.

Davis, Lee. *Scandals and Follies: The Rise and Fall of the Great Broadway Revue*. Limelight Editions, 2000.

Dudden, Faye E. *Women in the American Theatre: Actresses & Audiences, 1790–1870*. Yale University Press, 1997.

Earle, Marcelle, and Arthur C. Homme. *Midnight Frolic: A Ziegfeld Girl's True Story*. Twin Oaks Publishing Co., 1999.

Eghigian, Mars, and Frank Nitti. *After Capone: The Life and World of Chicago Mob Boss Frank "the Enforcer" Nitti*. Cumberland House, 2006.

Farnsworth, Marjorie. *The Ziegfeld Follies*. P. Davies, 1957.

Ganz, Cheryl. *The 1933 Chicago World's Fair: Century of Progress*. University of Illinois Press, 2012.

Gardner, Kara Anne. *Agnes De Mille*. Oxford University Press, 2016.

Glines, Karen. *Painting Missouri: The Counties En Plein Air*. Sweetgrass Books, an Imprint of Farcountry Press, 2017.

Golden, Eve. *Anna Held and the Birth of Ziegfeld's Broadway*. University of Pennsylvania Press, 2011.

Goldman, Herbert G. *Fanny Brice: The Original Funny Girl*. Oxford University Press, 1992.

Goodman, Jonathan. *The Passing of Starr Faithfull*. Kent State University Press, 1996.

Goss, Madeleine. *Bolero: The Life of Maurice Ravel*. Kessinger Publishing, 2008.

Hanley, Tullah. *Love of Art & Art of Love*. Piper Publishing, Inc., 1975.

Hatfield, Elaine, and Richard L. Rapson. *The G-String Murders*. Xlibris Corporation, 2009.

Hazelgrove, William Elliott. *Al Capone and the 1933 World's Fair: The End of the Gangster Era in Chicago*. Rowman & Littlefield, 2017.

Hirshey, Gerri. *Not Pretty Enough: The Unlikely Triumph of Helen Gurley Brown*. Sarah Crichton Books/FSG, 2017.

Hischak, Thomas S. *Broadway Plays and Musicals: Descriptions and Essential Facts of More Than 14,000 Shows Through 2007*. McFarland & Company, Inc., 2015.

Husum, Fred. *Chicago and the World's Fair, 1933*. Husum, F., Publishing Company, Inc., 1933. (Internet Archive, www.archive.org/details /chicagoworldsfai00husu)

Jones, Jan. *Billy Rose Presents—Casa Mañana*. TCU Press, 1999.

Jones, Jan. *Renegades, Showmen & Angels: A Theatrical History of Fort Worth, 1873–2001*. TCU Press, 2006.

Jordan, Teresa. *Cowgirls: Women of the American West*. University of Nebraska Press, 1992.

Joyce, Peggy Hopkins. *Men, Marriage, and Me*. Macauley Co., 1930.

Kachur, Lewis. *Displaying the Marvelous: Marcel Duchamp, Salvador Dalí, and Surrealist Exhibition Installations*. MIT Press, 2003.

Kennedy, Stetson. *Grits & Grunts: Folkloric Key West*. Pineapple Press, 2008.

Kirby, David. *Ultra-Talk: Johnny Cash, the Mafia, Shakespeare, Drum Music, St. Teresa of Avila, and 17 Other Colossal Topics of Conversation*. University of Georgia Press, 2007.

Knox, Holly. *Sally Rand: From Film to Fans*. Maverick Publications, 1988.

Koenig, Karl. *Jazz in Print (1856–1929): An Anthology of Selected Early Readings in Jazz History*. Pendragon Press, 2002.

Lafayette, Maximillien de. *Anthology and History of French Song and Music from 1730 to Present Day* (9th edition). Lulu.com, 2013.

Louvish, Simon. *Man on the Flying Trapeze: The Life and Times of W. C. Fields*. W. W. Norton, 1999.

Lynch, Christopher. *When Hollywood Landed at Chicago's Midway Airport: The Photos & Stories of Mike Rotunno*. History Press, 2012.

MacDonald, Laura, and William A. Everett. *The Palgrave Handbook of Musical Theatre Producers*. Palgrave Macmillan US, 2017.

McDougal, Dennis. *The Last Mogul: Lew Wasserman, MCA, and the Hidden History of Hollywood*. Da Capo Press, 2001.

McLellan, Diana. *Girls: Sappho Goes to Hollywood*. Booktrope Editions, 2013.

Mitchell, Joseph. *My Ears Are Bent*. Vintage Books, 2008.

Mordden, Ethan. *Ziegfeld: The Man Who Invented Show Business*. St. Martin's Press, 2008.

Moser, Margaret, et al. *Movie Stars Do the Dumbest Things*. St. Martin's, 2000.

Murray, Ken. *The Body Merchant*. 1976.

Nash, Jay Robert. *The Great Pictorial History of World Crime*. History, Inc., 2004.

Neiman, LeRoy. *All Told: My Art and Life Among Athletes, Playboys, Bunnies, and Provocateurs*. Lyons Press, 2012.

Noble, John Wesley, and Bernard Averbuch. *Never Plead Guilty: The Story of Jake Ehrlich*. Bantam Books, 1963.

Norton, Leslie, and Frederic Franklin. *Frederic Franklin: A Biography of the Ballet Star*. McFarland & Company, 2007.

Ott, Katherine. *Fevered Lives: Tuberculosis in American Culture Since 1870.* Harvard University Press, 1996.

Perry, Douglas. *Eliot Ness: The Rise and Fall of an American Hero.* Penguin Books, 2015.

Pfister, Fred. *Insiders' Guide to Branson and the Ozark Mountains.* Insiders' Guide, 2010.

Raeburn, John. *A Staggering Revolution: A Cultural History of Thirties Photography.* University of Illinois Press, 2006.

Richman, Harry, and Richard Gehman. *A Hell of a Life.* Duell, Sloan, and Pearce, 1966.

Rydell, Robert W. *World of Fairs: The Century-of-Progress Expositions.* University of Chicago Press, 1993.

Sann, Paul, and Howard V. Sann. *The Lawless Decade: Bullets, Broads & Bathtub Gin.* Dover Publications, 2010.

Sengstock, Charles A. *That Toddlin' Town: Chicago's White Dance Bands and Orchestras, 1900–1950.* University of Illinois Press, 2004.

Shafer, Yvonne. *Performing O'Neill.* St. Martin's, 2001.

Shteir, Rachel. *Striptease: The Untold History of the Girlie Show.* Oxford University Press, 2006.

Slide, Anthony. *The Encyclopedia of Vaudeville.* University Press of Mississippi, 2012.

Slide, Anthony. *Silent Players: A Biographical and Autobiographical Study of 100 Silent Film Actors and Actresses.* University Press of Kentucky, 2002.

Smith, Harry Allen. *Low Man on a Totem Pole.* World Distributors, 1961.

Sothern, Georgia. *Georgia: My Life in Burlesque.* New American Library, 1972.

Spivak, Jeffrey. *Buzz: The Life and Art of Busby Berkeley.* University Press of Kentucky, 2011.

Stagg, Jerry. *The Brothers Shubert.* Ballantine Books, 1969.

Stein, Sarah Abrevaya. *Plumes: Ostrich Feathers, Jews, and a Lost World of Global Commerce.* Yale University Press, 2010.

Stencell, A. W. *Girl Show: Into the Canvas World of Bump and Grind.* ECW Press, 1999.

Swan, June, et al. *Birds of Paradise: Plumes & Feathers in Fashion, Pluimen & Veren in De Mode.* Lannoo, 2014.

Sweet, Jill D. *Life as a Tarantella: A Memoir.* Lulu Publishing, 2015.

Terkel, Studs. *Hard Times: An Illustrated Oral History of the Great Depression.* New Press, 2013.

Vesely, James M. *Cadet Gray: Stories of Morgan Park Military Academy.* iUniverse, Inc., 2006.

Vogel, Michelle. *Olive Thomas: The Life and Death of a Silent Film Beauty.* McFarland & Co., 2007.

Ware, Susan, et al. *Notable American Women: A Biographical Dictionary.* Belknap, 1980.

Widmann, Otto. *A Preliminary Catalogue of the Birds of Missouri.* St. Louis, MO, 1907.

Wood, Larry. *Wicked Women of Missouri.* The History Press, 2016.

Zemeckis, Leslie. *Behind the Burly Q: The Story of Burlesque in America.* Skyhorse Publishing, 2013.

Zemeckis, Leslie, director. *Behind the Burly Q*, 2010.

Zemeckis, Leslie. *Goddess of Love Incarnate: The Life of Stripteuse Lili St. Cyr.* Counterpoint, 2015.

Ziegfeld, Richard, and Paulette Ziegfeld. *The Ziegfeld Touch: The Life and Times of Florenz Ziegfeld, Jr.* Harry N. Abrams, 1993.

LESLIE ZEMECKIS is an actress, filmmaker, and the author of *Goddess of Love Incarnate: The Life of Stripteuse Lili St. Cyr* and *Behind the Burly Q*, the definitive history of burlesque. She wrote, produced, and directed the critically acclaimed documentary based on the book, which has been championed by *USA Today* and *The New Yorker*. Her most recent documentary is *Mabel, Mabel, Tiger Trainer*. Find more at lesliezemeckis.com.

Printed in the United States
by Baker & Taylor Publisher Services